Relapse Prevention Therapy Workbook

Managing Core Personality and Lifestyle Issues

By Terence T. Gorski

Based on the GORSKI-CENAPS® Model

The Most Advanced Recovery Tools Available

Relapse Prevention Therapy Workbook

Managing Core Personality and Lifestyle Issues

Developed by

Terence T. Gorski

President
The CENAPS® Corporation

Edited, With Process Overviews by
Pamela Woll

Copyright © Terence T. Gorski, December 1995
Printed in the United States of America

Published by
Herald House/Independence Press
1001 West Walnut
P.O. Box 390
Independence, MO 64051-0390
1-800-767-8181 or 816-521-3015
Fax: 816-521-3066
Web site: www.relapse.org

Relapse Prevention Therapy Workbook Managing Core Personality and Lifestyle Issues

Table of Contents

Introduction by Terence T. Gorski

How often have you heard these myths?

- "People who relapse don't really want recovery badly enough."

- "Relapse just happens—everything's going fine, and then all of a sudden you've picked up a drink or a drug."

- "Once you get into a self-help program, that program will give you everything you need to stay clean and sober and get your life back on track."

- "There's something wrong with people who relapse."

- "You just haven't hit bottom yet. What you need is more pain in your life."

If you're one of the many people who have relapsed in spite of treatment and/or recovery efforts, you probably have plenty of pain in your life. You may have had many experiences that could have been your "bottom," but you ended up slipping back into active use anyway. You might even have learned to "live on the bottom," unable to believe that you have any hope of lasting recovery.

Well, you do have hope. Most people relapse because they don't understand what relapse is and how to prevent it. Relapse is a process that begins long before you start drinking or drugging. Most people return to alcohol or drug use because they experience a series of problems that causes them to be so dysfunctional in recovery that a return to chemical use seems like a reasonable choice.

With relapse prevention planning you can identify the warning signs that lead to relapse and learn to manage these signs while you're still in recovery. You can also learn to manage the irrational thoughts, unmanageable emotions, self-destructive urges, and self-defeating behaviors that drive those warning signs. With the *Brief Therapy* approach that this workbook takes, you can learn these skills as quickly and effectively as possible.

What Is Brief Therapy?

The field of chemical dependency and behavioral health care is moving rapidly toward brief, targeted, and strategic therapy. In this case, *brief* means that the goals need to be reached in a limited number of sessions. *Targeted* means that therapy has to directly address the central core problem. *Strategic* means that there are clearly defined tasks that are used to reach clearly defined goals.

This is important for two reasons. First, it helps people get well faster. When you're dealing with a potentially fatal problem like relapse, this difference in the speed of recovery might mean the difference between life and death. Second, most of the managed care organizations and public agencies that are paying for health care services now require brief, targeted, strategic approaches. More and more people are finding that they can't get insurance to cover traditional open-ended treatment.

I developed the CENAPS® Model of Relapse Prevention Therapy using the basic principles that built *Staying Sober: A Guide for Relapse Prevention, The Staying Sober Workbook,* and the full line of related books and tapes. However, in this workbook I've organized the material into clearly targeted processes that will help you learn to avoid relapse more quickly and effectively.

Do You Need Help in Using This Workbook?

The Relapse Prevention Therapy Workbook is meant to be used with the help of someone who understands chemical dependency and relapse prevention therapy, and is willing and able to support you through this process.

When you first learn about your personal relapse warning signs, you'll probably find these signs being "triggered" or activated automatically. This is normal and natural, but by yourself you probably won't be able to understand and manage them. You're more likely to refine and perfect your own denial. Instead, you need discussion and feedback from other people, especially from someone who understands the warning sign identification and management process.

I recommend that you find a Certified Relapse Prevention Specialist trained in the CENAPS® Model of Relapse Prevention (call the CENAPS® office at 708-799-5000 for names in your area). If that's not possible, you can use another therapist who understands chemical dependency and is willing to learn and use this model. Training and certification in Relapse Prevention Therapy are also available from the CENAPS® Corporation.

If you can't find or afford a therapist to guide you through this process, you can use a self-help group sponsor as your relapse prevention sponsor. However, that sponsor must be open to the principles of *Relapse Prevention Therapy* and willing to commit the time and effort needed to learn and use this model. If you do plan to use a sponsor, both of you should know up front that this process can be intense and time consuming, and it can change the nature of your relationship. It's important that you both know what you're getting into before you make this important commitment.

Relapse Prevention Therapy is designed to support your involvement in self-help recovery groups, *not* replace it. Much of the success of your relapse prevention efforts will depend on your ability to build an ongoing personal recovery program and a strong network within the recovering community. It's also a good idea to find or start a relapse prevention support group based on the CENAPS® Model in your community (your local CENAPS®-trained Relapse Prevention Specialists will know of any such groups). For information on starting groups, see *How to Start Relapse Prevention Support Groups* by Terence T. Gorski (Herald House/Independence Press, 800-767-8181).

Where Do You Start?

The first step is to get a general idea of what's involved in *Relapse Prevention Therapy.* The next two pages will help you with that. Then you'll need to start looking for a therapist or relapse prevention sponsor who can help you do this work. Whether you use a therapist or a sponsor who's willing to learn these techniques, make sure you schedule definite appointments and keep those appointments. As it is with anything, how much you get out of it will depend on how much you put into it.

What's Involved in Brief Therapy for Relapse Prevention?

There are five major phases to the comprehensive CENAPS® relapse-prevention process: Stabilization, Assessment, Warning Sign Identification, Warning Sign Management, and Recovery Planning. You don't do them all at once; you do them a little bit at a time. Your therapist or relapse prevention sponsor guides you through the whole process. First, here's the big picture of the five phases:

1. **Phase I: Stabilization** is a very important phase that has to come first. In this phase you fill out questionnaires that help you and your therapist decide what your core problems are, what kind of treatment you need, and how much your addiction is still affecting your mental status. Then you develop a schedule of recovery activities, an immediate relapse prevention plan, and an early intervention plan. These are all designed to keep you safe from relapsing again while you're going through the relapse prevention process.

2. **Phase II: Assessment** is the next step in relapse prevention. It's a chance to take a very thorough look at your life, addiction, and relapse patterns, to explore your beliefs about using and your reasons for addictive use. It starts with a history of your life and your addiction. That's followed by a calendar of past relapses and a deeper look at what that calendar shows. Then you compare what you've learned in both exercises, for new insights into the beliefs behind your addiction.

3. **Phase III: Warning Sign Identification** brings you into the heart of the relapse prevention process. It starts with a review of the common warning signs that lead from stable recovery to relapse, to help you identify three personal warning signs based on your own experiences. Then you look in depth at your own personal warning signs and the thoughts, feelings, urges, and actions that drive them. You identify "hidden warning signs"—signs that are less obvious, but all the more powerful in leading toward relapse—and your personal "hot responses," or emotional triggers. After that, you develop a final warning sign list that tells you how all your warning signs lead from one to another, toward relapse. Then you find three "critical warning signs"—places where you have the best chance of stopping the relapse process before you drink or drug again.

4. **Phase IV: Warning Sign Management** tells you how to stop the relapse warning signs you identified so carefully in Phase III. It gives you a chance to practice simple but powerful processes for managing the irrational thoughts, unmanageable feelings, self-destructive urges, and self-defeating behaviors that drive the relapse warning signs. In this phase you use those processes on all three of your critical warning signs.

5. **Phase V: Recovery Planning** helps you develop a structured recovery plan that's tailored to your individual needs, and test that plan against your critical relapse warning signs. This phase gives you a number of tools for planning and scheduling the recovery activities you need in order to keep identifying and managing your relapse warning signs and the thoughts, feelings, urges, and actions that drive them.

The five phases are made up of a total of 15 core "processes," and many of those processes are made up of several "parts," or individual exercises. All of these are listed in the Table of Contents (page 3). The therapist or sponsor who is guiding you through Relapse Prevention Therapy might assign all of the processes and parts, or might just choose some processes and parts within each phase. Those choices should be based on your individual needs and on the length of time you can spend in Relapse Prevention Therapy.

Before each session with your therapist, you'll be asked to complete all or part of a process as a homework assignment. Then you'll bring your completed assignment into the session with you. The two of you will review what you've done and talk about it. Each session will be structured, with certain work to be done. You'll leave with another assignment to finish before your next session.

If this sounds like a big commitment, think of it instead as a series of little commitments. You'll never have to do the WHOLE THING at once. You'll just be asked to do a manageable number of exercises. Each one will consist of a few sheets of paper where you'll read what's written and fill in the blanks. The only hard part will be looking inside yourself and being honest. But if you don't do that, what chance do you have of avoiding relapse?

Before you decide whether or not to make this commitment, ask yourself these questions:

• Has what you've been doing so far kept you from relapsing, or helped you enjoy recovery?

• How much of your life is lost every time you relapse? How much more are you willing to lose?

• Are you ready to make a commitment to staying in recovery, and do whatever it takes to keep that commitment?

People who stick with this process find themselves amazed at its results. It not only helps them prevent the pain of future relapses, but it also helps them understand and manage life problems that they didn't even know were related to their relapse patterns. This workbook will do much more than just help you understand what you've been doing wrong. It will show you choices where you now see only traps and dead-ends. It will show you solutions that are right there, within your reach, right now.

There's an old saying: If you're not part of the solution, you're part of the problem. If you're *not* willing to make this commitment to relapse prevention, then you're really making a commitment to the next relapse.

The choice is yours.

Foreword to Therapists

There's no such thing as a hopeless relapse-prone person. This might sound like an unlikely statement to you, if you've seen the repeated damage that relapse has done to so many lives.

CENAPS®-Trained and -Certified Relapse Prevention Specialists throughout the country—and the world—are reporting successful long-term recovery for countless people whom other methods have failed and other therapists have given up as lost causes. Now that this model has been improved and converted to a Brief Therapy format, even more people will have a chance to achieve lasting recovery. Depending on your client's needs, this process can be completed in 12-to-20 sessions—well within the limits set by managed care organizations.

The *Relapse Prevention Therapy Workbook* gives you and your client everything you need in order to work through this advanced, intensive psychotherapeutic and skill-building experience. Its five phases contain the 15 core processes for comprehensive relapse prevention, divided into manageable parts. The five phases and 15 processes are:

Phase I: Stabilization
- Process 1: Screening
- Process 2: Schedule of Recovery Activities
- Process 3: Immediate Relapse Prevention Plan
- Process 4: Early Intervention Plan

Phase II: Assessment
- Process 5: Life and Addiction History
- Process 6: Recovery and Relapse History

Phase III: Warning Sign Identification
- Process 7: Warning Sign Review
- Process 8: Warning Sign Analysis
- Process 9: Sentence Completion
- Process 10: The Final Warning Sign List

Phase IV: Warning Sign Management
- Process 11A: Thought Management for the First Critical Warning Sign
- Process 12A: Feeling Management for the First Critical Warning Sign
- Process 13A: Behavior and Situation Management for the First Critical Warning Sign
- Process 14A: Integrated TFUAR Management for the First Critical Warning Sign
- Process 11B: Thought Management for the Second Critical Warning Sign
- Process 12B: Feeling Management for the Second Critical Warning Sign
- Process 13B: Behavior and Situation Management for the Second Critical Warning Sign
- Process 14B: Integrated TFUAR Management for the Second Critical Warning Sign
- Process 11C: Thought Management for the Third Critical Warning Sign
- Process 12C: Feeling Management for the Third Critical Warning Sign
- Process 13C: Behavior and Situation Management for the Third Critical Warning Sign
- Process 14C: Integrated TFUAR Management for the Third Critical Warning Sign

Phase V: Recovery Planning
- Process 15: Recovery Planning

Clinical tools in the Appendices include the Screening Interview Form, the Strategic Treatment Plan for Relapse Prevention, the Session Documentation Form, the Stress Scale, the Global Assessment of Functioning (GAF) Scale, and the Magic Triangle Relaxation Technique.

If you haven't yet been trained in the CENAPS® Model of Relapse Prevention, I urge you to contact our office at 708-799-5000 to find out about training opportunities. We offer a Six-Day Advanced Certification School, a Three-Day Basic Certification School (which focuses on Warning Sign Identification and Management), One- and Two-Day Skills-Training Workshops, conference presentations, and consultation and inservice training. Training and certification in the CENAPS® Model will improve your effectiveness and stature in the field, as well as your clients' chances of lasting recovery.

If you'd like to find out more about this model from clinicians who are using it every day, call the CENAPS® office at 708-799-5000 for referral to a Certified Relapse Prevention Specialist in your area. For a full list of certified specialists, send a self-addressed, stamped envelope to The CENAPS® Corporation, 18650 Dixie Highway, Homewood, IL 60430.

If you're a self-help group sponsor who is planning to act as a relapse prevention sponsor, please be aware that you're about to make a big commitment in terms of the time and effort spent learning the model and conducting sessions with your sponsee. Please look carefully through the workbook before you make this commitment. If you aren't sure about your ability to keep the commitment—or about your openness to the processes contained in this workbook—it would be better to help your sponsee find someone who is committed to this process. If your sponsee can afford professional Relapse Prevention Therapy using this model, please urge him or her to take that step.

Your role in your client's or sponsee's journey through *Relapse Prevention Therapy* is an essential one. In order to be successful, the comprehensive relapse prevention process must awaken some difficult memories and insights. Without your help and vigilance, your client's or sponsee's success may be jeopardized. I urge you to learn as much as possible about the CENAPS® Brief Therapy Model before you begin this important work.

When you've had a chance to use this model, please let us know how it has worked for you and your clients. We at the CENAPS® Corporation will be happy to hear about your reactions to the workbook, and about the outcome of your efforts.

Thank you for the work that you're about to undertake. The hope that this model brings is very much needed by your clients, and by many others. I wish you the best of success.

Phase I: Stabilization

What?   Lowering your immediate risk of relapse

Beginning to manage your thoughts, feelings, and actions so you can complete the exercises in this workbook

Having a plan that will help you stop any future relapses quickly

Why?   If you're not stable, you can't do this work

Overview

Before you start doing the exercises in this workbook, it's important that you take an honest look at where you are right now. Are you still in active relapse? Are you stable enough physically and psychologically to figure out what went wrong and what you need to do differently next time? In other words, can you manage your thoughts, feelings, urges, and actions well enough to make it through the relapse prevention process?

The screening process is designed to get answers to those kinds of questions. It's the first step of "stabilization." Stabilization is just what it sounds like: making sure you're physically, mentally, and emotionally stable enough to do the work of relapse prevention. If you're not stable, then you'll have a hard time completing these exercises. They can bring up difficult and painful thoughts and feelings. That's why it's recommended that you go through this process with the help of a professional therapist.

Before you do any of the other exercises in this book, complete the four exercises in this section.

- The *Initial Evaluation* will help you find out if you're in recovery now and how stable your recovery is.

- The *Addiction Evaluation* will help you determine whether or not you're addicted, and your risk or stage of addiction.

- The *Assessment of Treatment Need* will show what kinds of help you'll need in order to begin the process of relapse prevention.

- The *Assessment of Mental Status* will help you find out if you're having problems managing your thoughts, feelings, urges, and actions—problems that many people experience in recovery, especially if they're under high levels of stress.

When you've finished these three exercises, show them to your therapist or sponsor. It's strongly recommended that the whole workbook be done under the guidance of your therapist or relapse prevention sponsor. But it's very important that at least this section be shared with someone in a strong position of help and support.

Depending on how serious your physical, mental, or emotional symptoms are, you might need professional help to get stable before you go on with the rest of the workbook. If that's the case, please get the help you need **now.** It would be useless and dangerous to skip over this all-important part of the stabilization process.

A recovery program is only as strong as its foundation.

> **It's strongly recommended that you complete this workbook with the help of a professional therapist trained in the CENAPS® Model of Relapse Prevention Therapy. For a list of names at no cost, send a self-addressed, stamped envelope to The CENAPS® Corporation, 18650 Dixie Highway, Homewood, IL 60430.**

Part 1:   Initial Evaluation

Instructions

Before you can develop a relapse prevention plan, you need to get back in recovery. You need to get stable enough in your abstinence from alcohol and other drugs to think clearly, manage your feelings, and control your behavior. The following questions are designed to help you find out if you're in recovery and how stable your recovery is. Answer each question as honestly as you can.

Section 1: Analysis of the Presenting Problem

The "presenting problem" is the problem that's causing trouble in your life right now—enough trouble to make you willing to get help.

1-1   What's the major problem that caused you to seek help at this time?

_____

_____

1-2   How long has this been a problem? _____

1-3   Why did you decide to seek help now? (Why not last week? Why not next week?)

_____

_____

_____

1-4   What have you done to try to solve this problem?

_____

_____

_____

a.   What approaches have you found helpful?

_____

_____

b.   What approaches have not been helpful?

_____

_____

Section 2: Assessment of Alcohol and Drug Use Patterns

2-1   How is this problem related to your alcohol or drug use?

_____

_____

2-2   Which of the following statements most accurately describes how alcohol and drug use is related to your current problems?

❑ a. Your alcohol or drug use has nothing to do with this problem.

❑ b. Your alcohol or drug use caused this problem.

❑ c. You use alcohol or drugs to manage the pain of having this problem.

❑ d. Your alcohol or drug use has sometimes made this problem worse.

❑ e. Your alcohol or drug use has kept you from solving this problem.

Please explain your answer: _____

_____

_____

2-3   Do you believe that you need to stop using alcohol and drugs in order to solve this problem? ❑ Yes   ❑ No   ❑ Unsure

Please explain your answer? _____

_____

_____

_____

Note: If you've had serious problems with alcohol or drug use, you need to abstain totally from use. This workbook is designed to help you learn how to prevent relapse. If you haven't made a firm decision to get sober and stay that way, it would be helpful for you to visit with a certified addictions counselor and talk about your objections to setting total abstinence as a goal.

2-4   Do you believe that you're addicted to alcohol or drugs? ❑ Yes   ❑ No   ❑ Unsure

Please explain:_____

_____

_____

Note: If you use alcohol or other drugs but you don't believe you're addicted, it will be helpful to complete Process 1, Part 2, *Addiction Evaluation*, (page 27) with a certified addictions counselor. This evaluation will help you determine whether or not you're addicted. If you're reading this book because you've tried unsuccessfully to control your drinking and drugging or stay sober, then you probably are addicted. Part 2 will help you to find out for sure.

2-5　**Denial** is an automatic and unconscious response to thinking about a problem. When you think about the possibility that you have a serious problem with alcohol and drugs, which of the following statements most accurately describes your thoughts?

❑ a. No, not me! My presenting problems have little or nothing to do with my use of alcohol or drugs. (This is called *Absolute Denial*)

❑ b. Yes, but it's not that bad. I have a small problem with alcohol and drugs, but it isn't so bad that I need to do anything about it. The whole thing is being exaggerated or blown out of proportion. (This is called *Minimizing*)

❑ c. Yes, but I have a good reason. My problems with alcohol and drugs are caused by other things that are happening in my life. Once I solve those other problems I'll stop drinking and drugging. (This is called *Rationalizing*)

❑ d. Yes, but it's not my fault. I only have problems with alcohol and drugs because other people are creating so much pain and problems that I have no choice but to use alcohol and drugs to cope with them. (This is called *Blaming*).

❑ e. Other: _____

_____

_____

2-6　Have you stopped using alcohol and drugs?　❑ Yes　❑ No

Note: If you've stopped drinking and using and are currently abstinent, congratulations. Abstinence is the first step toward recovery and relapse prevention. If you answered *no,* you need to get sober. If you can't do this by yourself, call a chemical dependence program in your area. People there can help you stop drinking and drugging. Then you can learn how to prevent relapse.

2-7　How long have you been abstinent?　_____ days, _____ months, _____ years

2-8　What made you decide to stop using alcohol and drugs?

_____

_____

Section 3: Abstinence-Based Symptoms of Addiction

3-1 **Acute Withdrawal** is a set of symptoms that people get when they stop using the alcohol or other drugs that they're addicted to. These symptoms usually start within 24 to 48 hours after people stop using alcohol and drugs, and last for a period of three to ten days.

Are you experiencing any of the following symptoms of acute withdrawal now?

❑ a. Rapid heartbeat   ❑ e. Confusion

❑ b. Shortness of breath   ❑ f. Hearing noises or seeing things that aren't there

❑ c. Nausea or vomiting   ❑ g. Anxiety

❑ d. Shakiness or tremors   ❑ h. Agitation

Note: If you're having any of these symptoms, you need to see a doctor who specializes in alcoholism or drug dependence, or get an evaluation from a certified addictions counselor. You may need medical treatment to help you recover from acute withdrawal.

3-2 **Post-Acute Withdrawal (PAW)** is a set of symptoms created by the long-term after-effects of alcohol and drug poisoning in the brain. These symptoms affect your *mental status* (how you think and feel, the urges you get, and how you act on those urges). The symptoms get worse when you're under high stress, and gradually improve the longer you're sober and working a recovery program.

Mark an "X" in the box in front of the symptoms you're experiencing now.

❑ a. *Difficulty in thinking clearly:* You have trouble concentrating, solving problems, or understanding why things happen. Your thoughts contradict one another, or you find yourself thinking the same things over and over.

❑ b. *Difficulty in managing feelings:* You feel either "numbed out" or overwhelmed by a jumble of emotions, and find it hard to tell others about your feelings when it would be appropriate to do so.

❑ c. *Difficulty remembering things:* You find yourself forgetting things that you learned or that happened a short time ago, or things that you've known a long time.

❑ d. *Difficulty with physical coordination and balance:* You feel dizzy, find yourself spilling or bumping into things, or have slow reflexes.

❑ e. *Difficulty sleeping restfully:* You have a hard time falling asleep, wake up a lot during the night, or have strange dreams. You get too much or too little sleep, and feel tired all the time.

❑ f. *Difficulty in managing stress:* You have a hard time recognizing minor signs of stress, have a hard time relaxing, feel tired or weak, or have a hard time functioning because of your stress. You fear that the stress will make you "fall apart" physically or mentally.

❑ g. *Difficulty staying in touch with reality:* You sometimes get confused about who you are or who other people are, where you are, what time or day it is, or what you're supposed to be doing. You feel dissociated, or disconnected from your body.

Note: If you checked any of these symptoms, you should complete Process 1, Part 4 "Assessment of Mental Status" (page 36). This exercise will help you find out which PAW symptoms you're experiencing and how serious they are.

3-3 **Addictive Preoccupation** is a set of symptoms that shows up in people who are psychologically dependent on alcohol or other drugs. These symptoms cause people to think about or become preoccupied with using or getting ready to use, even when it would be better for them to do other things. Most people who are physically addicted are also psychologically dependent.

Mark an "X" in the box in front of each symptom you're experiencing now.

❑ a. *Euphoric Recall:* When you think about your past experiences with addictive use, you tend to remember and exaggerate the good experiences and forget, block out, or minimize the bad experiences.

❑ b. *Awfulizing Abstinence:* When you think about what it's like to be abstinent, you tend to think about the bad experiences and forget about the good experiences.

❑ c. *Magical Thinking About Use:* When you think about what would happen if you started using in the future, you believe that using would somehow magically fix you or solve your problems.

3-4 **Urges to Use:** This is a set of symptoms that results in a strong and often overwhelming desire to start using again, even though you know it wouldn't be good for you. These urges can be intrusive. That means they force themselves into your consciousness when you don't want them, and they're hard to turn off.

Mark an "X" in the box in front of each symptom you're experiencing now.

❑ a. *Obsession With Alcohol and Drug Use:* Even though you're abstinent, you find that you can't stop thinking about using. (This is what's going on in your head.)

❑ b. *Compulsion to Use Alcohol and Drugs:* Even though you're abstinent, you still have a strong desire or urge to use. (This is an emotional response.)

❑ c. *Craving:* Even though you're abstinent, you still feel a strong physical craving for alcohol and drugs. (These are the signs your body may be giving you, like sweating, shaking, or churning in the pit of your stomach.)

Note: If you find that your addictive preoccupation is so strong that you have a hard time thinking about or concentrating on other things, you should talk to an alcohol and drug abuse counselor. You may need counseling to help you turn off these addictive thoughts.

Section 4: Mental and Emotional Problems

Many people experience mental and emotional problems that need to be addressed in recovery. Mental problems cause difficulty in thinking clearly, logically, and rationally. Emotional problems cause difficulty in recognizing, labeling, communicating, expressing, and managing feelings.

4-1   Have you ever experienced mental and emotional problems when you're not using alcohol or drugs?   ❑ Yes ❑ No   How Severe? (0-10): _____

Please explain: _____

_____

_____

4-2   Have you ever become so confused or disoriented when you weren't using that you had a hard time functioning?   ❑ Yes ❑ No   How Severe? (0-10): _____

Please explain: _____

_____

_____

4-3   Have you ever become so emotionally upset or over-reactive that you had a hard time functioning?   ❑ Yes ❑ No   How Severe? (0-10): _____

Please explain: _____

_____

_____

4-4   Have you ever become so emotionally numb, lethargic (don't care about anything), or dissociated (cut off from others or yourself) that you had a hard time functioning?

❑ Yes ❑ No   How Severe? (0-10): _____

Please explain: _____

_____

_____

4-5   Have you ever become so depressed that you had a hard time functioning?

❑ Yes ❑ No   How Severe? (0-10): _____

Please explain: _____

_____

_____

4-6   Have you ever felt like life isn't worth living, thought about killing yourself, or actually attempted suicide?   ❑ Yes ❑ No   How Severe? (0-10): _____

Please explain: _____

_____

_____

4-7   Have you ever become violent (for example, hit, choked, strangled, physically hurt, or killed another person) or attempted to physically hurt someone else?

❑ Yes ❑ No   How Severe? (0-10): _____

Please explain: _____

_____

_____

4-8   Have you ever forced another person to have sex with you when that person didn't want to?   ❑ Yes ❑ No   How Severe? (0-10): _____

Please explain: _____

_____

_____

4-9   Have you ever been physically or sexually abused by another person?

❑ Yes ❑ No   How Severe? (0-10): _____

Please explain: _____

_____

_____

4-10   If you have been physically or sexually abused, do you ever have painful or distressing memories or dreams of the abuse?

❑ Yes ❑ No   How Severe? (0-10): _____

Please explain: _____

_____

_____

4-11   Have you ever had trouble staying in touch with reality?

❑ Yes ❑ No   How Severe? (0-10): _____

Please explain: _____

_____

_____

4-12   Have you ever had hallucinations (begun seeing, hearing, or feeling things that weren't real)?   ❑ Yes ❑ No   How Severe? (0-10): _____

Please explain: _____

_____

_____

Section 5: Treatment Recommendations

5-1 **Type of Treatment Needed:** Now it's time for you to find out what type of treatment you need in order to recover. There are basically four types of treatment that may be right for you, depending on what you need right now. Please check the box in front of the statement (a through d) that comes closest to your true feelings right now.

❑ a. Other people are telling me that I have a problem and that I need treatment. I don't believe them. I'm not willing to follow through with treatment recommendations unless I'm forced to do it!

> **Note:** If this is how you feel, you probably need a *Motivational Counseling Program* that will help you find out for sure whether or not you're addicted and learn what you need to do to recover.

❑ b. I'm willing to stop using alcohol and drugs, but when I try to stop, my withdrawal, confusion, overreaction, or cravings are so strong that I return to using.

> **Note:** If this is how you feel, you probably need a *Stabilization Program* that will help you recover from acute withdrawal, post-acute withdrawal, and craving.

❑ c. I'm willing and able to stop using alcohol and drugs, but I don't understand what addiction is and I don't know what I need to do to build a recovery program that will keep me in recovery.

> **Note:** If this is how you feel, you probably need a *Primary Recovery Program* that will teach you about the symptoms of chemical dependency, the stages of recovery, how to build a recovery program, and the common warning signs that lead from stable recovery to relapse and how to manage them.

❑ d. I've stopped using alcohol and drugs before, learned what addiction is, and tried to use the recovery tools that were taught in treatment. But when I tried to stay sober, I experienced problems that caused me to relapse.

> **Note:** If this is how you feel, you probably need a *Relapse Prevention Program* that will focus on teaching you how to identify and manage the common warning signs that lead from stable recovery to relapse, and how to customize your recovery program so you can identify and manage critical warning signs as you experience them.

5-2 **Criteria for Entering a Relapse Prevention Program:** In order to benefit from a relapse prevention program, you need to be able to answer "yes" to the following questions:

a. Do you understand what addiction is?

❑ Yes ❑ No ❑ Unsure

b. Do you believe that you're addicted to alcohol and drugs?

❑ Yes ❑ No ❑ Unsure

c. Do you believe that you need to abstain from alcohol and other mood-altering drugs completely in order to recover? ❑ Yes ❑ No ❑ Unsure

d. Have you been able to totally abstain from using alcohol and drugs for a period of at least four weeks? ❑ Yes ❑ No ❑ Unsure

e. Did you try to use self-help programs or other recovery tools to help you abstain?

❑ Yes ❑ No ❑ Unsure

f. Did you become stable in your recovery? In other words, did you recover from acute and post-acute withdrawal, and had your cravings and urges diminished or disappeared to the point where you felt comfortable not using alcohol or drugs?

❑ Yes ❑ No ❑ Unsure

5-3 **Desired Treatment:** Based on what you learned about yourself and your problems by completing this evaluation, which of the following treatment recommendations do you believe would be best for you at this time?

❑ a. **No Treatment:** I'm not willing to accept any kind of treatment.

❑ b. **Motivational Counseling:** I don't really believe that I need treatment, but I'm willing to comply with attendance at an evaluation, education, and motivational counseling program.

❑ c. **Stabilization:** I'm willing to accept treatment, but I need a program that will help me get back in control of my urges to use and help me manage the thoughts, feelings, behaviors, and crises that are disrupting my life.

❑ d. **Primary Recovery:** I'm willing to accept treatment, and believe I need to focus primarily on how to understand my presenting problems and my addiction, and to learn how to build an effective recovery program.

❑ e. **Relapse Prevention:** I've already learned the basics about addiction and recovery, but I haven't been able to stay in recovery using the recovery skills I've already learned. I want to focus primarily on learning how to prevent relapse by learning to identify and manage relapse warning signs and setting up a plan to intervene early if I relapse again.

Part 2:   *Addiction Evaluation*

Instructions

This exercise will help you find out if you're addicted to alcohol or drugs, or if you're at high risk of becoming addicted. RPT is designed for people who have recognized and accepted their addiction and made a firm decision to stay abstinent. This means that they understand the symptoms of addiction and can apply this information to themselves. To complete the exercise:

• Read each question in Section 1 and answer "Yes" or "No" by checking the appropriate box.

• Read the scoring instructions that follow the exercise to find out what your answers mean.

Section 1: The Addiction Questionnaire

1.	Do you use alcohol more than twice a week?	☐ Yes	☐ No
2.	On the days when you use alcohol, do you usually have three drinks or more?	☐ Yes	☐ No
3.	Do you use mood-altering drugs not prescribed by a physician from time to time?	☐ Yes	☐ No
4.	Do you use prescription drugs that change your mood or personality?	☐ Yes	☐ No
5.	Do you sometimes use more than the amount prescribed?	☐ Yes	☐ No
6.	Do you get intoxicated on alcohol or drugs more than twice a year? (You're intoxicated if you use so much that you can't function safely or normally, or if other people think you can't function safely or normally).	☐ Yes	☐ No
7.	When you're not using alcohol or drugs, do you ever put yourself in situations that raise your risk of getting hurt or having problems?	☐ Yes	☐ No
8.	Have you ever felt that you should cut down on your drinking or drug use?	☐ Yes	☐ No
9.	Have other people ever criticized your drinking or drug use, or been annoyed by it?	☐ Yes	☐ No
10.	Have you ever felt bad or guilty about your drinking or drug use?	☐ Yes	☐ No
11.	Have you ever done things while you were using alcohol or drugs that you regretted or that made you feel guilty or ashamed?	☐ Yes	☐ No
12.	Have you ever used alcohol or drugs first thing in the morning to feel better, or to get rid of a hangover?	☐ Yes	☐ No
13.	Have you ever thought that you might have a problem with your drinking or drug use?	☐ Yes	☐ No
14.	Have you ever used alcohol or drugs in larger quantities than you intended? For example, have you ever used more than you wanted to or could afford to?	☐ Yes	☐ No
15.	Have you ever used alcohol or drugs more often than you intended? For example, have you ever planned not to use that day but done it anyway?	☐ Yes	☐ No
16.	Have you ever used alcohol or drugs for longer periods of time than you intended? In other words, have you ever not been able to stop when you planned to?	☐ Yes	☐ No
17.	Have you ever had a desire to cut down or control your use?	☐ Yes	☐ No
18.	Have you ever tried to cut down or control your use?	☐ Yes	☐ No

19.	Do you spend a lot of time getting ready to use alcohol or drugs, using, or recovering from using?	☐ Yes ☐ No
20.	Have you ever failed to meet a major life responsibility because you were intoxicated, hung over, or in withdrawal (having discomfort because you were no longer using)?	☐ Yes ☐ No
21.	Have you given up any work, social, or recreational activities because of alcohol or drug use?	☐ Yes ☐ No
22.	Have you had any physical, psychological, or social problems that were caused by, or made worse by, your alcohol or drug use?	☐ Yes ☐ No
23.	Have you ever continued to use alcohol or drugs even though you knew they were causing physical, psychological, or social problems, or making those problems worse?	☐ Yes ☐ No
24.	Did your tolerance (your ability to use a lot of alcohol and drugs without feeling intoxicated) increase after you started to use?	☐ Yes ☐ No
25.	Do you ever get physically uncomfortable or sick the day after using alcohol or drugs?	☐ Yes ☐ No
26.	Have you ever used alcohol or drugs to keep you from getting sick the next day, or to make a hangover go away?	☐ Yes ☐ No
27.	When you use alcohol or drugs, what do you want those substances to do for you that you believe you can't do without them? _____ _____	
28.	When you use alcohol or drugs, what do you want those substances to help you cope with or escape from that you believe you can't cope with or escape without them? _____ _____	

Section 2: Interpreting the Addiction Questionnaire

2-1   Count how many times you answered "Yes" to any of the questions numbered 1 through 13.

How many "Yes" answers did you check? _____.

2-2   Count how many times you answered "Yes" to any of the questions numbered 14 through 26.

How many "Yes" answers did you check? _____.

2-3   Check the box that most accurately describes your risk of addiction based upon your answers to the above questions.

☐ a. **Low Risk of Addiction:** If you answered "No" to all of the above questions, you're at low risk of addiction.

☐ b. **High Risk:** If you answered "yes" to three or more of the questions numbered 1 through 13, and answered "No" to all of the remaining questions, you are at high risk of addiction.

☐ c. **Early-Stage Addiction:** If you answered "Yes" to more than three of the questions numbered 1 through 13, and answered "Yes" to between three and six of the questions numbered 14 through 26, you are probably in the early stages of addiction.

☐ d. **Middle Stage Addiction:** If you answered "Yes" to more than three of the questions numbered 1 through 13, and answered "Yes" to between six and nine of the questions numbered 14 through 26, you are probably in the middle stages of addiction.

☐ e. **Late Stage Addiction:** If you answered "Yes" to more than three of the questions numbered 1 through 13, and answered "Yes" to more than nine of the questions numbered 14 through 26, you are probably in the late stages of addiction.

2-4   If you believe that alcohol and drugs can do things for you that you can't do without those substances, or believe that they can help you cope with things that you can't cope with unless you're using, you are probably dependent. Only people who are dependent on alcohol or drugs expect these substances to do things for them that they can't do without them.

Section 3: Personal Reaction to the Interpretation of the Addiction Questionnaire

Do you believe the results of this questionnaire accurately describe your current risk of addiction to alcohol or drugs?

☐ Yes   ☐ No ☐ Unsure

Please explain: _____

_____

_____

_____

_____

_____

Part 3:   *Assessment of Treatment Need*

Instructions

This exercise will help you find out if you can benefit from relapse prevention therapy (RPT). RPT is designed for people who have recognized and accepted their addiction, made a firm decision to stay abstinent, and used a recovery program to help them stay abstinent. To complete the exercise:

• Read each question and place a check mark in the box in front of the most appropriate answer.

• Read the scoring instructions that follow the exercise to find out what your answers mean.

_____ 1. How many times have you made serious attempts to stay abstinent?
- ❑ None (0)   ❑ Two (2)   ❑ Four (4)
- ❑ One (1)   ❑ Three (3)   ❑ Five (5)
- ❑ More than five (6)

_____ 2. What's the longest period of time you've been able to stay abstinent?
- ❑ Twelve weeks or more (4)   ❑ Fewer than four weeks (1)
- ❑ Six weeks (3)   ❑ I've never tried long-term abstinence (0)
- ❑ Four weeks (2)

_____ 3. How many times have you been admitted for detoxification from alcohol or drugs?
- ❑ None (0)   ❑ Two (2)   ❑ Four (4)
- ❑ One (1)   ❑ Three (3)   ❑ Five (5)
- ❑ More than five (6)

_____ 4. How many times have you left a detox program before successfully completing the program?
- ❑ None (0)   ❑ Two (2)   ❑ Four (4)
- ❑ One (1)   ❑ Three (3)   ❑ Five (5)
- ❑ More than five (6)

_____ 5. How many times have you been admitted to an inpatient or residential treatment program for chemical dependence (alcoholism or other drug addiction)?
- ❑ None (0)   ❑ Two (2)   ❑ Four (4)
- ❑ One (1)   ❑ Three (3)   ❑ Five (5)
- ❑ More than five (6)

_____ 6. How many times have you left one of those inpatient or residential treatment programs before successfully completing the program?
- ❑ None (0)   ❑ Two (2)   ❑ Four (4)
- ❑ One (1)   ❑ Three (3)   ❑ Five (5)
- ❑ More than five (6)

_____ 7. How many times have you been admitted to an outpatient treatment program for chemical dependence?

- ❑ None (0)
- ❑ Two (2)
- ❑ Four (4)
- ❑ One (1)
- ❑ Three (3)
- ❑ Five (5)
- ❑ More than five (6)

_____ 8. What's the longest time period that you've been continuously involved in an outpatient or aftercare program for chemical dependence?

- ❑ Sixteen weeks or more (4)
- ❑ One to four weeks (1)
- ❑ Nine to sixteen weeks (3)
- ❑ I never attended an outpatient/aftercare program (0)
- ❑ Five to eight weeks (2)

_____ 9. When you were most consistently involved in an outpatient/aftercare program, how many group therapy sessions did you attend in an average month?

- ❑ Ten or more a month (4)
- ❑ Fewer than two a month (1)
- ❑ Six to nine a month (3)
- ❑ I never attended an outpatient/aftercare program (0)
- ❑ Two to five a month (2)

_____ 10. When you were most consistently involved in an outpatient/aftercare program, how many individual therapy sessions did you attend in an average month?

- ❑ Ten or more a month (4)
- ❑ Fewer than two a month (1)
- ❑ Six to nine a month (3)
- ❑ I never attended an outpatient/aftercare program (0)
- ❑ Two to five a month (2)

_____ 11. How many times have you left an outpatient program before successfully completing it?

- ❑ None (0)
- ❑ Two (2)
- ❑ Four (4)
- ❑ One (1)
- ❑ Three (3)
- ❑ Five (5)
- ❑ More than five (6)

_____ 12. When you were most actively involved in your recovery, how many self-help group (AA, NA, etc.) meetings did you attend during an average week?

- ❑ Three or more meetings a week (4)
- ❑ Fewer than one meeting a week (1)
- ❑ Two meetings a week (3)
- ❑ I've never attended self-help group meetings (0)
- ❑ One meeting a week (2)

_____ 13. When you were most actively involved in your recovery, how many times a week did you have conversations with other recovering people, outside of self-help meetings or therapy?

- ❑ Seven or more times a week (3)
- ❑ One or two times a week (1)
- ❑ Three to six times a week (2)
- ❑ Less than once a week (0)

_____ 14. If you were involved in a twelve-step program when you were most actively involved in your recovery, how often did you do a tenth-step inventory (review and evaluate your daily problems and activities) outside of self-help group meetings or therapy?

- ❑ Seven or more times a week (3)
- ❑ One or two times a week (1)
- ❑ Three to six times a week (2)
- ❑ Less than once a week (0)

_____ 15. When you were most actively involved in your recovery, how often did you read recovery-oriented literature or listen to recovery-oriented tapes or speakers outside of self-help meetings or therapy?

❑ Seven or more times a week (3)   ❑ One or two times a week (1)

❑ Three to six times a week (2)   ❑ Less than once a week (0)

_____ 16. Did you have a self-help program sponsor?

❑ Yes (4)   ❑ No (0)

_____ 17. When you were most actively involved in your recovery, how often did you talk to your self-help program sponsor outside of self-help meetings or therapy?

❑ Seven or more times a week (4)   ❑ Less than once a week (1)

❑ Three to six times a week (3)   ❑ Didn't have a sponsor (0)

❑ One or two times a week (2)

_____ 18. If you were involved in a Twelve-Step program, choose the statement that most accurately describes your experience with the fourth and fifth steps of AA.

❑ I completed a written fourth step and talked about it with my sponsor. (3)

❑ I completed a written fourth step but didn't talk about it with my sponsor. (2)

❑ I did a fourth step in my mind, but never wrote it down or talked to anyone about it. (1)

❑ I never did a fourth or fifth step. (0)

_____ 19. How long after you stopped going to self-help meetings did you return to alcohol and drug use?

❑ I was actively attending meetings when I started using again. (5)

❑ Less than a week after I stopped (4)

❑ Between one and three weeks after I stopped (3)

❑ Between four and seven weeks after I stopped (2)

❑ Eight or more weeks after I stopped (1)

_____ 20. Choose the statement that best describes your understanding of and ability to discuss the basic information about chemical dependence.

❑ I can explain it clearly without help. (3)

❑ I can explain it clearly to others with help. (2)

❑ I understand it but can't explain it. (1)

❑ I don't understand it. (0)

_____ 21. Choose the statement that best describes how strongly you believe you're suffering from chemical dependence or your other target problem.

❑ Totally Convinced (3)   ❑ Partially Convinced (1)

❑ Mostly Convinced (2)   ❑ Not Convinced (0)

_____ 22. Choose the statement that best describes the level of pain or inner conflict you experience when you think or talk about your addiction.

❑ No inner conflict when I think or talk about my addiction (3)

❑ Mild discomfort when I talk about it (2)

❑ Serious discomfort when I talk about it (1)

❑ So uncomfortable that I refuse to talk about it (0)

_____ 23. Are you currently in recovery and experiencing pain or having a hard time functioning?

❑ Yes, and I'm afraid I might relapse soon. (3)

❑ Yes, and I'm worried about relapse. (2)

❑ Yes, but I'm not in any immediate danger of relapse. I just want to lower my risk. (1)

❑ No. I'm not experiencing any pain or trouble functioning, and I'm not worried about the immediate risk of relapse. (0)

_____ 24. In the past have you experienced periods of pain or trouble functioning when you were abstinent?

❑ Yes, and it caused me to use in spite of my honest desire not to. (3)

❑ Yes, and it caused me to feel a compulsion to use in spite of my honest desire not to, but I didn't use. (2)

❑ Yes, and it caused me to think about using but not to feel a compulsion to use. I didn't use. (1)

❑ I never experienced periods of pain or difficulty functioning. (0)

_____ 25. When you've been abstinent in the past, have you ever experienced any progressive problems (problems that kept getting worse) that caused you to think about using for relief?

❑ Yes, and it caused me to use in spite of my honest desire not to. (3)

❑ Yes, and it caused me to feel a compulsion to use in spite of my honest desire not to, but I didn't use. (2)

❑ Yes, and it caused me to think about using but not to feel a compulsion to use. I didn't use. (1)

❑ I never experienced progressive problems. (0)

Scoring and Interpretation

1. A number appears after each answer on the questionnaire. For each answer that you selected, write the number assigned to it in the space provided in front of the question (at the left edge of the page).

2. Add all of the numbers on the left side of the page, and write the total score below.

Total Score = _____ out of 52

If your score is:	You probably need:
0 - 24 _____	Primary treatment and active self-help group involvement
25-41 _____	Relapse prevention, self-help group involvement, and primary treatment
41-52 _____	Relapse prevention therapy

Primary Treatment is designed to help people understand, recognize, and accept their addiction and develop a recovery plan.

Relapse Prevention Therapy is designed to help people understand the relapse process, identify and manage warning signs, and set up a revised recovery program that allows for the identification and management of the warning signs that lead to relapse. Most people who relapse need to review a number of basic recovery skills, then develop a relapse prevention plan.

Part 4:   *Assessment of Mental Status*

About This Exercise

The regular and heavy use of alcohol and other drugs can damage the brain. It can take between six and eighteen months of sobriety for the brain to heal. While the brain is healing it's common for recovering people to have a hard time thinking clearly, managing feelings, remembering things, sleeping restfully, being physically coordinated, managing stress, and staying in touch with reality. These are symptoms of a short-term brain impairment that is sometimes called Post-Acute Withdrawal (PAW). During times of high stress these PAW symptoms can get so bad that they get in the way of normal living and working a recovery program. As a result, they can increase the risk of relapse.

If you have serious problems with PAW symptoms, you might need special help to complete the relapse prevention exercises in this workbook. The following questions will help you decide if you are having PAW symptoms and find out how serious your symptoms are. If you find that you are having PAW symptoms often, or that these symptoms are causing problems for you, there are steps you can take. You can make an appointment with a doctor who understands chemical addiction, and with a certified alcohol and drug abuse counselor who can help you set up a plan to manage these symptoms.

Instructions

Answer each of the following questions by checking one or more boxes, according to the individual question instructions. This exercise doesn't give a numerical score like the last two exercises do. But when you read your answers, look for any area where you've checked off more than one symptom, or where you've checked off a box that indicates that this problem occurs even when it isn't triggered by outside stress. Underline those areas. It's important that you show the answers to your therapist and talk about what they mean.

Section 1: Difficulty Thinking Clearly

1-1 **How often do you have difficulty thinking clearly?** (Check only one.)

a. ❑ Less than once a week   d. ❑ Once a day

b. ❑ Once a week   e. ❑ More than once a day

c. ❑ Several times a week

1-2 **When you have difficulty thinking clearly, which of the following do you experience?** (Check all that apply.)

a. ❑ I can't concentrate or pay attention for more than a few minutes.

b. ❑ I can't solve problems that I used to be able to solve easily.

c. ❑ I start thinking the same things over and over again and I have a hard time thinking about anything else.

d. ❑ I have a hard time understanding words or ideas unless they describe people or things that I can actually see or touch.

e. ❑ My thoughts contradict each other and I can't seem to think in an orderly or logical way.

f. ❑ I can't see the causes of problems, even when their causes should be obvious to me.

g. ❑ I can't set priorities or figure out the most important thing to do.

h. ❑ I can't predict the logical consequences of my own or other people's behavior, even when those consequences should be obvious to me.

i. ❑ I can't take appropriate action based on my judgment, or do what I tell myself I need to do.

j. ❑ I can't stop doing things that I know will hurt me or others.

1-3 **Which of the following statements most accurately describes the relationship between stress and the trouble you have in thinking clearly?** (Check only one.)

a. ❑ I find it hard to think clearly, but only when I'm under high stress. In times of low stress my thinking returns to normal.

b. ❑ I have a hard time thinking clearly in times of high stress and in times of low stress. It seems like when I'm sober I can never think clearly.

1-4 **How long do these problems with thinking usually last?** (Check only one.)

a. ❑ Less than 15 minutes   e. ❑ One to three days

b. ❑ 15 minutes to one hour   f. ❑ Four to seven days

c. ❑ One to six hours   g. ❑ Eight days or longer

d. ❑ Seven to 23 hours

1-5 **How well do you function during the times when you have a hard time thinking clearly?** (Check only one.)

a. ❑ I can function normally without extra effort.

b. ❑ I can function normally, but it takes extra effort.

c. ❑ Sometimes I can't function normally, even with extra effort.

d. ❑ Most of the time I can't function normally, even with extra effort.

Section 2: Difficulty Managing Feelings

2-1　**How often do you have a hard time managing feelings?** (Check only one.)

    a. ❑ Less than once a week   d. ❑ Once a day

    b. ❑ Once a week   e. ❑ More than once a day

    c. ❑ Several times a week

2-2　**What feelings do you have the most trouble managing?** (Check all that apply.)

    a. ❑ Strength   g. ❑ Weakness   Others:_____

    b. ❑ Anger   h. ❑ Caring   _____

    c. ❑ Happiness   i. ❑ Sadness   _____

    d. ❑ Safety   j. ❑ Fear   _____

    e. ❑ Satisfaction   k. ❑ Frustration   _____

    f. ❑ Pride   l. ❑ Shame   _____

2-3　**When you have trouble managing feelings, which of the following do you experience?** (Check all that apply.)

    a. ❑ I emotionally overreact (the feelings I have are stronger than I think they should be, considering the problem I'm having or the situation I'm in).

    b. ❑ I feel emotionally numb (I don't know what I'm feeling).

    c. ❑ I shift between emotional overreaction and emotional numbness.

    d. ❑ I'm unable to tell other people what I'm feeling even when it's appropriate or important to do so.

2-4　**Which of the following statements most accurately describes the relationship between stress and your difficulty in managing feelings?** (Check only one.)

    a. ❑ I have trouble managing feelings, but only when I'm under very high stress. During periods of low stress my feelings return to normal.

    b. ❑ I have trouble managing feelings in times of high stress, and in times of low stress. It seems like when I'm sober I can never manage my feelings.

2-5　**How long does this trouble with managing feelings usually last?** (Check only one.)

    a. ❑ Less than 15 minutes   e. ❑ One to three days

    b. ❑ 15 minutes to one hour   f. ❑ Four to seven days

    c. ❑ One to six hours   g. ❑ Eight days or longer

    d. ❑ Seven to 23 hours

2-6　**How well do you function when you're having trouble managing your feelings?** (Check only one.)

    a. ❑ I can function normally without extra effort.

    b. ❑ I can function normally, but it takes extra effort.

    c. ❑ Sometimes I can't function normally, even with extra effort.

    d. ❑ Most of the time I can't function normally, even with extra effort.

Section 3: Difficulty Remembering Things

3-1　**How often do you have a hard time remembering things?**　(Check only one.)

a. ❑ Less than once a week

d. ❑ Once a day

b. ❑ Once a week

e. ❑ More than once a day

c. ❑ Several times a week

3-2　**When you have a hard time remembering things, which of the following do you experience?**　(Check all that apply.)

a. ❑ I forget things that I learn shortly after I learn them.

b. ❑ I can't remember things I knew before.

c. ❑ I can't remember important childhood events.

d. ❑ I can't remember important events in adulthood.

3-3　**Which of the following statements most accurately describes the relationship between stress and your difficulty remembering things?**　(Check only one.)

a. ❑ I have trouble remembering things, but only when I'm under very high stress. During periods of low stress my ability to remember things returns to normal.

b. ❑ I have trouble remembering things in times of high stress and in times of low stress. It seems like when I'm sober I can never remember things.

3-4　**How long does this difficulty remembering things usually last?**　(Check only one.)

a. ❑ Less than 15 minutes

e. ❑ One to three days

b. ❑ 15 minutes to one hour

f. ❑ Four to seven days

c. ❑ One to six hours

g. ❑ Eight days or longer

d. ❑ Seven to 23 hours

3-5　**How well do you function during the times when you're having trouble remembering things?**　(Check only one.)

a. ❑ I can function normally without extra effort.

b. ❑ I can function normally, but it takes extra effort.

c. ❑ Sometimes I can't function normally, even with extra effort.

d. ❑ Most of the time I can't function normally, even with extra effort.

Section 4: Difficulty With Physical Coordination

4-1 **How often do you have trouble with physical coordination?** (Check only one.)

a. ❏ Less than once a week   d. ❏ Once a day

b. ❏ Once a week   e. ❏ More than once a day

c. ❏ Several times a week

4-2 **When you have trouble with physical coordination, which of the following do you experience?** (Check all that apply.)

a. ❏ Dizziness

b. ❏ Trouble with balance

c. ❏ Hand-eye coordination problems

d. ❏ Slow reflexes

e. ❏ Clumsiness

f. ❏ Being accident prone

4-3 **Which of the following statements most accurately describes the relationship between stress and your difficulty with physical coordination?** (Check only one.)

a. ❏ I only have trouble with physical coordination when I'm under very high stress. During periods of low stress, my physical coordination returns to normal.

b. ❏ I have trouble with physical coordination in times of high stress and in times of low stress. It seems like when I'm sober I always have trouble with physical coordination.

4-4 **How long does this difficulty with physical coordination usually last?** (Check only one.)

a. ❏ Less than 15 minutes   e. ❏ One to three days

b. ❏ 15 minutes to one hour   f. ❏ Four to seven days

c. ❏ One to six hours   g. ❏ Eight days or longer

d. ❏ Seven to 23 hours

4-5 **How well do you function during the times when you're having trouble with physical coordination?** (Check only one.)

a. ❏ I can function normally without extra effort.

b. ❏ I can function normally, but it takes extra effort.

c. ❏ Sometimes I can't function normally, even with extra effort.

d. ❏ Most of the time I can't function normally, even with extra effort.

Section 5: Difficulty Sleeping Restfully

5-1   How often do you have a hard time sleeping restfully? (Check only one.)

a. ❑ Less than once a week   d. ❑ Once every night

b. ❑ Once a week   e. ❑ More than once every night

c. ❑ Several times a week

5-2   When you have a hard time sleeping restfully, which of the following do you experience? (Check all that apply.)

a. ❑ Difficulty in falling asleep

b. ❑ Unusual or disturbing dreams

c. ❑ Waking up many times during the night

d. ❑ Not being rested after sleeping

e. ❑ Always feeling tired

f. ❑ Changes in the time of day when I sleep

g. ❑ Sleeping for very long periods of time

h. ❑ None of the above

5-3   Which of the following statements most accurately describes the relationship between stress and your difficulty in sleeping restfully? (Check only one.)

a. ❑ I have trouble sleeping restfully, but only when I'm under very high stress. During periods of low stress my sleep patterns return to normal.

b. ❑ I have trouble sleeping restfully in times of high stress and in times of low stress. It seems like when I'm sober I can never sleep restfully.

5-4   How long does this difficulty with sleeping restfully usually last? (Check only one.)

a. ❑ Less than one night   c. ❑ Four to seven nights

b. ❑ One to three nights   d. ❑ Eight nights or longer

5-5   How well do you function during the times when you're having trouble sleeping restfully? (Check only one.)

a. ❑ I can function normally without extra effort.

b. ❑ I can function normally, but it takes extra effort.

c. ❑ Sometimes I can't function normally, even with extra effort.

d. ❑ Most of the time I can't function normally, even with extra effort.

Section 6: Difficulty Managing Stress

6-1   **How often do you have a hard time managing stress?** (Check only one.)

a. ❑ Less than once a week   d. ❑ Once a day

b. ❑ Once a week   e. ❑ More than once a day

c. ❑ Several times a week

6-2   **When you have trouble managing stress, which of the following do you experience?** (Check all that apply.)

a. ❑ I can't recognize minor signs of stress

b. ❑ I can't relax when I realize I'm under stress

c. ❑ I'm always tired or weak

d. ❑ I'm afraid the stress will make me "fall apart" physically

e. ❑ I'm afraid the stress will make me "fall apart" mentally

f. ❑ I can't function normally because of severe stress

6-3   **Which of the following statements most accurately describes the relationship between stress and your difficulties in managing your stress?** (Check only one.)

a. ❑ I have trouble managing stress, but only when I'm under very high stress. During periods of low stress my ability to manage my stress returns to normal.

b. ❑ I have trouble managing stress in times of high stress and in times of low stress. It seems like when I'm sober I can never manage my stress.

6-4   **How long does this trouble with managing stress usually last?** (Check only one.)

a. ❑ Less than one day   c. ❑ Four to seven days

b. ❑ One to three days   d. ❑ Eight days or longer

6-5   **How well do you function when you're having trouble managing stress?** (Check only one.)

a. ❑ I can function normally without extra effort.

b. ❑ I can function normally, but it takes extra effort.

c. ❑ Sometimes I can't function normally, even with extra effort.

d. ❑ Most of the time I can't function normally, even with extra effort.

Section 7: Difficulty Staying in Touch With Reality

7-1   **How often do you have a hard time staying in touch with reality?** (Check only one.)

a. ❑ Less than once a week   d. ❑ Once a day

b. ❑ Once a week   e. ❑ More than once a day

c. ❑ Several times a week

7-2   **When you have trouble staying in touch with reality, which of the following do you experience?** (Check all that apply.)

a. ❑ I get confused about who I am

b. ❑ I get confused about who the people I'm with are

c. ❑ I get confused about where I am

d. ❑ I get confused about when it is, or what time or day it is

e. ❑ I get confused about what I'm supposed to be doing

f. ❑ I feel dissociated, or disconnected from my body

7-3   **Which of the following statements most accurately describes the relationship between stress and your difficulty staying in touch with reality?** (Check only one.)

a. ❑ I have trouble staying in touch with reality, but only when I'm under very high stress. During periods of low stress my ability to stay in touch with reality returns to normal.

b. ❑ I have trouble staying in touch with reality in times of high stress, and in times of low stress. It seems like when I'm sober I can never stay in touch with reality.

7-4   **How long does this trouble staying in touch with reality usually last?** (Check only one.)

a. ❑ Less than one day   c. ❑ Four to seven days

b. ❑ One to three days   d. ❑ Eight days or longer

7-5   **How well do you function when you're having trouble staying in touch with reality?** (Check only one.)

a. ❑ I can function normally without extra effort.

b. ❑ I can function normally, but it takes extra effort.

c. ❑ Sometimes I can't function normally, even with extra effort.

d. ❑ Most of the time I can't function normally, even with extra effort.

Section 8: Personal Evaluation

8-1 **What's the most important thing you learned about yourself by completing this evaluation of mental status?**

_____

_____

_____

_____

8-2 **What are you feeling as a result of completing this evaluation, and how strongly** (on a scale of one to ten)?

_____

☐ Strong	or ☐ Weak	_____	☐ Safe	or ☐ Threatened	_____
☐ Angry	or ☐ Caring	_____	☐ Fulfilled	or ☐ Frustrated	_____
☐ Happy	or ☐ Sad	_____	☐ Proud	or ☐ Ashamed, guilty	_____

8-3 **What problems do you see as a result of completing this evaluation that could put you at risk of relapse?**

_____

_____

_____

_____

The first step in finding out what went wrong with past recovery efforts is to look at the kinds of things you did to stay in recovery. If your recovery program wasn't strong enough to support continuing recovery, that tells you at least part of the reason you relapsed. On the other hand, if your recovery program was strong, then you can be sure there were some other important problems that led to relapse.

A recovery program is much more than a few meetings each week. An effective recovery program touches every aspect of your life. It involves what you eat, how much you sleep, who you talk to and what you talk about, how you spend your time, and what you expect of yourself and other people. It's the good part of your life that makes all the other good parts possible.

So in taking stock of past recovery efforts, you need to look at a wide variety of things. The two exercises in this process do just that.

- The *Review of Recovery Activities* looks at your past involvement in therapy and self-help groups, your diet and exercise, your ability to relieve stress, your work and recreational activities, and your use of quiet time.

- In *Evaluating Strengths, Weaknesses, and Expectations,* you'll be asked to think about the strong and weak points of past recovery programs, whether you expected too much or too little of yourself, and what you'd like to do differently in future recovery efforts.

As you go through this process you might find a number of ways in which you didn't do all you could to protect your recovery. This isn't meant to make you feel guilty. It's meant to help you understand what went wrong, so you can do it differently in the future. Please don't waste time kicking yourself over this. You have work to do.

The next process (*Immediate Relapse Prevention Plan*) will help you work out a detailed plan for protecting your recovery while you're in Relapse Prevention Therapy. And the final phase of Relapse Prevention Therapy will help you build a strong personal recovery program for ongoing safety and growth. So don't worry about the holes in your past recovery programs. They'll be filled in, many times over, through the work you do in Relapse Prevention Therapy.

Your job right now is to be as honest as possible about past recovery efforts, not judging yourself and not fearing the truth. The truth will be your best friend throughout the relapse prevention process. It's your one true hope for continuing recovery and a happy, productive life.

Schedule of Recovery Activities

Process 2

Part 1:   Review of Recovery Activities

Instructions

Please answer the following questions. Think carefully about what you did to manage your recovery during your last efforts to stay sober. For each question:

1. check the appropriate box(es),

2. add up the numbers of points indicated for the box(es) you checked, and

3. write the total number of points on the line for that question at the left edge of the page.

_____   **1. How often did you attend group or individual counseling sessions?**

   ❑ Never (0)   ❑ Sometimes (1)   ❑ Often (2)   ❑ Very Often (3)

Please describe the type of counseling you participated in and your personal reactions to that counseling:

_____

_____

_____

_____

_____   **2. How often did you regularly attend self-help recovery group meetings?**

   ❑ Never (0)   ❑ Sometimes (1)   ❑ Often (2)   ❑ Very Often (3)

   a. How many meetings a week did you attend? _____

   b. What types of meetings did you attend most often?

      ❑ Open   ❑ Closed   ❑ Speaker   ❑ Step   ❑ Discussion

   c. Did you have a home group? ❑ Yes   ❑ No

   d. Please describe your personal reaction to the meetings.

_____

_____

_____

_____

_____

_____

_____ 3. **How often did you talk to your sponsor in your self-help group (AA, NA, etc.)? If you didn't have a sponsor, check "never."**

❑ Never (0)   ❑ Sometimes (1)   ❑ Often (2)   ❑ Very Often (3)

If you had a sponsor, please describe your relationship with him or her, including the good and bad points of that relationship.

_____

_____

_____

_____

_____

_____

_____ 4. **The following is a list of the Twelve Steps (of AA, NA, CA, etc.). For each step, check the answer that most clearly describes your past completion of the tasks required for that step.**

Step 1: We admitted we were powerless over alcohol—that our lives had become unmanageable.

❑ Fully completed (2)   ❑ Partially completed (1)   ❑ Didn't start (0)

Step 2: Came to believe that a Power greater than ourselves could restore us to sanity.

❑ Fully completed (2)   ❑ Partially completed (1)   ❑ Didn't start (0)

Step 3: Made a decision to turn our will and our lives over to the care of God *as we understood Him.*

❑ Fully completed (2)   ❑ Partially completed (1)   ❑ Didn't start (0)

Step 4: Made a searching and fearless moral inventory of ourselves.

❑ Fully completed (2)   ❑ Partially completed (1)   ❑ Didn't start (0)

Step 5: Admitted to God, to ourselves, and to another human being the exact nature of our wrongs.

❑ Fully completed (2)   ❑ Partially completed (1)   ❑ Didn't start (0)

Step 6: Were entirely ready to have God remove all these defects of character.

❑ Fully completed (2)   ❑ Partially completed (1)   ❑ Didn't start (0)

Step 7: Humbly asked Him to remove our shortcomings.

❑ Fully completed (2)   ❑ Partially completed (1)   ❑ Didn't start (0)

Step 8: Made a list of all persons we had harmed, and became willing to make amends to them all.

❑ Fully completed (2)   ❑ Partially completed (1)   ❑ Didn't start (0)

Step 9: Made direct amends to such people wherever possible, except when to do so would injure them or others.

❑ Fully completed (2)   ❑ Partially completed (1)   ❑ Didn't start (0)

Step 10: Continued to take personal inventory and when we were wrong promptly admitted it.

❑ Fully completed (2)   ❑ Partially completed (1)   ❑ Didn't start (0)

Step 11: Sought through prayer and meditation to improve our conscious contact with God *as we understood Him*, praying only for knowledge of His will for us and the power to carry it out.

❑ Fully completed (2) ❑ Partially completed (1) ❑ Didn't start (0)

Step 12: Having had a spiritual awakening as the result of these steps, we tried to carry this message to alcoholics, and to practice these principles in all our affairs.

❑ Fully completed (2) ❑ Partially completed (1) ❑ Didn't start (0)

Total Points _____ + _____ = _____

Please describe how you felt about working the steps, which steps you found helpful, and which steps you found not to be helpful.

_____

_____

_____

_____

_____

_____

5. **How often did you eat three well balanced meals a day?**

❑ Never (0) ❑ Sometimes (1) ❑ Often (2) ❑ Very Often (3)

Please describe your average daily eating habits at that time.

Breakfast: _____

Morning Snack: _____

Lunch: _____

Dinner: _____

Evening Snack: _____

Other: _____

6. **How often did you eat foods that were high in sugar (candy, chocolate, cakes, ice cream, etc.)?**

❑ Very Often (0) ❑ Often (1) ❑ Sometimes (2) ❑ Never (3)

Please describe your favorite high-sugar or binge foods and how you feel before, during, and after an episode of heavy eating.

_____

_____

_____

_____ **7. How often did you drink beverages containing caffeine?**

❑ Very Often (0)   ❑ Often (1)   ❑ Sometimes (2)   ❑ Never (3)

a. How much caffeine would you consume in a normal day?

❑ Cups of coffee   = _____.

❑ Cans of caffeinated soft drinks   = _____.

❑ Other (specify): _____ = _____.

b. How often did you notice a change in mood (becoming more stimulated, energized, alert, or wired) as a result of your use of caffeine?

❑ Never (0)   ❑ Sometimes (1)   ❑ Often (2)   ❑ Very Often (3)

_____ **8. How often did you use nicotine (including cigarettes, cigars, and smokeless tobacco)?**

❑ Very Often (0)   ❑ Often (1)   ❑ Sometimes (2)   ❑ Never (3)

_____ **9. How often did you exercise at least three times a week for at least 20 to 30 minutes at a time, in a way that was strenuous enough to make you breathe hard and start to sweat?**

❑ Never (0)   ❑ Sometimes (1)   ❑ Often (2)   ❑ Very Often (3)

Please describe your regular exercise habits.

_____

_____

_____

_____

_____ **10. How often did you use relaxation techniques?**

❑ Never (0)   ❑ Sometimes (1)   ❑ Often (2)   ❑ Very Often (3)

Please check the types of relaxation exercises you used, and how often you used them.

Types of Relaxation Exercises Used	How Often You Used Them			
	Never	Sometimes	Very Often	Often
a. Breathing exercises	❑	❑	❑	❑
b. Muscle relaxation	❑	❑	❑	❑
c. Guided Imagery	❑	❑	❑	❑
d. Conscious relaxation of parts of your body	❑	❑	❑	❑
e. Biofeedback	❑	❑	❑	❑

_____ **11. How often did you use prayer and meditation on a regular basis to help you recover?**

❑ Never (0)   ❑ Sometimes (1)   ❑ Often (2)   ❑ Very Often (3)

Please describe the types of prayer and meditation you found most helpful and least helpful.

_____

_____

_____

_____

_____ 12. **How often did you talk to people about your life and ask for feedback on a regular basis?**

❏ Never (0)   ❏ Sometimes (1)   ❏ Often (2)   ❏ Very Often (3)

Please describe the main people you talked to and what you talked to them about.

_____ 13. **How often did you try to solve problems as soon as they came up?**

❏ Never (0)   ❏ Sometimes (1)   ❏ Often (2)   ❏ Very Often (3)

a. Please describe the types of problems you tried to solve as they came up.

_____

_____

_____

_____

_____

_____

_____

b. Please describe the types of problems you tended to put off solving.

_____

_____

_____

_____

_____

_____

_____

_____ 14. **How often did you schedule time for recreational activities? (Recreational activities should be activities that you consider fun.)**

❏ Never (0)   ❏ Sometimes (1)   ❏ Often (2)   ❏ Very Often (3)

a. Please describe the recreational activities you enjoyed most.

_____

_____

_____

_____

b. Please describe the recreational activities you least enjoyed and why you didn't enjoy them.

_____

_____

_____

_____

Did you take part in many recreational activities that you didn't enjoy? ❏ Yes ❏ No

If so, why?

_____

_____

_____

_____

___ **15. How often did you schedule time for activities with your family?**

❏ Never (0) ❏ Sometimes (1) ❏ Often (2) ❏ Very Often (3)

Please describe your current relationship with the members of your family. Describe how your addiction and tendency to relapse has affected your relationship with your family.

_____

_____

_____

_____

_____

_____

_____

___ **16. How often did you schedule time to spend with friends?**

❏ Never (0) ❏ Sometimes (1) ❏ Often (2) ❏ Very Often (3)

Please list your current friends and how close you feel to them.

_____

_____

_____

_____

_____

_____

_____

_____

_____

_____

_____

_____ **17. How often did you work on a regular schedule that didn't interfere with recovery or recreational activities?**

❑ Never (0)   ❑ Sometimes (1)   ❑ Often (2)   ❑ Very Often (3)

Please describe your typical work week during that period. If you tended to over-work (more than 8 hours a day or 40 hours a week), please describe how many hours you worked and why you worked so many hours.

_____

_____

_____

_____

_____

_____

_____

_____

_____

_____

_____ **18. How often did you schedule some quiet time on a regular basis to think and plan your recovery program?**

❑ Never (0)   ❑ Sometimes (1)   ❑ Often (2)   ❑ Very Often (3)

Please describe your feelings and reactions to planning periods of quiet time for yourself and your recovery.

_____

_____

_____

_____

_____

_____

_____

_____

Scoring and Interpretation

1. A number appears after each answer on the questionnaire. For each answer that you selected, write the number assigned to it in the space provided in front of the question (at the left edge of the page).

2. Add all of the numbers on the left side of the page, and write the total score below.

   Total Score = _____ out of 75

If your score is:

0 - 25 points	A lack of recovery support activities was probably a primary factor in your relapse.
26 - 50 points	A lack of recovery support activities was probably a strong influence on your past relapse, but there are probably other areas that need to be considered in terms of stresses, problems, and relapse warning signs.
51 - 75 points	Other problems probably interfered with the effectiveness of your recovery program.

Schedule of Recovery Activities

Part 2: *Evaluating Strengths, Weaknesses, and Expectations*

1. **Strengths in Past Recovery Programs:** What things did you do in your past recovery programs that were helpful and can act as a foundation as you plan a new and more effective program?

    _____

    _____

    _____

    _____

    _____

    _____

    _____

    _____

    _____

    _____

2. **Weaknesses in Past Recovery Programs:** What things did you do or fail to do in your past recovery programs that weakened you or set you up to relapse?

    _____

    _____

    _____

    _____

    _____

    _____

    _____

    _____

    _____

    _____

3. **Unrealistic Expectations:** Did you expect too much of yourself and try to do too much, too quickly in your past recovery efforts?

❑ Yes   ❑ No

Please explain why you answered the question as you did.

_____

_____

_____

_____

_____

_____

_____

_____

_____

_____

4. **Low Expectations:** Did you expect too little of yourself and fail to practice the basics of recovery?

❑ Yes   ❑ No

Please explain why you answered the question as you did.

_____

_____

_____

_____

_____

_____

_____

_____

_____

_____

5. **Inappropriate Focus:** Did you try to do the wrong kinds of things in your past recovery efforts? In other words, did you focus on the easy parts of recovery by doing things that made you look good, while you avoided or denied the harder parts of recovery that would have dealt with your major problems?

❑ Yes   ❑ No

Please explain why you answered the question as you did.

_____

_____

_____

_____

_____

_____

_____

_____

_____

_____

_____

6. **Desired Change:** Please list the things you'll need to do differently in your recovery if you want to avoid relapse in the future.

_____

_____

_____

_____

_____

_____

_____

_____

_____

_____

_____

Overview

The *Immediate Relapse Prevention Plan* is an important part of Stabilization. It gives you some solid ground to stand on while you do the often-challenging work of Relapse Prevention Therapy. The *Immediate Relapse Prevention Plan* is made up of five parts:

- A list of *Telephone Contacts,* people you can call if you feel emotionally shaky or if you feel an urge to start using.

- An exercise for *Identifying Immediate High-Risk Situations,* situations you might be involved in within the next several weeks that might make you feel like using.

- A technique for *Managing Immediate High-Risk Situations* and an opportunity to practice this technique on each of the high-risk situations you've identified. This exercise helps you identify the thoughts, feelings, urges, and actions you tend to have in those situations; and think about safer ways of managing those thoughts, feelings, urges, and actions.

- A technique for *Challenging Relapse Justifications,* the irrational thoughts you use to talk yourself into relapsing. This technique includes identifying your personal relapse justifications and the logical form that these statements take, and finding meaningful ways of challenging these justifications.

- A *Relapse Prevention Pledge* that you can use on a regular basis to renew and strengthen your commitment to recovery, and to lower your levels of stress, craving, and addictive thinking when those problems come up.

No matter how strong your resolve to avoid relapse is, you will be faced with high-risk situations. You might daily find yourself in a family, a job, or a neighborhood where alcohol or drugs are an important part of the culture. You might go to a wedding—or have dinner in a restaurant that serves drinks—with friends, co-workers, or family members who are drinking. Or you might have to deal with people whose words or actions raise painful or difficult emotions in you. You might feel like exploding or melting into the woodwork.

Sooner or later the relapse justifications set in. They seem so reasonable at first. "I can never relax and enjoy myself while I'm in recovery ..." "Since I've been in recovery my problems with my family have gotten worse, not better ..." "My boss still doesn't trust me even though I'm in recovery ..." And the next step is always something like, "... so I might as well start using again." That's when the relapse prevention pledge and the list of telephone contacts come in handy.

While you're dialing the phone you can say the pledge to yourself over and over, to quiet your thoughts, calm your feelings, and lower your craving levels. Then you can talk to people you trust, telling them where you've been, what you've been doing, what you're thinking, what you're feeling, and what you have an urge to do. They can help you get your thoughts, feelings, urges, and actions back on track so you can stay in recovery and continue to do this work.

As time goes on in Relapse Prevention Therapy, you'll have many more—and more powerful—tools for coping with high-risk situations and relapse justifications. It will get easier. Meanwhile, these few tools can keep you going, keep you safe, and keep renewing your hope.

Instructions

List the names and telephone numbers of five people you can call if you feel an urge to start addictive use, people who will support you in staying in recovery. Be sure to list at least two people you can call at night.

1.   Name: _____   Home phone: _____

     Available: ❑ Day ❑ Evening ❑ Night   Work phone: _____

2.   Name: _____   Home phone: _____

     Available: ❑ Day ❑ Evening ❑ Night   Work phone: _____

3.   Name: _____   Home phone: _____

     Available: ❑ Day ❑ Evening ❑ Night   Work phone: _____

4.   Name: _____   Home phone: _____

     Available: ❑ Day ❑ Evening ❑ Night   Work phone: _____

5.   Name: _____   Home phone: _____

     Available: ❑ Day ❑ Evening ❑ Night   Work phone: _____

Part 2:   *Identifying Immediate High-Risk Situations*

List three situations that you may be involved in within the next several weeks that could cause you to feel like using alcohol or drugs.

1.   **Immediate High-Risk Situation #1**   **Title:** _____

   Description: _____

_____

_____

_____

_____

_____

   How likely is it that this situation will cause you to relapse?

   ❑ Very High Risk   ❑ High Risk   ❑ Low Risk   ❑ Very Low Risk

2.   **Immediate High-Risk Situation #2**   **Title:** _____

   Description: _____

_____

_____

_____

_____

_____

   How likely is it that this situation will cause you to relapse?

   ❑ Very High Risk   ❑ High Risk   ❑ Low Risk   ❑ Very Low Risk

3.   **Immediate High-Risk Situation #3**   **Title:** _____

   Description: _____

_____

_____

_____

_____

_____

   How likely is it that this situation will cause you to relapse?

   ❑ Very High Risk   ❑ High Risk   ❑ Low Risk   ❑ Very Low Risk

Section 1: Managing Immediate High Risk Situation #1

Title of High-Risk Situation #1: _____

1-1   General Mismanagement

a. How have you mismanaged this kind of situation in the past in a way that increased your risk of relapse?

_____

_____

_____

_____

b. How could you manage this kind of situation more effectively in the future to lower your risk of relapse?

_____

_____

_____

_____

1-2   Thought Management

a. What irrational thoughts are you likely to have in this situation that might lead you to relapse?

_____

_____

_____

_____

b. What's another way of thinking about this situation that can help you stay sober and avoid relapse?

_____

_____

_____

_____

1-3   Feeling Management

a. What feelings are you likely to have in this situation that might lead you to relapse?

_____

_____

_____

_____

b. What's another way of managing your feelings in this situation that can help you stay sober and avoid relapse?

_____

_____

_____

_____

1-4   Self-Destructive Urges

a. What are you likely to have an urge to do in this situation that might cause you to relapse?

_____

_____

_____

_____

b. What might be an effective way of fighting self-destructive urges in this situation?

_____

_____

_____

_____

1-5   Self-Defeating Actions

a. What have you done in this kind of situation that has increased your risk of relapse?

_____

_____

_____

_____

b. What's another way of acting in this situation that can help you stay sober and avoid relapse?

_____

_____

_____

_____

Section 2: Managing Immediate High-Risk Situation #2

Title of High-Risk Situation #2: _____

2-1   General Mismanagement

    a. How have you mismanaged this kind of situation in the past in a way that increased your risk of relapse?

_____

_____

_____

_____

_____

    b. How could you manage this kind of situation more effectively in the future to lower your risk of relapse?

_____

_____

_____

_____

2-2   Thought Management

    a. What irrational thoughts are you likely to have in this situation that might lead you to relapse?

_____

_____

_____

_____

    b. What's another way of thinking about this situation that can help you stay sober and avoid relapse?

_____

_____

_____

_____

2-3   Feeling Management

    a. What feelings are you likely to have in this situation that might lead you to relapse?

_____

_____

_____

b. What's another way of managing your feelings in this situation that can help you stay sober and avoid relapse?

_____

_____

_____

_____

2-4   Self-Destructive Urges

a. What are you likely to have an urge to do in this situation that might cause you to relapse?

_____

_____

_____

_____

b. What might be an effective way of fighting self-destructive urges in this situation?

_____

_____

_____

_____

_____

2-5   Self-Defeating Actions

a. What have you done in this kind of situation that has increased your risk of relapse?

_____

_____

_____

_____

b. What's another way of acting in this situation that can help you stay sober and avoid relapse?

_____

_____

_____

_____

Section 3: Managing Immediate High-Risk Situation #3

Title of High-Risk Situation #3: _____

3-1   General Mismanagement

   a. How have you mismanaged this kind of situation in the past in a way that increased your risk of relapse?

   _____
   _____
   _____
   _____

   _____

   b. How could you manage this kind of situation more effectively in the future to lower your risk of relapse?

   _____
   _____
   _____

   _____

3-2   Thought Management

   a. What irrational thoughts are you likely to have in this situation that might lead you to relapse?

   _____
   _____
   _____

   b. What's another way of thinking about this situation that can help you stay sober and avoid relapse?

   _____
   _____
   _____
   _____

3-3   Feeling Management

   a. What feelings are you likely to have in this situation that might lead you to relapse?

   _____
   _____
   _____
   _____

b. What's another way of managing your feelings in this situation that can help you stay sober and avoid relapse?

_____

_____

_____

_____

3-4   Self-Destructive Urges

a. What are you likely to have an urge to do in this situation that might cause you to relapse?

_____

_____

_____

_____

b. What might be an effective way of fighting self-destructive urges in this situation?

_____

_____

_____

_____

3-5   Self-Defeating Actions

a. What have you done in this kind of situation that has increased your risk of relapse?

_____

_____

_____

b. What's another way of acting in this situation that can help you stay sober and avoid relapse?

_____

_____

_____

_____

Part 4:   Challenging Relapse Justifications

A "relapse justification" is an irrational way of thinking that convinces you that relapsing will somehow make you a better person or solve your problems.

Section 1: Relapse Justification #1

1-1   Identifying Relapse Justification #1

I can convince myself that I'm justified in using alcohol and/or drugs by saying to myself:

_____

_____

_____

_____

Relapse justifications often start with a belief that life is somehow more difficult or painful in recovery, and end with a conclusion that you must relapse in order to be a better person or solve your problems.

Rewrite Relapse Justification #1 in that two-part format:

Since I believe that ... _____

_____

_____

_____

... this means I have to relapse in order to ..._____

_____

_____

_____

1-2   Challenging Relapse Justification #1

I can challenge this relapse justification and talk myself into staying sober by saying to myself :

_____

_____

_____

_____

_____

_____

Section 2: Relapse Justification #2

2-1 Identifying Relapse Justification #2

I can convince myself that I'm justified in using alcohol and/or drugs by saying to myself:

_____

_____

_____

_____

Relapse justifications often start with a belief that life is somehow more difficult or painful in recovery, and end with a conclusion that you must relapse in order to be a better person or solve your problems.

Rewrite Relapse Justification #2 in that two-part format:

Since I believe that ... _____

_____

_____

_____

... this means I have to relapse in order to ..._____

_____

_____

_____

2-2 Challenging Relapse Justification #2

I can challenge this relapse justification and talk myself into staying sober by saying to myself :

_____

_____

_____

_____

_____

_____

Section 3: Relapse Justification #3

3-1   Identifying Relapse Justification #3

I can convince myself that I'm justified in using alcohol and/or drugs by saying to myself:

_____

_____

_____

_____

Relapse justifications often start with a belief that life is somehow more difficult or painful in recovery, and end with a conclusion that you must relapse in order to be a better person or solve your problems.

Rewrite Relapse Justification #3 in that two-part format:

Since I believe that ... _____

_____

_____

_____

... this means I have to relapse in order to ..._____

_____

_____

_____

3-2   Challenging Relapse Justification #3

I can challenge this relapse justification and talk myself into staying sober by saying to myself :

_____

_____

_____

_____

_____

_____

Part 5:   Relapse Prevention Pledge

In recovery you might not create as many problems for yourself as you did in relapse or before recovery started. But problems still happen, and for a while they can seem more painful or upsetting in recovery because you're feeling your emotions instead of trying to escape them with alcohol or drugs. To get through these painful and upsetting times without relapsing, you need to make a firm commitment to recovery.

The following pledge can help you remind yourself that recovery is a promise you've made to yourself, a promise that you can't afford to break. It can help you remember that alcohol and drugs actually make things much worse, even though you might feel like they'll make things better.

Copy this pledge in your own handwriting on a piece of paper, on a three-by-five card, or wherever you'll be likely to find it most easily. Read it out loud to yourself every morning and every night. Read it more often in times of stress, or when you feel the cravings or addictive thinking coming back. You can read it every hour, or even every five minutes—whatever it takes to lower your levels of stress and craving.

**No matter what happens today,
I won't relapse.**

**I won't relapse, because if I do
it will make things worse, not better.**

**If I don't relapse,
this pain will pass
and I will be free in recovery.**

Overview

Many people mistakenly believe that, if they do relapse, they have no choice but to keep using addictively until they lose everything and "hit bottom" again. That's not true. It's one of the lies your addictive thinking would like you to believe: "Well, since you've already blown it, you might as well really knock yourself out," says the addictive thinking. "Once you've had enough of the relapse you'll be more motivated to get back into recovery."

The trouble is there's no such thing as "enough," no matter how long your relapse lasts. And it's harder to recover from a longer relapse that's done more damage to your body, brain, emotions, relationships, finances, and work history. It's much better to stop the relapse early, when you still have hope, dignity, and friends you haven't pushed away.

The process of *Early Intervention Planning* has one central aim: to recruit and train a small team of people who will help you get back into recovery quickly if you do relapse in the future—your *Early Intervention Team*. This process has four parts:

- The *Client Intervention Worksheet,* in which you examine the things you can do to get back in recovery quickly if you should relapse, the three people you'd choose to support you in your efforts to get back in recovery, and the things that those people could do or say that would really help you accept the help you need to get back on track.

- The *Intervention Worksheet for Team Members,* which helps your support people examine the ways in which your past relapses have affected them, the things they can do to take care of themselves if you relapse again, and the things they'd be willing to do to help you get back into recovery.

- The *Final Intervention Agreement,* a signed commitment that you and each of your intervention team members make to one another. This commitment addresses the thoughts, feelings, urges, and actions that would otherwise threaten to keep you out of recovery.

- *Intervention Letters,* written to you—one letter from yourself, and one from each of your Early Intervention Team members. Guidelines are provided, along with sample intervention letters.

Effective intervention is much different from the nagging, guilt-trips, and angry responses you may have received in the past from people who were concerned about your use. It's likely that those kinds of responses usually made things worse. Effective intervention is a process that you set in motion long before the relapse happens.

First you hold a training for the three people you've chosen to be on your Early Intervention Team. At that training, your therapist or relapse prevention sponsor helps your team members understand how addiction, recovery, relapse, and intervention work. With the help of the *Client Intervention Worksheet,* you tell your team members how you believe they can best help you if you should relapse again. With the help of the *Intervention Worksheet for Team Members,* they explore their own reactions to your relapse patterns, their own needs for self-care, and what they would be willing and able to do to help you if you relapse in the future.

At the training you fill out and sign a copy of the *Final Intervention Agreement* with each of your Intervention Team members. Then your therapist or relapse prevention sponsor explains the intervention letter-writing process and passes out copies of the intervention letter instructions, the sample intervention letters, and an early intervention letter that you've written to yourself following those instructions. Each member is instructed to send you a copy of that letter, along with his or her own intervention letter to you, if you relapse in the future.

Choosing Early Intervention Team Members

It's important to choose your team members carefully. Not everyone wants to be involved, and not everyone who wants to be involved will be able to help you. Look for people who:

- Have a solid recovery program, or have never had a problem with chemical dependency.
- Understand chemical dependence as a disease, or are willing to learn about the disease and recovery from it.
- Support your need to abstain from all self-defeating behavior.
- Support relapse prevention planning as part of your recovery plan.
- You should **not** involve people who:
- Are chemically dependent and actively using alcohol or other drugs (this includes heavy drinkers and illegal drug users who deny that they're addicted).
- Don't understand chemical dependence as a disease or aren't willing to learn about it.
- Don't support your need to abstain from all self-defeating behavior.
- Don't support relapse prevention planning as part of your recovery plan.

Members of your Intervention Team must be willing to make commitments, not only to helping you recover, but also to practicing their own programs of personal recovery. Remember, your addiction has affected everyone who has been involved with you. Family members, close friends, employers, even people in your self-help groups may have been hurt by your relapse history.

Some of the people who care most deeply about you may have developed their own problems with anger, resentment, trying to control your addictive use, or trying to protect you from the consequences of your use. Until they can resolve those kinds of issues, they won't be in a good position to help you. They might try to control your recovery and do for you some of the things you'll need to do for yourself.

If any of the people you're considering for your Early Intervention Team are members of Al-Anon, they might be concerned when you first invite them, thinking that their involvement might violate their Al-Anon recovery. You can reassure them that it won't violate their Al-Anon program. Detachment from the symptoms of addictive disease is an important part of the Al-Anon program, but it's possible for people to detach and still warn you if they see signs of relapse. Working with you to plan a course of action, they can detach with love, and still take all the necessary steps to protect themselves from the consequences of your relapse.

One of the biggest problems in the past may have been ineffective communication about addiction, recovery, and relapse—ineffective communication by all concerned. Working on your *Early Intervention Plan* together will give you and those who care about you a chance to heal your communication and restore dignity to all who are involved in this process.

Early Intervention Plan

Part 1:   *Client Intervention Worksheet*

Section 1: Actions That You Can Take

1-1   As someone who has had a tendency to relapse, think about what you can do to stop the relapse early, should it occur. This might include things like calling your self-help program sponsor, going to a treatment program, or calling your counselor. Write out the things that you could do on your own to stop a relapse early.

_____

_____

_____

_____

1-2   If you relapse, what thoughts might motivate you to stop the relapse?

_____

_____

_____

1-3   How could you manage your feelings in ways that would help you stop the relapse?

_____

_____

_____

1-4   How could you fight or resist your urges or cravings?

_____

_____

_____

1-5   Where could you go to help you stop the relapse?

_____

_____

_____

1-6   What things could you do to help you stop the relapse?

_____

_____

_____

Section 2: Choosing Relapse Support People

When addicts start using substances addictively they're often out of control. And even if a relapse starts with a plan to carefully control use, it can reach this out-of-control stage very quickly. Loss of control means that you can't control your thinking, judgment, or behavior. As a result, you can't stop drinking and drugging by yourself. The good news is that other people can do things to help you stop addictive use and get back in control. Name three people you can contact if you relapse—possibly a spouse or significant other, a close friend, and a self-help group sponsor.

2-1   **Person #1:** _____ Day Phone: _____

Evening Phone: _____

Why did you choose this person?_____

_____

_____

_____

_____

2-2   **Person #2:** _____ Day Phone: _____

Evening Phone: _____

Why did you choose this person?_____

_____

_____

_____

_____

2-3   **Person #3:** _____ Day Phone: _____

Evening Phone: _____

Why did you choose this person?_____

_____

_____

_____

_____

On the next three pages you'll be asked to think about things each of these people can say or do if you relapse. However, addiction is a disease of denial. **When addicts are actively using, they can rationalize and resist even the most honest and persuasive argument.** As a result, they can sabotage others' ability to help them. So as you write about each person, you'll also be asked to think about how you might sabotage their efforts to help you get back into recovery. Write down advice or recommendations on how they can effectively help you stop your relapse if you try to refuse their help.

Section 3: Actions for Person #1

3-1   If you relapse, how could Person #1 help you get back in recovery?

_____

_____

_____

3-2   How could this person help you start thinking in ways that might help stop the relapse?

_____

_____

3-3   How could this person help you manage your feelings in ways that might stop the relapse?

_____

_____

3-4   How could this person help you fight or resist your urges or cravings?

_____

_____

3-5   What things could this person do, or suggest that you do, to help stop the relapse?

_____

_____

3-6   If Person #1 tried to get you into treatment and you refused, what would be the most effective strategies for getting you into treatment, even if you didn't want to go?

_____

_____

_____

3-7   How could this person help you think in ways that might help you accept treatment?

_____

_____

3-8   How could this person help you manage your feelings so you could accept treatment?

_____

_____

3-9   How could this person help you fight or resist your urge to stay out of treatment?

_____

_____

3-10   What things could this person do, or suggest that you do, to help you accept treatment?

_____

_____

Section 4: Actions for Person #2

4-1　If you relapse, how could Person #2 help you get back in recovery?

_____

_____

_____

4-2　How could this person help you start thinking in ways that might help stop the relapse?

_____

_____

4-3　How could this person help you manage your feelings in ways that might stop the relapse?

_____

_____

4-4　How could this person help you fight or resist your urges or cravings?

_____

_____

4-5　What things could this person do, or suggest that you do, to help stop the relapse?

_____

_____

4-6　If Person #2 tried to get you into treatment and you refused, what would be the most effective strategies for getting you into treatment, even if you didn't want to go?

_____

_____

_____

4-7　How could this person help you think in ways that might help you accept treatment?

_____

_____

4-8　How could this person help you manage your feelings so you could accept treatment?

_____

_____

4-9　How could this person help you fight or resist your urge to stay out of treatment?

_____

_____

4-10　What things could this person do, or suggest that you do, to help you accept treatment?

_____

_____

Section 5: Actions for Person #3

5-1   If you relapse, how could Person #3 help you get back in recovery?

_____

_____

5-2   How could this person help you start thinking in ways that might help stop the relapse?

_____

_____

5-3   How could this person help you manage your feelings in ways that might stop the relapse?

_____

_____

5-4   How could this person help you fight or resist your urges or cravings?

_____

_____

5-5   What things could this person do, or suggest that you do, to help stop the relapse?

_____

_____

5-6   If Person #3 tried to get you into treatment and you refused, what would be the most effective strategies for getting you into treatment, even if you didn't want to go?

_____

_____

5-7   How could this person help you think in ways that might help you accept treatment?

_____

_____

5-8   How could this person help you manage your feelings so you could accept treatment?

_____

_____

5-9   How could this person help you fight or resist your urge to stay out of treatment?

_____

_____

5-10   What things could this person do, or suggest that you do, to help you accept treatment?

_____

_____

Section 1: Responding to Someone Else's Relapse

When someone we care about relapses, it's important to respond to the relapse effectively. In order to do that, we first need to understand and manage our own thoughts, emotional reactions, urges, and actions. The relapse of someone we love can stir up some very painful or upsetting emotions—fear, anger, guilt, mistrust, anxiety, sadness, etc. If we don't know how to manage those emotions we often try to control the relapse; or we react in ways that hurt us, that violate our own values, or that keep the relapse going longer by protecting the person from its consequences. Instead, we need to find ways to stay centered in our own lives, and be supportive without neglecting our own self-care.

1-1　　　When this person has relapsed in the past, how has the relapse itself directly affected you?

_____

_____

_____

1-2　　　How have you reacted to those consequences in ways that seemed to make things worse for you, even though you only wanted to make things better?

_____

_____

_____

1-3　　　What kinds of thoughts have you had before you reacted that way?

_____

_____

1-4　　　What kinds of feelings have those thoughts brought out in you?

_____

_____

1-5　　　What have you had an urge to do in response to these feelings?

_____

_____

1-6　　　What actions have you taken that have seemed to make things worse for you?

_____

_____

1-7   If this person relapses in the future, how can you protect yourself from the consequences of the relapse—from the ways in which the relapse itself directly affects you?

_____

_____

_____

1-8   How can you protect yourself from your own emotional reactions to the relapse?

_____

_____

1-9   What thoughts might help you react more calmly and productively?

_____

_____

1-10   What can you do to manage your feelings more effectively?

_____

_____

1-11   What can you do to resist any urges to do things that might hurt you, to try to control the relapse, to violate your own values, or to protect the person from the consequences of the relapse?

_____

_____

1-12   What actions can you take to make sure that you keep taking good care of your own needs?

_____

_____

_____

Section 2: Intervention

Even if your reactions to past relapses haven't turned out to be helpful, you can learn new ways of responding that can help the person get back into recovery sooner, with less damage.

2-1   Think about what you could do that might help the person stop early if a relapse occurs in the future. This might include calling attention to the relapse, encouraging the person to call a counselor or self-help program sponsor, or suggesting a treatment program. What kinds of things would you be willing to do to help this person stop a relapse early?

_____

_____

_____

2-2   What kinds of things could you say or do to help the person think more clearly or honestly about the relapse and the need for treatment?

_____

_____

2-3   What could you do or say to help the person manage his or her feelings more effectively?

_____

_____

2-4   What could you do or say to help the person fight or resist cravings or self-defeating urges?

_____

_____

2-5   What could you suggest that the person do to stop the relapse?

_____

_____

_____

2-6   Who else could you suggest that the person contact for help?

_____

_____

_____

2-7   If the person resists help or treatment, what do you think would be an effective response?

_____

_____

_____

2-8   If your efforts are unsuccessful, what do you need to remember in order to keep your emotional balance and keep taking care of your own needs?

_____

_____

_____

Name of Client: _____

Name of Intervention Team Member: _____

In the event of a relapse, the following things will happen:

Section 1: General

Intervention Team Member

If you relapse in the future, I will do the following things to take care of myself:

_____

_____

_____

I also agree to do the following to help you accept help and get back into recovery:

_____

_____

_____

Client

If I relapse and you respond to the relapse in that way, I agree to respond as follows:

_____

_____

_____

Section 2: Thoughts

Intervention Team Member

I agree to do or say the following things to help you straighten out your thinking:

_____

_____

Client

If you do or say those things, I agree to respond as follows:

_____

_____

Section 3: Feelings

Intervention Team Member

I agree to do or say the following things to help you manage your feelings:

_____

_____

Client

If you do or say those things, I agree to respond as follows:

_____

_____

Section 4: Urges

Intervention Team Member

I agree to do or say the following things to help you resist your self-destructive urges:

_____

_____

Client

If you do or say those things, I agree to respond as follows:

_____

_____

Section 5: Actions

Intervention Team Member

I agree to do, or suggest that you do, the following things to help you get back in recovery:

_____

_____

Client

If you do or say those things, I agree to respond as follows:

_____

_____

Signatures

_____   _____
Client   **Date**   **Intervention Team Member**   **Date**

Section 1: Instructions for Writing an Intervention Letter

An intervention letter is a letter that you send to a person you care about who has relapsed. Its purpose is to persuade the person to get the help needed to return to recovery.

1-1 **Statement of Caring:** Tell the person how much you love and care for him or her, and that you can't just sit by and watch the relapse process happen again without doing something. This is a very important part of the intervention letter because it helps the person remember why you're writing it. It confirms that you're trying to help, rather than to criticize.

1-2 **Evidence of Relapse:** The person may be in denial about the relapse process, and need real evidence that tells what's going on and how it's affecting him or her. In this section, stick to things, behavior, or events that you've actually seen, heard, etc., rather than your own opinions or feelings about what the person is doing. For example, if you believe you saw the person drunk or high, tell exactly what behaviors made you think that. If the relapse has had negative consequences, describe those consequences objectively, without using emotional language.

1-3 **Personal Impact:** Tell the person how the relapse and all the associated behaviors are affecting you, and how his or her past relapse patterns have affected you. Talk about any problems those patterns have caused you in your own life. This is the part of the letter that should describe your emotions in seeing the person go through another relapse.

1-4 **Personal Protection:** Tell the person what you need to do to protect yourself from the consequences of his or her relapse. Make a commitment to take these steps to protect yourself.

1-5 **Statement of Faith:** Tell the person that you know if he or she weren't relapsing these things wouldn't be happening, and you know that the person has a deep-down commitment to recovery.

1-6 **Request and Commitment:** Tell the person what you believe he or she needs to do to get help, and what you're willing to do if he or she gets that help. For this part of the letter, use the information on your *Intervention Worksheet* and *Final Intervention Agreement*.

Writing this letter is one of the most effective things you can do to help stop relapse before it causes great physical, mental, social, and professional damage. It can be a powerful tool in helping this person make a new commitment to recovery.

Section 2: Sample Intervention Letter–Client to Him- or Herself

(Date)

Dear Me,

It feels strange to be writing a letter to myself, but I need a way for my sober self to communicate with my addictive self. So this letter is for you, addictive self. You seem to be in charge right now. I'm writing this letter because you've relapsed, something you never wanted to do again. I want you to get help and get back in recovery, no matter what it takes to do it right.

I really do care about you. I care about what happens to you, although it probably hasn't always seemed that way. I've let you hurt yourself and those you love many times in the past, but I can't sit by now and let you go through it all again. Every time it gets worse, and you don't deserve the pain.

I know what's happening. You're telling yourself you have it under control this time, but you don't. You're thinking about using all the time, even if you're still trying to pretend you can be moderate in your use. You've already broken the limits you set up for yourself when the relapse began. What makes you think you'll keep the promises you're making now? You've become very dishonest again, conning people, hiding your use, and making excuses when you do things that violate your values. You're less loving with your family and less productive in your work. You're feeling nervous or angry most of the time, except when you're drunk or high.

I'm suffering a lot as a result of this relapse. I feel ashamed and afraid. I'm sad for all the life that's being wasted. I'm afraid this might be the one you don't come back from.

I know you didn't really want to relapse, and I know that underneath it all you really are committed to recovery. I believe in you. I believe in your ability to accept help and get your life back. I believe in your strength, and in your ability to get past the pain and be free in recovery.

In order to get through this you'll need to get help right away, no matter what else seems more important. First I want you to say the Relapse Prevention Pledge to yourself, out loud, three times. Then I want you to get rid of any alcohol or drugs. Trust that you'll be okay without them. Then call your relapse prevention therapist and talk about whether or not you'll need treatment in order to stabilize. Then call your sponsor. Go to a meeting together today, no matter what. If you need treatment, start it as soon as possible. When you get stable, start right back into the relapse prevention work.

You can do it. You have to do it. You deserve to be free.

Sincerely,

(Date)

Dear _____,

I'm writing to you about your relapse. I really love and care about you, and I value you very highly as a person. I can't watch this happen without letting you know where I stand.

Of course I'd noticed that you hadn't been calling me much lately, and I haven't seen you at meetings. When I've talked to you lately you've sounded like you wanted to end the conversation as soon as possible, and you didn't want to talk about how things were going for you. I could tell something was wrong, but when I confronted you, you made excuses to get out of the conversation. You kept telling me everything was fine.

Today I got a call as part of your Early Intervention Team, and learned that you've been in a relapse, probably for a few weeks. I understand that you're still not back to full-time use, but that your efforts to hide your use aren't working any more.

It really hurts to see you in relapse again. I've found so much peace and happiness in recovery, and I want you to have the same. It hurts to see a really good person in pain, and I know that this is leading toward a lot of pain for you. I'm very worried about your family, and about your job. I know that right now it probably feels like the pain of not using would be worse than the pain of continuing the relapse. But think about all your past relapses. They've all ended in pain that's much worse than the pain of early recovery.

I'm not going to try to rescue you from this relapse, but I do want you to know I'm here for you. I know that, deep down inside, you really want recovery. I've enclosed a copy of a letter you wrote to yourself in case you relapsed again. That letter tells me you really want to live.

I want you to get rid of any alcohol or drugs that you might have around, to call your relapse prevention therapist, and to call me, as soon as possible. Let's go to a meeting together and talk about what to do next to get some help. We can talk about any parts of your life that are feeling out-of-control right now, and steps you can take to stabilize them. I'm willing to spend more time with you working on the new skills you're building in therapy.

I know you have it in you to succeed, if you choose to do the work necessary to get here. I really hope you do.

Sincerely,

(Date)

Dear _____,

I'm writing because I love you very much, and I can't just sit by and watch you destroy yourself. You've been acting funny for a while, kind of nervous and defensive, but I told myself you were just under a lot of stress. I know that's true, but that wasn't the whole story. You were handling your stress in ways that made the stress worse. I ran into your boss, and he mentioned that you've missed work a lot lately—something you hadn't told me. Now it's clear that you've started using again. In the past couple of weeks I've found evidence of drugs and alcohol around the house (I found a half-empty bottle in the back of the hall closet that wasn't there before, and a couple of joints in your car ashtray).

When I realized you were in relapse, I got a big knot in my gut. I don't know if I can go through that again, as bad as it gets near the end. I don't know if I could stand to lose you, but I'm not willing to lose myself in your relapse either. I worry about the kids more than I do about myself. They deserve two parents who are capable of giving their best.

As we all agreed when we met for the Intervention Team Training, I've called your relapse prevention therapist. I've increased the number of self-help recovery group meetings that I go to, in order to get more strength and support to get me through this. I'm going to take steps to make sure that I don't let this relapse affect my work or my role as a parent, or otherwise put me off balance.

I love you, but I'm not blinded by my love for you. I see so much goodness and strength in you that I know it's real. I know you really want to recover and live a full and responsible life. I know you can.

I'm asking you to get rid of any substances that you might have hidden, to call your relapse prevention therapist, and to call your sponsor, as soon as possible. I'm willing to do anything I can to support your getting help, including listening, being with you if you need me there, taking care of the kids while you get well, and anything else I can do without hurting the kids or my own recovery.

Please know that I'm here for you.

Sincerely,

Section 5: Sample Intervention Letter–Friend to Client

(Date)

Dear _____,

I'm writing because I'm worried about you. I really care about you, and I've just heard that you're in relapse. I want to offer you my support in your efforts to get back into recovery.

I could tell something was wrong lately. You haven't seemed like the same person. You've seemed pretty close to the edge. You've also acted like you were hiding something—side-stepping my questions whenever I expressed concern. Today your relapse prevention therapist let me know about your current situation, so I'm writing this letter, as we agreed I would do.

I really miss the friend I've come to know since you've been in recovery. That friend has been very open and honest, someone I could trust. You were always there for me, ready to listen even if you didn't have any answers. I knew you cared. I haven't felt that way lately, and I miss that closeness. I feel shut out of your life, just when you need help the most. That hurts.

I know that friend is still there inside you. I know you want recovery and I know you can do whatever it takes to recover and stay well.

I'm not going to push my help on you, but I'm offering it if you want it. You know where to reach me, and you know that I care very much.

Sincerely,

Phase II: Assessment

What?

Figuring out what really caused you to relapse

Recognizing the excuses for relapse that haven't been helpful

Replacing those excuses with an accurate understanding of the real causes of relapse

Why?

If you try to stop relapsing by doing the same things that failed in the past—for the same reasons you did them before—you'll fail again

You need to do different things, and do them for different reasons

In order to succeed, you need to correct the problems that you failed to correct before

Overview

The next step in relapse prevention planning, and the first step in the *Assessment* phase, is to look at your life history and how it relates to your use of alcohol and other drugs.

Addictive use isn't an isolated process, disconnected from the rest of life. Addictive thinking is very much a part of life, influenced by everything you experience. Even in early childhood, before you started your most destructive addictive patterns, you were forming beliefs about alcohol and other drugs that would continue to shape your life long after.

Behind every choice to use addictively are two kinds of beliefs: (1) What you believe alcohol or drugs will allow you to do that you can't do without them; and (2) What you believe alcohol or drugs will allow you to stop doing, escape from, or cope with that you can't stop doing, escape from, or cope with without them.

The *Life and Addiction History* process has four parts:

- The *Childhood* history explores the family relationships that affected you as a child, your strengths and weaknesses and significant childhood experiences, and the beliefs about alcohol and drugs that you formed from watching the people around you.

- The history of *Adolescence* explores your strengths, weaknesses, and significant life experiences in adolescence, the role that you wanted alcohol and other drugs to play in those experiences, and the benefits and disadvantages of using alcohol and drugs in adolescence.

- The history of *Adulthood* explores your strengths, weaknesses, and significant life experiences in adulthood, the role that you wanted alcohol and other drugs to play in those experiences, and the benefits and disadvantages of using alcohol and drugs to cope with those experiences.

- The *Summary* gives you a chance to find patterns in the life histories you've completed. You'll be asked to summarize your beliefs about what alcohol and drugs can do for you, and to describe the most important thing you learned about yourself while you were completing your history of childhood, adolescence, and adulthood.

Exploring these life experiences will be very useful when you get to Process 6, *Recovery and Relapse History*. It will also give you a stronger grasp on the old beliefs behind your addictive thinking—an important foundation for the Warning Sign Identification and Management processes that form the core of relapse prevention.

As you begin the *Life and Addiction History,* make sure you keep in close contact with your support network and your therapist or relapse prevention sponsor. No matter how much you've thought and talked about your past experiences, there's always the chance that some painful or upsetting memory will catch you off guard.

If that happens, please don't hesitate to call someone you trust. There's no shame in feeling the hurt left by the past. It's something everyone goes through, and we don't have to go through it alone. Understanding people can help you grieve the past and go forward into the future with new hope.

Life and Addiction History

Part 1:   *Childhood*

Instructions

Many people relapse because they have life problems that they've never learned to cope with, problems that keep coming back over and over. The purpose of completing a life and addiction history is to identify the pattern of recurring problems that set you up to relapse. The following questions will help you think about your life and how you used alcohol or drugs to help you cope with those problems.

Section 1: Description of Childhood

Describe your childhood by answering the following questions based on how you remember your family *before you reached the age of twelve.*

1-1   Write three words that describe your mother.

_____

1-2   Write three words that describe your relationship with your mother.

_____

1-3   Write three words that describe your father.

_____

1-4   Write three words that describe your relationship with your father.

_____

1-5   Write three words that describe the relationship between your mother and your father.

_____

1-6   List your brothers and sisters in the order in which they were born. Include yourself in the correct order. Next to each name, write a few words describing that brother or sister as a person, and a few words describing your relationship with that brother or sister.

Names of Brothers and Sisters in Order of Birth	Words Describing the Brother or sister	Words Describing Your Relationship

1-7   Write three words that describe what you were like as a child.

_____

1-8   List the three primary strengths and weaknesses that you had as a child.

Primary Strengths as a Child	Primary Weaknesses as a Child
1. _____	1. _____
2. _____	2. _____
3. _____	3. _____

1-9   List the three most significant life experiences that you had as a child, the role that alcohol and drug use played in those experiences, and what you learned as a result.

Significant Childhood Experiences	The role alcohol and drug use played was ...	What I learned as a result was ...
1. _____	_____	_____
2. _____	_____	_____
3. _____	_____	_____

Section 2: Addictive Use During Childhood

Children learn important lessons from seeing how parents, other family members, and friends of the family use alcohol and drugs. Think back to your childhood and answer these questions based on what you learned from these examples.

2-1   What members of your family used alcohol or other drugs and what do you remember about their use?

_____

_____

2-2   From watching others use alcohol and drugs, what did you come to believe that alcohol or drugs would allow you do that you couldn't do without those substances?

_____

_____

2-3   From watching others use alcohol and drugs, what did you come to believe that alcohol or drugs would allow you to stop doing, escape from, or cope with as an adult that you couldn't without those substances?

_____

_____

Life and Addiction History

Process 5

Part 2:   Adolescence

Section 1: Life Events in Adolescence

Describe your adolescence by answering the following questions based on how you remember your life *between the ages of 12 and 21*.

1-1   List the three primary strengths and weaknesses that you had as an adolescent.

Primary Strengths as an Adolescent	Primary Weaknesses as an Adolescent
1. _____	1. _____
2. _____	2. _____
3. _____	3. _____

1-2   List the three most significant life experiences that you had as an adolescent, the role that alcohol and drug use played in those experiences, and what you learned as a result.

Significant Adolescent Experiences	The role alcohol and drug use played was ...	What I learned as a result was ...
1. _____	_____	_____
2. _____	_____	_____
3. _____	_____	_____

Section 2: Addictive Use During Adolescence

2-1   Describe your alcohol or other drug use during adolescence.

_____

_____

_____

_____

_____

_____

2-2   List the three life experiences you identified in Question 1-2. Describe what you wanted alcohol and drugs to do for you, and what you wanted them to help you stop doing or escape from.

Significant Adolescent Experiences	What I wanted alcohol and drugs to do for me was ...	What I wanted alcohol and drugs to help me stop doing or escape from was ...
Experience #1 (Refer to 1-2)		
Experience #2 (Refer to 1-2)		
Experience #3 (Refer to 1-2)		

2-3   What were the benefits and disadvantages of using alcohol and drugs to cope with each of those life experiences?

Significant Adolescent Experiences	The benefits of using alcohol and drugs to cope with that experience were ...	The disadvantages in using alcohol and drugs to cope with that experience were ...
Experience #1 (Refer to 1-2)		
Experience #2 (Refer to 1-2)		
Experience #3 (Refer to 1-2)		

2-4   What did you want alcohol or drugs to allow you to do that you couldn't do without them? Did you get what you wanted?

_____

_____

_____

_____

2-5   What did you want alcohol or drugs to allow you to stop doing, escape from, or cope with that you couldn't when not using? Did you get what you wanted?

_____

_____

_____

_____

2-6   What were the benefits and disadvantages of using alcohol and drugs?

Benefits of Alcohol and Drug Use	Disadvantages of Alcohol and Drug Use
1.	1.
2.	2.
3.	3.

Life and Addiction History

Process 5

Part 3:   Adulthood

Section 1:   Life Events in Adulthood

Describe your experiences in adulthood by answering the following questions based on your life *after age 21*.

1-1   List the three primary strengths and weaknesses that you've had as an adult.

Primary Strengths as an Adult	Primary Weaknesses as an Adult
1. _____	1. _____
2. _____	2. _____
3. _____	3. _____

1-2   List the three most significant life experiences that you've had as an adult, the role that alcohol and drug use has played in those experiences, and what you've learned as a result.

Significant Experiences in Adulthood	The role alcohol and drug use played was ...	What I learned as a result was ...
1. _____	_____	_____
2. _____	_____	_____
3. _____	_____	_____

Section 2: Addictive Use During Adulthood

2-1   Describe your alcohol or other drug use as an adult.

_____

_____

_____

_____

_____

_____

_____

_____

2-2   List the three life experiences you identified in Question 1-2. Describe what you wanted alcohol and drugs to do for you, and what you wanted them to help you stop doing or escape from.

Significant Adult Experiences	What I wanted alcohol and drugs to do for me was ...	What I wanted alcohol and drugs to help me stop doing or escape from was ...
Experience #1 (Refer to 1-2)		
Experience #2 (Refer to 1-2)		
Experience #3 (Refer to 1-2)		

2-3   What were the benefits and disadvantages of using alcohol and drugs to cope with each of those life experiences?

Significant Adult Experiences	The benefits of using alcohol and drugs to cope with that experience were ...	The disadvantages in using alcohol and drugs to cope with that experience were ...
Experience #1 (Refer to 1-2)		
Experience #2 (Refer to 1-2)		
Experience #3 (Refer to 1-2)		

Instructions

Review your answers to all of the questions about your life and how you used alcohol and drugs. Answer these last two questions as they apply to your overall use of alcohol and drugs during the course of your whole life.

1.   Describe the positive things that you believed alcohol or drugs would allow you to do or become.

_____

_____

_____

_____

_____

_____

2.   Describe the negative or painful things that you used to believe that alcohol or drugs would help you to stop doing, escape from, or cope with.

_____

_____

_____

_____

_____

_____

3.   Describe the most important thing that you learned about yourself by completing this history.

_____

_____

_____

_____

_____

_____

Overview

Process 6, the *Recovery and Relapse History,* adds another dimension to the work you started with your *Life and Addiction History.* This process will give you a precise picture of the rise and fall of recovery and relapse in your life. You'll begin to see important patterns that you couldn't see while you were riding that roller coaster.

This history has three parts:

- In completing *The Relapse Calendar,* you'll "map" your periods of recovery and relapse throughout the history of your addiction. This will give you a "big-picture" view of your relapse history that will help you see how all your past relapses fit together. It shows you the whole proverbial forest, where you're used to seeing just a bunch of trees. This part has detailed directions, a sample calendar, and a blank calendar for your use.

- The *Relapse Episode List* gives you a chance to look in depth at your three most recent attempts at recovery and the relapses that followed them, pinpointing what you wanted the periods of recovery and relapse to do for you, your thoughts and feelings before relapsing or trying recovery once again, and what you did to try to stay in recovery. Going back to our forest metaphor, you'll be taking a much closer look at the trees you most recently banged your head on.

- The *Summary of Relapse History* helps you step back from the picture and find the overall patterns that will help you understand what went wrong and how it might relate to your life events. Here you'll see clearly the path you've taken through the forest and how it's brought you where you are today.

Many people believe that relapse just "happens" out of nowhere, but it doesn't. There are long chains of thoughts, feelings, and urges that lead to the action of picking up a drink or a drug. Often people aren't aware that they have any choice because they aren't aware of the belief systems that drive their thoughts, feelings, urges, and actions.

Like the *Life and Addiction History,* this process focuses heavily on what you believed addictive use could help you do; and what you believed it could help you stop doing, escape from, or cope with. By the end of these exercises you'll have a clearer idea of how all these patterns have fit together, and how they've pulled you away from successful recovery and into relapse.

This sets the stage for the *Warning Sign Identification* process, in which you'll take a much closer look at the individual thoughts, feelings, urges, and actions that drive your relapse patterns.

Part 1:   The Relapse Calendar

Many relapse-prone people minimize or "awfulize" their memories of relapse. Those who minimize say to themselves, "I don't relapse very often, and when I do, it isn't very bad at all." Those who awfulize say to themselves, "I've relapsed so many times I couldn't even count them, and when I do relapse, I always lose everything."

The Relapse Calendar will help you remember how many relapse episodes you've had, what started them, and how long they lasted. A relapse episode is a period of time when you used alcohol or drugs that was followed by at least ten days of abstinence.

Here's how you complete the calendar:

1.   Enter the date of your first serious attempt at abstinence in the space indicated on the first line.

2.   The first column gives you a place to enter the year. Starting with the year of your first serious attempt at abstinence, enter all the following years down to the present.

3.   Following each year is a time-line, with the months printed across the top. Locate the date of your first serious attempt at abstinence on the time-line and mark it with a hash mark (l).

4.   Identify the point on the time-line when you returned to addictive use. Place another hash mark (l) at that point on the time line. Connect the two hash marks with a solid horizontal line (————————————) to represent this first period of abstinence.

5.   Identify the next point on the time-line when you became abstinent, and mark it with a hash mark. Connect that with the previous hash mark using a jagged line (ᑎᐯᐯᐯ) to indicate this period of addictive use.

6.   Mark all periods of abstinence with solid lines and all periods of addictive use with jagged lines. Be sure to include all periods of abstinence and all relapse episodes.

7.   At the start of each period of abstinence, write a title for that abstinence period above the line.

8.   At the start of each period of addictive use, write a title above the start of the jagged line.

Section 1: Sample Relapse Calendar

First Serious Attempt at Abstinence: March 1, 1980

Year	Jan	Feb	Mar	Apr	May	June	July	Aug	Sept	Oct	Nov	Dec
1980							First try.					
1981						Got arrested.		Beat the charge.		Try again.		
1982			Now I know I'm an addict.						I really want recovery.			
1983												
1984	Now I've got it made.							This is harder than I thought.				
1985												
1986												
1987												
1988												
1989												

Year	Jan	Feb	Mar	Apr	May	June	July	Aug	Sept	Oct	Nov	Dec
1990	I'll try again.											
1991								Depressed.				
1992	This time for sure.											
1993									My wife died.			
1994												
1995	Entered relapse prevention therapy.											

Section 2: The Relapse Calendar

First Serious Attempt at Abstinence: _____

Year	Jan	Feb	Mar	Apr	May	June	July	Aug	Sept	Oct	Nov	Dec

Year	Jan	Feb	Mar	Apr	May	June	July	Aug	Sept	Oct	Nov	Dec

Recovery and Relapse History
Part 2:   Relapse Episode List

Instructions

This exercise will help you notice what happened when you tried not to use alcohol and drugs in the past. By understanding what happened during these times, you can see what to change. Refer to your completed relapse calendar while you do this exercise.

On the relapse calendar, find your three most recent relapse episodes and the periods of recovery before those episodes. When you're looking at a relapse episode, it's important also to look at the period of recovery right before it, because the period of recovery contains clues that help you understand why you relapsed. Just as we "hit a bottom" in addiction that leads into recovery, we can also "hit a bottom" in recovery if we don't have the right kind of support and skill training.

In this exercise each relapse episode and the period of recovery before it is called an "Attempt at Recovery/Relapse Episode." If you've had only two relapses, start with Section 2. If you've had only one relapse, start with Section 3.

Section 1: Third Most Recent Attempt at Recovery/Relapse Episode

1-1   Look at your relapse calendar. When did the period of recovery before your third most recent relapse begin?

_____ (Month and year)

1-2   Remember what you were thinking and feeling right before you decided to get into recovery. What made you decide to get in recovery that time?

_____

_____

_____

    a. What did you want recovery to do for you that you couldn't do for yourself while you were actively using?

_____

_____

    b. What did you want to escape from or cope with in recovery that you couldn't while you were actively using?

_____

_____

1-3   What did you do to stop using and get into recovery?

_____

_____

_____

1-4   What did you do on an ongoing basis to help yourself stay in recovery?

_____

_____

_____

1-5   Remember what you were thinking and feeling right before you decided to relapse (your third most recent relapse). What made you decide to relapse?

_____

_____

_____

a. What did you want the relapse to do for you that you couldn't do for yourself while you were in recovery?

_____

_____

b. What did you want to escape from or cope with in relapse that you couldn't while you were in recovery?

_____

_____

1-6   When did you relapse? _____ (Month and year)

1-7   What was the main thing you wanted the relapse to help you do?

_____

_____

_____

1-8   What happened to you after you relapsed?

_____

_____

_____

Section 2: Second Most Recent Attempt at Recovery/Relapse Episode

2-1   Look at your relapse calendar. When did the period of recovery before your second most recent relapse begin?

_____ (Month and year)

2-2   Remember what you were thinking and feeling right before you decided to get into recovery. What made you decide to get in recovery that time?

_____

_____

_____

a. What did you want recovery to do for you that you couldn't do for yourself while you were in relapse?

_____

_____

b. What did you want to escape from or cope with in recovery that you couldn't while you were in relapse?

_____

_____

2-3   What did you do to stop the relapse and get into recovery?

_____

_____

_____

2-4   What did you do on an ongoing basis to help yourself stay in recovery?

_____

_____

_____

2-5   Remember what you were thinking and feeling right before you decided to relapse (your second most recent relapse). What made you decide to relapse?

_____

_____

_____

a. What did you want the relapse to do for you that you couldn't do for yourself while you were in recovery?

_____

_____

b. What did you want to escape from or cope with in relapse that you couldn't while you were in recovery?

_____

_____

2-6   When did you relapse? _____ (Month and year)

2-7   What was the main thing you wanted the relapse to help you do?

_____

_____

_____

2-8   What happened to you after you relapsed?

_____

_____

_____

Section 3: Most Recent attempt at Recovery/Relapse Episode

3-1   Look at your relapse calendar. When did the period of recovery before your most recent relapse begin?

_____ (Month and year)

3-2   Remember what you were thinking and feeling right before you decided to get into recovery. What made you decide to get in recovery that time?

_____

_____

_____

   a. What did you want recovery to do for you that you couldn't do for yourself while you were in relapse?

_____

_____

   b. What did you want to escape from or cope with in recovery that you couldn't while you were in relapse?

_____

_____

3-3   What did you do to stop the relapse and get into recovery?

_____

_____

_____

3-4   What did you do on an ongoing basis to help yourself stay in recovery?

_____

_____

_____

3-5   Remember what you were thinking and feeling right before you decided to relapse (your most recent relapse). What made you decide to relapse?

_____

_____

_____

a. What did you want the relapse to do for you that you couldn't do for yourself while you were in recovery?

_____

_____

b. What did you want to escape from or cope with in relapse that you couldn't while you were in recovery?

_____

_____

3-6   When did you relapse? _____ (Month and year)

3-7   What was the main thing you wanted the relapse to help you do?

_____

_____

_____

3-8   What happened to you after you relapsed?

_____

_____

3-9   Remember what you were thinking and feeling right before you decided to get into recovery. What made you decide to get in recovery this time?

_____

_____

_____

a. What did you want recovery to do for you that you couldn't do for yourself while you were in relapse?

_____

_____

b. What did you want to escape from or cope with in recovery that you couldn't while you were in relapse?

_____

_____

3-10   What did you do to stop the relapse and get into recovery?

_____

_____

_____

Recovery and Relapse History

Process 6

Part 3:   Summary of Relapse History

Instructions

In this exercise you'll look for any patterns in your reasons for returning to alcohol or drug use in the past. Review your Relapse Calendar and Relapse Episode List, and answer the following questions.

1.   When was your first attempt at recovery? _____ (Month and year)

2.   Since that time, how many times have you tried to recover and relapsed? _____

3.   What's the longest period of time you've stayed in recovery? _____

4.   What were your major reasons for stopping the relapses and getting back in recovery?

_____

_____

_____

5.   What were the major things you wanted recovery to do for you that you couldn't do for yourself in relapse?

_____

_____

_____

6.   What were the major things you wanted to escape from or cope with in recovery that you couldn't escape from or cope with in relapse?

_____

_____

_____

7.   What were the major things you wanted relapse to do for you that you couldn't do for yourself in recovery?

_____

_____

_____

8.   What were the major things you wanted to escape from or cope with by relapsing that you couldn't escape from or cope with in recovery?

_____

_____

_____

9. Look at the summary section of your Life and Addiction History (page 95). List the positive things you believed that addictive use could do for you.

_____

_____

_____

10. How do those things compare with what you wanted relapse to do for you? (Question 7, above.)

_____

_____

_____

11. Look again at the summary section of your Life and Addiction History (page 95). List the negative or painful things you believed that addictive use could help you stop doing, escape from, or cope with.

_____

_____

_____

12. How do those things compare with the negative or painful things you wanted to escape from or cope with by relapsing? (Question 8, above.)

_____

_____

_____

13. What are the most important things you learned by completing this exercise?

_____

_____

_____

14. What things have you identified in this exercise that increase your risk of relapsing while you're in recovery?

_____

_____

_____

_____

Phase III: Warning Sign Identification

What?

Identifying the exact sequence of problems that moves you from stable recovery to relapse

Identifying the related thoughts, feelings, urges, and actions that drive that sequence of problems

Why?

You can't solve a problem that you don't understand

You need to know the exact sequence of problems that has hurt your recovery in the past

You need to identify your thoughts, feelings, urges, and actions before you can change them

Overview

The first step in Phase III, *Warning Sign Identification,* is a review of the common warning signs that have been identified by other people who have had a tendency to relapse. In the following pages you'll probably find a lot of things that you've experienced, and some that you're experiencing right now. More than any other portion of this workbook, the *Warning Sign Review* process will let you know you're not alone.

These common relapse warning signs tend to progress in ten phases: (1) Internal Change, (2) Denial, (3) Avoidance and Defensiveness, (4) Crisis Building, (5) Immobilization, (6) Confusion and Overreaction, (7) Depression, (8) Loss of Control, (9) Thinking About Relapse, and (10) Relapse. Within each of those phases are a number of common warning signs.

You might find yourself identifying with most of the warning signs in one phase, or with some in several phases. What matters is that you read them with an open mind and honestly search yourself to see where they do or don't fit your experience.

The *Warning Sign Identification* process has three parts:

- The *Relapse Warning Sign List—Reading Assignment* is a long, detailed list of all the common warning signs in all ten phases. You'll read this list as an assignment between sessions, marking the warning signs that you've experienced. You can also use special symbols to mark the ones that confuse or upset you, and those that cause you to "space out" or start daydreaming while you read them. Then you'll bring your completed list to your next session, to talk about it with your therapist or relapse prevention sponsor.
- The *Brief Warning Sign List—For In-Session Review* gives a one-paragraph summary of the warning signs in each of the ten phases of relapse. You'll read this list aloud in session with your therapist or sponsor.
- The *Initial Warning Sign List* gives you an opportunity to select three warning signs from the *Relapse Warning Sign List* or the *Brief Warning Sign List* and look closely at those three signs. For each of the three signs you'll be asked to think about why you chose it, identify the word or phrase that stands out to you, and write a personal title and description of that sign.

As you read the common warning sign lists, you might find yourself feeling uncomfortable about some of the signs that you identify with. If you do, make a note of these signs on the list, and talk to your therapist or relapse prevention sponsor about them.

If you find yourself identifying with many of the signs, don't worry. It doesn't mean you're in worse shape than other relapse-prone people. It just means you're willing to be honest about your experience. That honesty will serve you well throughout the relapse prevention process.

Part 1: Relapse Warning Sign List—Reading Assignment

Instructions

The following list of relapse warning signs has been developed to help you recognize the typical sequence of problems that leads you from a comfortable and stable recovery back to relapse. Please read the list carefully as a homework assignment between sessions. After you read each paragraph, pause for a moment and notice what you're thinking and feeling. Put a check mark (✓) next to any warning sign that you've experienced. Put a question mark (?) next to any warning sign you have difficulty understanding. Put an asterisk (*) next to any warning sign that causes you to "space out" or to start daydreaming while you're reading it. At your next session, please be prepared to discuss the warning signs that stood out to you.

Phase 1: Internal Change

I start to notice that something is going wrong. I'm still working a recovery program and look good on the outside, but I'm using old ways of thinking and managing feelings that make me feel bad on the inside. I'm concerned, but I don't know what's wrong or what to do about it. The most common relapse warning signs are:

☐ 1-1   *Increased Stress:* I begin to feel more stressed than usual. Sometimes this is the result of a problem or situation that's easy to see. At other times it's the result of little problems that cause stress to build up slowly over time.

☐ 1-2   *Change in Thinking:* I begin to think that my recovery program isn't as important as it used to be. Sometimes things are going so well that I don't believe I need to put a lot of effort into my program. At other times I have problems that my recovery program doesn't seem to help, and I ask myself "why bother?"

☐ 1-3   *Change in Feeling:* I start having unpleasant feelings that I don't like. Sometimes I feel euphoric, like everything is going my way when I know that it really isn't. At other times I feel depressed, like nothing is working out. I know that these mood sweeps aren't good for me.

☐ 1-4   *Change in Behavior:* I start acting different. I still look and sound good on the outside, but I know deep inside that I'm not practicing my recovery program the way I used to, and that something is going wrong.

Stop reading and take a moment to identify one of the warning signs that you've just read that stood out to you most.

1. Which warning sign stood out to you?

   _____

2. Why did it stand out? _____

   _____

Phase 2: Denial

I stop paying attention to others or honestly telling them what I'm thinking and feeling. I convince myself that everything is okay when it really isn't. The most common relapse warning signs are:

☐ 2-1 *Worrying About Myself:* I feel uneasy about the changes in my thinking, feelings, and behavior. This uneasiness comes and goes and usually lasts only a short time. Sometimes I feel afraid that I won't be able to stay in recovery, but I don't want to think about it.

☐ 2-2 *Denying That I'm Worried:* I deal with this uneasiness by using old self-defeating ways of thinking and acting. I start lying to myself about what's happening and try to convince myself that everything is okay when it really isn't. Sometimes I believe the lies I tell myself and I can forget my problems and feel better for a little while. I usually can't tell when I'm lying to myself until later. It's only when I think or talk about the situation later that I'm able to recognize how bad I was feeling and how I denied those feelings.

Stop reading and take a moment to identify one of the warning signs that you've just read that stood out to you most.

1. Which warning sign stood out to you?

    _____

2. Why did it stand out? _____

    _____

Phase 3: Avoidance and Defensiveness

I try to avoid anyone or anything that will force me to be honest about how my thinking, feelings, and behavior have changed. If I'm directly confronted, I get defensive and can't hear what others are trying to tell me. The most common relapse warning signs are:

☐ 3-1 *Believing I'll Never Relapse:* I convince myself that I don't need to put a lot of energy into my recovery program because I'll never relapse. I don't tell the people involved in my recovery program about this because I know they'll give me a hard time. I tell myself that it's none of their business.

☐ 3-2 *Focusing on Others Instead of Myself:* I take the focus off of myself by becoming more concerned about the recovery of others than about my own recovery. I privately judge my friends, spouse, and other recovering people. I keep these judgments to myself unless others confront me. Then I try to turn the tables by criticizing them. This is often called working the other guy's program.

☐ 3-3 *Getting Defensive:* I don't want to tell others what I'm thinking and doing because I'm afraid they'll criticize or confront me. I feel scared, angry, and defensive when other people ask me questions or point out things about my recovery that I don't want to see. I tend to get defensive even when no defense is necessary.

☐ 3-4 *Getting Compulsive:* I start using compulsive behaviors to keep my mind off of how uncomfortable I'm feeling. I get stuck in old, rigid, and self-defeating ways of thinking and acting. I try to control conversations, either by talking too much or by not talking at all. I start working more than I need to and get over-involved in many activities. Other people think I'm the model of recovery because of my heavy involvement in self-help groups. I tend to act like a therapist to others but I'm reluctant to talk about my personal problems. I avoid casual or informal involvement with people unless I can be in control.

☐ 3-5 *Acting Impulsively:* I start creating problems for myself by using poor judgment and impulsively doing things without thinking them through. This usually happens in times of high stress. Sometimes I privately feel bad but I tend to make excuses and blame others for my problems.

☐ 3-6 *Getting Lonely:* I start spending more time alone because I feel uncomfortable around others. I usually have good reasons and excuses for staying away from other people. I start feeling lonely. Instead of dealing with the loneliness by trying to meet and be around other people, I get more compulsive about doing things alone.

Stop reading and take a moment to identify one of the warning signs that you've just read that stood out to you most.

1. Which warning sign stood out to you?

   _____

2. Why did it stand out? _____

   _____

Phase 4: Crisis Building

I start having problems in recovery that I don't understand. Even though I want to solve these problems and I work hard at it, two new problems pop up to replace every problem that I solve. The most common warning signs are:

☐ 4-1 *Seeing Only a Small Part of the Problem:* I start thinking that my life is made up of separate and unrelated parts. I focus on one small part of my life and block out everything else. Sometimes I focus only on the good things and block out or ignore the bad. In this way I can mistakenly believe everything is fine when it really isn't. At other times I see only the things that are going wrong and blow them out of proportion. This causes me to feel like nothing is going my way even when there are many good things happening in my life. I can't see the "big picture" or figure out how the things I do in one part of my life can cause problems in other parts of my life. When problems develop, I don't know why.

☐ 4-2 *Getting Depressed:* I believe that life is unfair and that I have no power to do anything about it. I feel depressed, down, blue, listless, and empty of feelings. I lack energy, tend to sleep too much, and rarely feel good or full of life. At times I'm able to distract myself from these moods by getting busy with other things and not talking about the depression.

☐ 4-3 *Poor Planning:* I feel so bad about myself that I can't make realistic plans. Sometimes I make grandiose plans and try to do more than is possible. At other times I sell myself short by planning to do too little, because I don't believe in myself. At still other times I don't make any plans at all. I refuse to think about what I'm going to do next. I interpret the slogan "One Day at a Time" to mean that I shouldn't plan ahead or think about what I'm going to do next. My plans are based more on wishful thinking (how I wish things would be) than on reality (how things actually are).

☐ 4-4 *Plans Begin to Fail:* My plans begin to fail and each failure causes new problems. I tend to overreact to or mismanage each problem in a way that creates a new and bigger problem. I start having the same kinds of problems with work, friends, family, and money that I used to have before I got into recovery. I feel guilty and remorseful when I have these problems. I work hard to try to solve them, but something always seems to go wrong that creates an even bigger or more depressing problem.

Stop reading and take a moment to identify one of the warning signs that you've just read that stood out to you most.

1. Which warning sign stood out to you?

    _____

2. Why did it stand out? _____

    _____

Phase 5: Immobilization

During this phase I feel trapped in an endless stream of unmanageable problems and feel like giving up. I can't seem to get started or make myself do the things that I know I need to do. Even when I try, nothing seems to work out. The most common relapse warning signs are:

☐ 5-1 *Daydreaming and Wishful Thinking:* It becomes more difficult to concentrate or figure things out. I have fantasies of escaping or "being rescued from it all" by an event that's unlikely to happen. I start daydreaming and wishing that I could get the things that I want without having to do anything to get them. I want something magical to happen that will rescue me from it all.

☐ 5-2 *Feeling That Nothing Can be Solved:* I begin to feel like a failure who will never be able to get anything right. My failures may be real or imagined. I exaggerate small problems and blow them out of proportion while failing to notice anything that I do right. I start to believe that "I've tried my best and recovery isn't working out."

☐ 5-3 *Immature Wish to be Happy:* I have a vague desire to "be happy" or to have "things work out," but I don't set up any plans to make those things happen. I want to be happy, but I have no idea what I can do to make myself happy. I'm not willing to work hard or pay the price for the happiness that I want. I start wishing that something magical would happen to rescue me from my problems.

Stop reading and take a moment to identify one of the warning signs that you've just read that stood out to you most.

1. Which warning sign stood out to you?
    _____

2. Why did it stand out? _____

    _____

Phase 6: Confusion and Overreaction

I have trouble thinking clearly and managing my thoughts, feelings, and actions. I'm irritable and I tend to overreact to small things. The most common relapse warning signs are:

☐ 6-1 *Difficulty In Thinking Clearly:* I have trouble thinking clearly and solving simple problems. Sometimes my mind races and I can't shut it off, and at other times it seems to shut off or go blank. My mind tends to wander and I have difficulty thinking about something for more than a few minutes. I get confused and have trouble figuring out how one thing relates to or affects other things. I also have difficulty deciding what to do next in order to manage my life and recovery. As a result I tend to make bad decisions that I wouldn't have made if I were thinking clearly.

☐ 6-2 *Difficulty In Managing Feelings And Emotions:* I start to have difficulty managing my feelings and emotions. Sometimes I overreact emotionally and feel too much. At other times I become emotionally numb and can't figure out what I'm feeling. Sometimes I feel strange or have "crazy feelings" for no apparent reason. I start to think I might be going crazy. I have strong mood swings and periodically feel depressed, anxious, and scared. As a result of this, I don't trust my feelings and emotions and often try to ignore, stuff, or forget about them. My mood sweeps start causing me new problems.

☐ 6-3 *Difficulty Remembering Things:* At times I have problems remembering things and learning new information and skills. Things I want to remember seem to dissolve or evaporate from my mind within minutes. I also have problems remembering key events from my childhood, adolescence, or adulthood. At times I remember things clearly, but at other times these same memories won't come to mind. I feel blocked, stuck, or cut off from these memories. At times, my inability to remember things causes me to make bad decisions that I wouldn't have made if my memory were working properly.

☐ 6-4 *Periods of Confusion:* I start getting confused more often. The confusion is more severe and lasts longer. I'm not sure what's right or wrong. I don't know what to do to solve my problems, because everything I try seems to make them worse. I get angry at myself, because I can't solve my problems and I just keep making things worse.

☐ 6-5 *Difficulty Managing Stress:* I start having trouble dealing with stress. Sometimes I feel numb and can't recognize the minor signs of daily stress. At other times I seem overwhelmed by severe stress for no real reason. When I feel stressed out, I can't relax no matter what I do. The things other people do to relax either don't work for me or they make the stress worse. It seems I get so tense that I'm not in control. The stress starts to get so bad that I can't do the things I normally do. I get afraid that I'll collapse physically or emotionally.

☐ 6-6 *Irritation With Friends:* My relationships with friends, family, counselors, and other recovering people become strained. Sometimes I feel threatened when others talk about the changes they're noticing in my behavior and moods. At other times I just don't care about what they say. The arguments and conflicts get worse in spite of my efforts to resolve them. I start to feel guilty.

☐ 6-7   *Easily Angered:* I feel irritable and frustrated. I start losing my temper for no real reason and feeling guilty afterwards. I often overreact to small things that really shouldn't make any difference. I start avoiding people because I'm afraid I might lose control and get violent. The effort to control myself adds to the stress and tension.

Stop reading and take a moment to identify one of the warning signs that you've just read that stood out to you most.

1.   Which warning sign stood out to you?

    _____

2.   Why did it stand out? _____

    _____

Phase 7: Depression

During this phase, I become so depressed that I can't do the things I normally do. At times I feel that life is not worth living, and sometimes I think about killing myself or relapsing as a way to end the depression. I'm so depressed that I can't hide it from others. The most common relapse warning signs are:

☐ 7-1 *Irregular Eating Habits:* Either I start to overeat or I lose my appetite and eat very little. As a result I start gaining or losing weight. I skip meals and stop eating at regular times. I replace a well-balanced, nourishing diet with "junk food."

☐ 7-2 *Lack of Desire to Take Action:* I can't get started or get anything done. At those times I'm unable to concentrate; I feel anxious, fearful, and uneasy. I often feel trapped, with no way out.

☐ 7-3 *Difficulty Sleeping Restfully:* I have difficulty sleeping restfully. I can't fall asleep. When I do sleep, I have unusual or disturbing dreams, awaken many times, and have difficulty falling back to sleep. I sleep fitfully and rarely experience a deep, relaxing sleep. I wake up from a night of sleep feeling tired. The times of day during which I sleep change. At times, I stay up late due to an inability to fall asleep, and then over-sleep because I'm too tired to get up in the morning. At times I become so exhausted that I sleep for extremely long periods, sometimes sleeping around the clock for one or more days.

☐ 7-4 *Loss of Daily Structure:* My daily routine becomes haphazard. I stop getting up and going to bed at regular times. I start skipping meals and eating at unusual times. I find it hard to keep appointments and plan social events. I feel rushed and overburdened at times and then have nothing to do at other times. I'm unable to follow through on plans and decisions, and I experience tension, frustration, fear, and anxiety that keep me from doing what I know needs to be done.

☐ 7-5 *Periods of Deep Depression:* I feel depressed more often. The depression becomes worse, lasts longer, and interferes with living. The depression is so bad that it's noticed by others and can't be easily denied. The depression is most severe during unplanned or unstructured periods of time. Fatigue, hunger, and loneliness make the depression worse. When I feel depressed, I separate from other people, become irritable and angry with others, and often complain that nobody cares or understands what I'm going through.

Stop reading and take a moment to identify one of the warning signs that you've just read that stood out to you most.

1. Which warning sign stood out to you?

   _____

2. Why did it stand out? _____

   _____

Phase 8: Loss of Control

I can't control my thoughts, feelings, or behaviors. My life becomes so unmanageable that I start to believe there are only three ways out—insanity, suicide, or relapse. I no longer believe that anyone or anything can help me. The most common warning signs are:

☐ 8-1   *Hiding My Problems:* I feel guilty because I believe I'm doing things wrong. I hide my problems and stop telling others what's happening to me. The more I hide my problems, the worse they get.

☐ 8-2   *Feeling Powerless and Helpless:* I start to believe that there's nothing I can do to handle my problems in recovery. I make up my mind to get back on track and try to do things differently, but I fall back into the same patterns of dysfunctional behavior. I have trouble getting started. I have difficulty thinking clearly and paying attention to things. I start to believe that I can't do anything right and that there's no way out. I feel sorry for myself and use self-pity to get attention from others. I feel ashamed, crazy, and defective. I don't believe I'll ever feel normal again.

☐ 8-3   *Refusing Help:* I avoid talking with people who care about me and want to help me. Sometimes I drive them away by getting angry and criticizing them. At other times I quietly withdraw from them. I feel helpless and start to lose respect for myself. I have no confidence that I can do anything to solve my problems. I try to hide these feelings by acting as if I don't care.

☐ 8-4   *Breaking My Recovery Program:* I find excuses to miss scheduled recovery activities because they don't make me feel better. I start to tell myself that I don't have to keep my recovery program as a number-one priority. Other things seem more important. Eventually I stop attending all scheduled recovery activities, even though I need help and I know it.

☐ 8-5   *Going Against My Values:* I begin to do things that I believe are wrong. I know that I'm lying, using denial, and making excuses for my behavior, but I can't stop myself. I feel out of control. I start doing things on a regular basis that I normally wouldn't do, things that violate my values. I just can't seem to stop myself or control my behavior.

☐ 8-6   *Complete Loss of Self-Confidence:* I feel trapped and overwhelmed because I can't think clearly or do the things that I know I need to do to solve my problems. I feel powerless and hopeless. I start to believe that I'm useless and incompetent, and that I'll never be able to manage my life.

☐ 8-7   *Unreasonable Resentment:* I feel angry because of my inability to behave the way I want to. Sometimes my anger is with the world in general, sometimes with someone or something in particular, and sometimes with myself.

☐ 8-8   *Overwhelming Loneliness, Frustration, Anger, and Tension:* I feel completely overwhelmed. I feel like I'm helpless, desperate, and about to go crazy. It keeps getting harder and harder to control my thoughts, feelings, and behavior. My problems keep getting worse. No matter how hard I try to get back in control, I can't do it.

Stop reading and take a moment to identify one of the warning signs that you've just read that stood out to you most.

1. Which warning sign stood out to you?
   _____

2. Why did it stand out? _____

   _____

Phase 9: Thinking About Relapse

I start to think that relapsing will help me solve my problems and feel better. Things seem so bad that I begin to think I might as well relapse because things couldn't get worse. I want to believe that I can have a short-term, low-consequence relapse without experiencing major problems, even though deep inside I know I can't. I try to put these thoughts out of my mind, but sometimes they're so strong that I can't stop them. I start to believe that relapsing is the only way to keep myself from going crazy or killing myself. It actually looks like a sane and rational alternative.

☐ 9-1 *Thinking About Relapse:* I start hoping that I can be normal and not have to worry about working a recovery program. I imagine what it would be like if I could go back to my old way of doing things without experiencing any pain or problems. I start to think that a relapse will help me feel better. I start to believe I might really be able to control it next time.

☐ 9-2 *Getting Dissatisfied With Recovery:* I look at my recovery and notice all of the pain and problems I'm experiencing. Things seem so bad that I begin to think that I might as well relapse because things couldn't get any worse. Life seems to have become unmanageable even though I'm in recovery.

☐ 9-3 *Getting Obsessed With Relapse:* The thoughts about relapse keep popping into my head. Sometimes I'm able to put these thoughts out of my mind, but often they're so strong that I can't stop them. I begin to believe that relapsing is the only alternative to going crazy or committing suicide. Relapsing actually looks like a sane and rational alternative, and I can't stop thinking about it

☐ 9-4 *Convincing Myself To Relapse:* I mistakenly believe that relapsing will somehow make my problems better or allow me to escape from them for a little while. I tell myself that the relapse will be controlled and time-limited. I think about relapsing, getting relief, and then getting back into recovery before I lose control.

Stop reading and take a moment to identify one of the warning signs that you've just read that stood out to you most.

1. Which warning sign stood out to you?

    _____

2. Why did it stand out? _____

    _____

Phase 10: Relapse

I start the relapse and try to control it. I feel disappointed because the relapse isn't doing for me what I thought it would. I feel guilty because I know that I mismanaged my recovery. My relapse spirals out of control, creating severe problems with my life and health. The problems continue to get worse until I realize that I need help and decide to try recovery one more time.

☐ 10-1 *Starting The Relapse:* I try to solve my problems and feel better by relapsing. Although I try to rationalize my behavior, deep inside I know that the relapse won't work and that it will hurt me in the long run. I convince myself that I have no choice. I try to tell myself that relapsing is a normal behavior and that I can handle it this time.

☐ 10-2 *Attempting To Control:* I try to focus on the positive aspects of the relapse and keep the problems under control. I convince myself that I feel better when I'm using my relapse behaviors. I deny or block out the pain and problems caused by the relapse. I start moving in and out of various self-destructive behaviors related to the relapse. I convince myself that I can handle it.

☐ 10-3 *Feeling Disappointed:* I feel disappointed because the relapse isn't doing for me what I thought it would. I feel guilty because I believe I've done something wrong. I feel ashamed because I start to believe that I'm defective and worthless as a person and my relapse proves it.

☐ 10-4 *Loss of Control:* My relapse spirals out of control. At times I feel that I can handle it, and then I lose it and get into trouble. I try to control again and start to cycle in and out of the problems caused by the relapse. I feel the relapse gathering momentum and I can see that I'm losing control. Sometimes I lose control slowly. At other times, the loss of control is very rapid. No matter how hard I try, I can't stop and get back into recovery.

☐ 10-5 *Life and Health Problems:* I start having severe problems with my life and health. Marriage, jobs, and friendships are seriously damaged. Eventually, I hit a crisis that forces me to seek treatment and start all over again.

Stop reading and take a moment to identify one of the warning signs that you've just read that stood out to you most.

1. Which warning sign stood out to you?

   _____

2. Why did it stand out? _____

   _____

Part 2:   *Brief Warning Sign List—For In-Session Review*

Instructions

In a session with your therapist or sponsor, read the following list of warning signs that lead from stable recovery to relapse. This list should be familiar to you because it's a summary of the warning signs that you read as a homework assignment. When you've finished reading, select a warning sign that applies to you and answer the discussion questions at the end of the list.

1. **Internal Change:** I start using old ways of thinking, managing feelings, and behaving that make me look good on the outside but leave me feeling bad on the inside. I get more stressed than usual and my recovery program seems less important. My moods swing from feeling on top of the world to feeling like nothing is working out. Deep inside I start to feel like something is wrong, but I try to cover it up.

2. **Denial:** I stop paying attention to or honestly telling others what I'm thinking and feeling. I start worrying about the changes in my thinking, feelings, and behavior. I don't want to think about it or talk about it. I go into denial and try to convince myself that everything is okay when I know that it really isn't.

3. **Avoidance and Defensiveness:** I avoid people who will honestly point out the problems that I don't want to see. When they do, I get defensive, scared, and angry. I blame them for making me feel bad. I take the focus off of myself by criticizing their problems and faults instead of honestly looking at my own problems. I start using compulsive behaviors to keep my mind off of how uncomfortable I'm feeling. I start creating problems for myself by using poor judgment and impulsively doing things without thinking them through. I start feeling uncomfortable around others, I spend more time alone, and I start to feel lonely and isolated.

4. **Crisis Building:** I start having problems that I don't understand. Even though I want to solve these problems and I work hard at it, two new problems pop up to replace every problem that I solve. I can't see the big picture and I start doing things that won't really help. I start to feel depressed, and try to distract myself by getting busy with other things and not talking about the depression. I stop planning ahead. Things keep going wrong, and I feel like nothing is going my way. No matter how hard I try, nothing seems to work.

5. **Immobilization:** I feel trapped in an endless stream of unmanageable problems. I get tired of putting time and energy into things that aren't working. I feel like giving up. I can't seem to get started or make myself do the things that I know I need to do. I exaggerate small problems and blow them out of proportion. I can't force myself to deal with the major things that could really make a difference. I begin to feel like a failure who can't do anything right. I start wishing that I could run away or that something magical would happen to rescue me from my problems.

6. **Confusion and Overreaction:** I have trouble thinking clearly and solving usually simple problems. Sometimes my mind races and I can't shut it off. At other times I go blank and can't concentrate on anything. I have trouble remembering things. I switch from overreacting to feeling emotionally numb. I start to think that I might be going crazy. I stop trusting my feelings and try to ignore, stuff, or forget about them. I start making bad decisions that I wouldn't have made if I were thinking clearly. I become easily angered and start to take it out on my friends and family. I get irritated with other people because they don't understand me and can't seem to help me.

7. **Depression:** I get so depressed that I can't do the things I normally do. I feel that life is not worth living, and sometimes I think about killing myself or relapsing as a way to end the depression. I'm so depressed that I can't hide it from others. I stop eating right. I can't get started or get anything done. I sleep fitfully and rarely experience a deep, relaxing sleep. I can't stick to a productive daily schedule. I find it hard to keep appointments and plan ahead. I isolate myself and convince myself that nobody cares and that there's no one who can help me. I feel trapped with no way out.

8. **Loss of Control:** I start doing things that violate my values, hurt me, and hurt those I love. As a result, I start losing respect for myself. I find excuses to miss therapy and self-help group meetings. I cut myself off from others by ignoring them, getting angry with them, or criticizing and putting them down. I get so isolated that it seems there's no one to turn to for help. I start to feel sorry for myself and use self-pity to get attention. I feel ashamed and guilty. I know that I'm out of control but I keep lying, using denial, and making excuses for my behavior. I feel trapped by the pain and start to believe that I'll never be able to manage my life. I see only three possible ways out—insanity, suicide, or relapse. I no longer believe that anyone or anything else can help me. No matter how hard I try to regain control, I'm unable to do so.

9. **Thinking About Relapse:** I start to think that having a relapse will help me solve my problems and feel better. Things seem so bad that I begin to think I might as well relapse because things couldn't get worse. I try to convince myself that I can use relapse behaviors without losing control or developing serious problems, even though deep inside I know I can't. I try to put these thoughts about relapse out of my mind, but sometimes they're so strong that I can't stop them. I start to believe that relapsing is the only way to keep myself from going crazy or killing myself. Relapsing actually looks like a sane and rational alternative.

10. **Relapse:** I try to solve my problems and feel better by relapsing. Although I rationalize my behavior, deep inside I know that relapsing won't work and will hurt me in the long run. I start the relapse and try to control my behavior. I feel myself losing control and get disappointed because the relapse isn't doing for me what I thought it would. My relapse spirals out of control, creating severe problems with my life and health. The problems continue to get worse until I realize that I need help and decide to try recovery one more time.

Part 3:   *The Initial Warning Sign List*

Instructions

Review the warning signs on the Relapse Warning Sign List and the Brief Warning Sign List. Select three of those warning signs that apply to you and answer the following questions about them:

Section 1: Warning Sign #1

1-1   What is the title of the first warning sign that you selected? (Copy it directly from the Brief Warning Sign List)

_____

1-2   Why did you select that warning sign?

_____

_____

_____

1-3   Read the warning sign description again and underline what you consider the most important word or phrase. What word or phrase did you underline?

_____

1-4   What does that word or phrase mean to you?

_____

_____

_____

1-5   Write a personal title for the warning sign that will be easy for you to remember. This title shouldn't be longer than two or three words.

_____

1-6   Write a personal description of this warning sign. Make sure the description is a single sentence that begins with the words I know *I'm in trouble with my recovery when ...* It's important not to use any words from your personal title in this description.

_____

_____

_____

Section 2: Warning Sign #2

2-1   What is the title of the second warning sign that you selected? (Copy it directly from the Brief Warning Sign List)

_____

2-2   Why did you select that warning sign?

_____

_____

_____

_____

2-3   Read the warning sign description again and underline what you consider the most important word or phrase. What word or phrase did you underline?

_____

2-4   What does that word or phrase mean to you?

_____

_____

_____

2-5   Write a personal title for the warning sign that will be easy for you to remember. This title shouldn't be longer than two or three words.

_____

2-6   Write a personal description of this warning sign. Make sure the description is a single sentence that begins with the words I know *I'm in trouble with my recovery when ...* It's important not to use any words from your personal title in this description.

_____

_____

_____

Section 3: Warning Sign #3

3-1 What is the title of the third warning sign that you selected? (Copy it directly from the Brief Warning Sign List)

_____

3-2 Why did you select that warning sign?

_____

_____

_____

_____

3-3 Read the warning sign description again and underline what you consider the most important word or phrase. What word or phrase did you underline?

_____

3-4 What does that word or phrase mean to you?

_____

_____

_____

3-5 Write a personal title for the warning sign that will be easy for you to remember. This title shouldn't be longer than two or three words.

_____

3-6 Write a personal description of this warning sign. Make sure the description is a single sentence that begins with the words _I know I'm in trouble with my recovery when ..._ It's important not to use any words from your personal title in this description.

_____

_____

_____

Your next job will be to analyze each of the three warning signs that you selected by writing about situations in which you managed these warning signs poorly, and about other situations in which you managed them well. Then you'll figure out how you change when you experience those warning signs, and how those warning signs increase your risk of relapse. After that, you'll look for hidden warning signs that can lead to relapse.

Overview

For many people who go through Relapse Prevention Therapy, this process is where all the pieces start to fall together and the whole thing starts to make sense. Many people suddenly start to understand why they've been doing all this work, and find new faith in the relapse prevention process.

In many ways the *Warning Sign Analysis* process is very much like a chapter from a detective novel. You start with three main clues, the three warning signs that you identified in your *Initial Warning Sign List*. The process is divided into three parts, each for one of your initial warning signs. You follow these exercises from beginning to end for each sign:

- In the *Description of a Past Experience* sections, you'll complete a "situation map" for this warning sign. In a situation map, you talk or write about an experience as if it were a story with a beginning, a middle, and an end. You answer certain questions about it to try to identify specific, concrete behaviors. In each of these sections you'll complete a situation map for a situation in which you managed this warning sign poorly or ineffectively.

- In the *Description of Personal* Change sections, you'll think about how you tend to change when this warning sign is turned on—how your thoughts, feelings, urges, and actions change; and how other people's reactions to you change as a result.

- In the final section of each part, you'll be given a technique for *Finding Hidden Warning Signs* in that particular situation. A hidden warning sign is something you do that increases your risk of relapse, but that you might not be consciously aware of as part of your relapse pattern. In these sections you begin to create your warning sign list, using the *Warning Sign Identification Cards* in the back of the workbook.

One of the greatest benefits of the situation mapping process is that it helps you see the "structure" or pattern that your behaviors tend to take. A map of a situation that you managed poorly will show a self-defeating structure of problems and symptoms. That structure will also tend to be "self-reinforcing"—meaning that one problem leads to another, and the last problem leads back to the first, starting the whole cycle over and over. Your *Description of Personal Change* shows how it tends to affect you and your relationships when you get dragged down in that cycle.

On the other hand, if you were to map a well-managed situation, it would show a "solution structure"—a straight line going from problems to solutions. Unlike a problem structure, a solution structure isn't a vicious circle that leads back into itself. It's a path that leads up and out of the problem.

By the time you've examined your situation and personal change for a warning sign, you'll be ready to look more deeply into your experience of that warning sign and find the hidden warning signs inside it. Finding those hidden warning signs is an important step in the healing process that is recovery. From this point on you'll have a much clearer picture of your own part in the problems that you experience—the part that you can actually do something about.

Warning Sign Analysis

Process 8

Part 1: Working With the First Warning Sign

Section 1: Description of a Past Experience With the First Warning Sign

1-1 Pick one of the three warning signs from the *Initial Warning Sign List* (page 126) that you'd like to learn more about. Find your personal title and description for that warning sign on the *Initial Warning Sign List* and copy them in the spaces provided below.

a. Personal Title: _____

b. Personal Description: I know I'm in trouble with my recovery when ...

_____

_____

1-2 Think of a specific past situation in which you experienced this warning sign while in recovery and *managed it poorly or ineffectively*. Tell the experience as if it were a story with a beginning, a middle, and an ending.

Sequencing Statements	Clarifying Questions
1. The warning sign was triggered when ...	1. Who were you with and what were they doing?
2. The first thing I did was ...	2. What were you doing?
3. The next thing I did was ...	3. What was going on around you?
4. The next thing I did was ...	4. Where did this happen?
5. What finally happened was ...	5. When did this happen? (Month, day, time)

The warning sign was triggered when ... _____

_____

_____

_____

_____

_____

_____

_____

_____

_____

_____

_____

_____

_____

1-3   What did you want to accomplish by managing this situation the way you did?

_____

_____

_____

1-4   Did you get what you wanted by managing the situation this way?
        ❏ Yes   ❏ No   ❏ Unsure   Please Explain:

_____

_____

_____

Section 2: Description of Personal Change With the First Warning Sign

Review the story of the past experience with the relapse warning sign that you described in Section 1 (Description of a Past Experience With the First Warning Sign).

2-1   Write the personal title of the warning sign you're analyzing.

_____

2-2   How do you change when you're experiencing this warning sign?

_____

_____

_____

_____

2-3   How does your thinking change when you're experiencing this warning sign?

_____

_____

_____

_____

        a. What is your thinking like when this warning sign is turned off?

_____

_____

        b. What is your thinking like when this warning sign is turned on?

_____

_____

2-4   How do your feelings change when you're experiencing this warning sign?

_____

_____

_____

a. What are you feeling when this warning sign is turned off, and how strongly (on a scale of one to ten)?

☐ Strong or ☐ Weak _____	☐ Safe or ☐ Threatened _____
☐ Angry or ☐ Caring _____	☐ Fulfilled or ☐ Frustrated _____
☐ Happy or ☐ Sad _____	☐ Proud or ☐ Ashamed, guilty _____

b. What are you feeling when this warning sign is turned on, and how strongly?

☐ Strong or ☐ Weak _____	☐ Safe or ☐ Threatened _____
☐ Angry or ☐ Caring _____	☐ Fulfilled or ☐ Frustrated _____
☐ Happy or ☐ Sad _____	☐ Proud or ☐ Ashamed, guilty _____

2-5   What do you have an urge to do when you're experiencing this warning sign?

_____

_____

_____

_____

a. What do you have an urge to do when the warning sign is turned off?

_____

_____

b. What do you have an urge to do when the warning sign is turned on?

_____

_____

2-6   What do you actually do when you're experiencing this warning sign?

_____

_____

_____

_____

a. What do you usually do when this warning sign is turned off?

_____

_____

b. What do you usually do when this warning sign is turned on?

_____

_____

2-7   How do other people usually react when you're experiencing this warning sign?

_____

_____

_____

_____

   a. How do other people usually react to you when the warning sign is turned off?

_____

_____

   b. How to other people usually react to you when this warning sign is turned on?

_____

_____

Section 3: Finding Hidden Warning Signs in the First Warning Sign

3-1   Review the descriptions of your past experience when you managed your first warning sign ineffectively, and your analysis of how you changed when you experienced it. As you review these things, see if you can notice any *hidden warning signs*. A hidden warning sign is something that you do that increases your risk of having a relapse, but that you might not be consciously aware of as part of your relapse pattern. For example, a hidden warning sign might be "I start working long hours" or "I start losing my temper a lot." In the space below, list any hidden warning signs that you can see in your descriptions of this warning sign.

_____

_____

_____

_____

_____

_____

_____

_____

_____

_____

3-2   Turn to the back of the manual and find the *Warning Sign Identification Cards.* Tear out these cards and put them in a pile next to you.

3-3   Now you're going to start creating a list of your own personal warning signs, but you're going to have that list on a series of cards, rather than on a single sheet of paper.

3-4   Notice that the front of each card has a place for a title and a description of a relapse warning sign.

- Use one card for each of the hidden warning signs that you identified above.

- For each hidden warning sign that you identified in question 3-1, write a personal title on the card.

- Then write a personal description on the card, on the line that starts with the words *I know I'm in trouble with my recovery when ...* (Remember: Write the title and description of each hidden warning sign on a separate warning sign card.)

- Take a deep breath and read the sentence out loud to yourself several times, to make sure it feels right to you. If it doesn't feel right when you read it out loud, write it again on a new card, using different words that feel better to you.

Keep starting new cards until you have one for each hidden warning sign.

3-5   Arrange the cards in the order in which the warning signs generally happen. If you have two or more cards that are obviously describing the same warning sign, throw away all but one.

3-6   Go through your cards one by one and read their titles and descriptions. Try to imagine yourself going through the sequence of activities that they describe. Notice if there are any *gaps in the action.* These are places where you've failed to describe things you've actually done that have been part of the pattern. For example, the gap between "I start working long hours" and "I start losing my temper a lot" might be filled with the warning sign "I start getting less and less sleep." If you find any gaps in the action in your warning sign cards, start new cards to fill in the gaps.

Warning Sign Analysis **Process 8**

Part 2:   Working With the Second Warning Sign

Section 1: Description of a Past Experience With the Second Warning Sign

1-1   Pick another of the three warning signs from the *Initial Warning Sign List* (page 126) that you'd like to learn more about. Find your personal title and description for that warning sign on the *Initial Warning Sign List* and copy them in the spaces provided below.

a. Personal Title: _____

b. Personal Description: I know I'm in trouble with my recovery when ...

_____

_____

1-2   Think of a specific past situation in which you experienced this warning sign while in recovery and *managed it poorly or ineffectively*. Tell the experience as if it were a story with a beginning, a middle, and an ending.

Sequencing Statements	Clarifying Questions
1. The warning sign was triggered when ...	1. Who were you with and what were they doing?
2. The first thing I did was ...	2. What were you doing?
3. The next thing I did was ...	3. What was going on around you?
4. The next thing I did was ...	4. Where did this happen?
5. What finally happened was ...	5. When did this happen? (Month, day, time)

The warning sign was triggered when ... _____

_____

_____

_____

_____

_____

_____

_____

_____

_____

_____

_____

_____

_____

_____

_____

1-3   What did you want to accomplish by managing this situation the way you did?
_____
_____
_____

1-4   Did you get what you wanted by managing the situation this way?
❑ Yes   ❑ No   ❑ Unsure   Please Explain:
_____
_____
_____

Section 2: Description of Personal Change With the Second Warning Sign

Review the story of the past experience with the relapse warning sign that you described in Section 1 (Description of a Past Experience With the Second Warning Sign).

2-1   Write the personal title of the warning sign you're analyzing.

_____

2-2   How do you change when you're experiencing this warning sign?
_____
_____
_____
_____

2-3   How does your thinking change when you're experiencing this warning sign?
_____
_____
_____

a. What is your thinking like when this warning sign is turned off?
_____
_____

b. What is your thinking like when this warning sign is turned on?
_____
_____

2-4   How do your feelings change when you're experiencing this warning sign?
_____
_____
_____

a. What are you feeling when this warning sign is turned off, and how strongly (on a scale of one to ten)?

☐ Strong or ☐ Weak _____	☐ Safe or ☐ Threatened _____
☐ Angry or ☐ Caring _____	☐ Fulfilled or ☐ Frustrated _____
☐ Happy or ☐ Sad _____	☐ Proud or ☐ Ashamed, guilty _____

b. What are you feeling when this warning sign is turned on, and how strongly?

☐ Strong or ☐ Weak _____	☐ Safe or ☐ Threatened _____
☐ Angry or ☐ Caring _____	☐ Fulfilled or ☐ Frustrated _____
☐ Happy or ☐ Sad _____	☐ Proud or ☐ Ashamed, guilty _____

2-5　What do you have an urge to do when you're experiencing this warning sign?

_____

_____

_____

_____

a. What do you have an urge to do when the warning sign is turned off?

_____

_____

b. What do you have an urge to do when the warning sign is turned on?

_____

_____

2-6　What do you actually do when you're experiencing this warning sign?

_____

_____

_____

_____

a. What do you usually do when this warning sign is turned off?

_____

_____

b. What do you usually do when this warning sign is turned on?

_____

_____

2-7   How do other people usually react when you're experiencing this warning sign?

_____

_____

_____

_____

_____

     a. How do other people usually react to you when the warning sign is turned off?

_____

_____

     b. How to other people usually react to you when this warning sign is turned on?

_____

_____

Section 3: Finding Hidden Warning Signs in the Second Warning Sign

3-1   Review the descriptions of your past experience when you managed your second warning sign ineffectively, and your analysis of how you changed when you experienced it. As you review these things, see if you can notice any *hidden warning signs*. In the space below, write any hidden warning signs that you haven't yet identified.

_____

_____

_____

_____

_____

_____

_____

_____

_____

_____

3-2   Use your blank warning sign cards, and fill in a card for each new hidden warning sign you've identified.

    • Use one card for each of the new hidden warning signs.

    • For each hidden warning sign, write a personal title on the card.

    • Then write a personal description on the card, on the line that starts with the words *I know I'm in trouble with my recovery when* ... (Remember: Write the title and description of each hidden warning sign on a separate warning sign card.)

- Take a deep breath and read the sentence out loud to yourself several times, to make sure it feels right to you. If it doesn't feel right when you read it out loud, write it again on a new card, using different words that feel better to you. Keep starting new cards until you have one for each new hidden warning sign.

3-3   Put these cards in with the cards you filled out for the first warning sign (Part 1, Section 3), arranging them in the order in which the warning signs generally happen. If you have two or more cards that are obviously describing the same warning sign, throw away all but one.

3-4   Go through your cards one by one and read their titles and the descriptions. Try to imagine yourself going through the sequence of activities that they describe. Notice if there are any *gaps in the action*. If you find any gaps in the action in your warning sign cards, start new cards to fill in the gaps.

Part 3:   *Working With the Third Warning Sign*

Section 1: Description of a Past Experience With the Third Warning Sign

1-1   Take the remaining warning sign from the *Initial Warning Sign List* (page 126) that you'd like to learn more about. Find your personal title and description for that warning sign on the *Initial Warning Sign List* and copy them in the spaces provided below.

      a. Personal Title: _____

      b. Personal Description: I know I'm in trouble with my recovery when ...

      _____

      _____

1-2   Think of a specific past situation in which you experienced this warning sign while in recovery and *managed it poorly or ineffectively*. Tell the experience as if it were a story with a beginning, a middle, and an ending.

Sequencing Statements	Clarifying Questions
1. The warning sign was triggered when ...	1. Who were you with and what were they doing?
2. The first thing I did was ...	2. What were you doing?
3. The next thing I did was ...	3. What was going on around you?
4. The next thing I did was ...	4. Where did this happen?
5. What finally happened was ...	5. When did this happen? (Month, day, time)

The warning sign was triggered when ... _____

_____

_____

_____

_____

_____

_____

_____

_____

_____

_____

_____

_____

_____

_____

1-3   What did you want to accomplish by managing this situation the way you did?

_____

_____

_____

1-4   Did you get what you wanted by managing the situation this way?
       ❑ Yes   ❑ No   ❑ Unsure   Please Explain:

_____

_____

_____

Section 2: Description of Personal Change With the Third Warning Sign

Review the story of the past experience with the relapse warning sign that you described in Section 1 (Description of a Past Experience With the Third Warning Sign).

2-1   Write the personal title of the warning sign you're analyzing.

_____

2-2   How do you change when you're experiencing this warning sign?

_____

_____

_____

_____

2-3   How does your thinking change when you're experiencing this warning sign?

_____

_____

_____

_____

       a. What is your thinking like when this warning sign is turned off?

_____

_____

       b. What is your thinking like when this warning sign is turned on?

_____

_____

2-4   How do your feelings change when you're experiencing this warning sign?

_____

_____

_____

a. What are you feeling when this warning sign is turned off, and how strongly (on a scale of one to ten)?

☐ Strong or ☐ Weak _____	☐ Safe or ☐ Threatened _____
☐ Angry or ☐ Caring _____	☐ Fulfilled or ☐ Frustrated _____
☐ Happy or ☐ Sad _____	☐ Proud or ☐ Ashamed, guilty _____

b. What are you feeling when this warning sign is turned on, and how strongly?

☐ Strong or ☐ Weak _____	☐ Safe or ☐ Threatened _____
☐ Angry or ☐ Caring _____	☐ Fulfilled or ☐ Frustrated _____
☐ Happy or ☐ Sad _____	☐ Proud or ☐ Ashamed, guilty _____

2-5 What do you have an urge to do when you're experiencing this warning sign?

_____

_____

_____

_____

a. What do you have an urge to do when the warning sign is turned off?

_____

_____

b. What do you have an urge to do when the warning sign is turned on?

_____

_____

2-6 What do you actually do when you're experiencing this warning sign?

_____

_____

_____

_____

a. What do you usually do when this warning sign is turned off?

_____

_____

b. What do you usually do when this warning sign is turned on?

_____

_____

2-7   How do other people usually react when you're experiencing this warning sign?

_____

_____

_____

_____

_____

   a. How do other people usually react to you when the warning sign is turned off?

_____

_____

   b. How do other people usually react to you when this warning sign is turned on?

_____

_____

Section 3: Finding Hidden Warning Signs in the Third Warning Sign

3-1   Review the descriptions of your past experience when you managed your third warning sign ineffectively, and your analysis of how you changed when you experienced it. As you review these things, see if you can notice any *hidden warning signs*. In the space below, write any hidden warning signs that you haven't yet identified.

_____

_____

_____

_____

_____

_____

_____

_____

_____

_____

_____

3-2   Use your blank warning sign cards, and fill in a card for each new hidden warning sign you've identified.

   • Use one card for each of the new hidden warning signs.

   • For each hidden warning sign, write a personal title on the card.

   • Then write a personal description on the card, on the line that starts with the words *I know I'm in trouble with my recovery when ...* (Remember: Write the title and description of each hidden warning sign on a separate warning sign card.)

- Take a deep breath and read the sentence out loud to yourself several times, to make sure it feels right to you. If it doesn't feel right when you read it out loud, write it again on a new card, using different words that feel better to you. Keep starting new cards until you have one for each new hidden warning sign.

3-3 Put these cards in with the cards you filled out for the first warning sign (Parts 1 and 2, Section 3), arranging them in the order in which the warning signs generally happen. If you have two or more cards that are obviously describing the same warning sign, throw away all but one.

3-4 Go through your cards one by one and read their titles and the descriptions. Try to imagine yourself going through the sequence of activities that they describe. Notice if there are any *gaps in the action*. If you find any gaps in the action in your warning sign cards, start new cards to fill in the gaps.

Overview

A *Sentence Completion* exercise is a technique that can help you uncover hidden warning signs that have been "repressed," or blocked from your conscious awareness.

It's important to your relapse patterns that you stay unaware of some of your most important hidden warning signs. If you were aware of them, you'd be less likely to act them out, and less likely to relapse. So your conscious mind has grown very good at sorting through your thoughts and memories, deciding which ones it is or isn't okay to be aware of. That's how denial works.

When you use *Sentence Completion* exercises you can often get past that conscious sorting and blocking function. Instead, you get into the "automatic" part of your mind that just says what it thinks without questioning or judging it. You can learn a lot more about what's really going on inside you.

One thing you'll often run into when you reach that automatic part of your mind is something called a "hot response." A hot response is a thought that stirs up an unpleasant memory, starts a strong feeling, or causes you to start a private argument with yourself. A hot response is your conscious blocking function's way of saying, "Back off! You're getting too close!"

Sometimes the thing you're getting too close to might be a repressed memory that you aren't psychologically ready to deal with now without losing some of your ability to "function"—to take care of yourself and do the things you need to do in your life. If that happens, don't try to deal with the memory alone. Call your therapist immediately. If you don't have a therapist, find one who specializes in the types of memories you're having. This is important, no matter how strong you are.

Most often, though, the thing you're getting too close to will be an awareness that would ruin your relapse game. It might expose a lie you're telling yourself or point out how you're keeping yourself locked into the relapse cycle. As painful or upsetting as that awareness is, it might be your only hope of avoiding the next relapse. You need to let the awareness come up. With the help of your therapist or relapse prevention sponsor, you can cope with the uncomfortable feelings and take an honest and courageous look at this new truth. It might save your life.

The *Sentence Completion* process has five parts, each one giving you a chance to look deeper into the tangle of lies and games that makes up the relapse process. In each part, though, you decide which awareness to look at, so you have control over the process. You can take as many risks, or as few risks, as you choose. Here are the parts in this process:

- In *Warning Sign Review,* you'll be asked to take some time to relax, then read through the titles and descriptions on your warning sign cards, paying attention to how you feel as you read through the cards. Then you'll list all of the personal titles on your warning sign cards.

- In *Working With the First Sentence Stem,* you'll write down the automatic thoughts you have when you complete, over and over, the sentence that begins "I know I'm in trouble with my recovery when ..." Then you'll look for hot responses in those automatic thoughts, and create a new sentence stem from one of those hot responses.

- In *Working With the Second Sentence Stem,* you'll go through the same process with your new sentence stem, and create another new sentence stem from one of your new hot responses.

- In *Working With the Third Sentence Stem,* you'll complete the last new sentence stem that you created, and identify new hot responses.

- In *Working With the Final Sentence Stem,* you'll complete the sentence that begins "I'm now becoming aware that ..." and find hot responses in your answers. Then you'll go through all of your sentence completion exercises, find all the hot responses, and make sure you have warning signs describing all of those responses. If you don't, you'll create new cards to cover them.

As you can see, the final goal of this process is to flesh out your warning sign cards, adding cards that take you into a deeper and clearer awareness of your personal relapse patterns.

Part 1:   Warning Sign Review

In this exercise, you'll use a technique called "sentence completion" to help identify hidden warning signs that have been *repressed,* or blocked from conscious awareness.

1.   **Centering Technique:** Take a deep breath, hold it, and let it out slowly. Relax and notice how your stomach, chest, and throat feel. Take a final deep breath, let it out, and notice how you're feeling.

2.   **Read Your Warning Sign Cards:** Read the front of your Warning Sign Identification Cards and notice how you're feeling as you read each warning sign. Make note of your personal warning sign titles below:

_____

_____

_____

_____

_____

_____

_____

_____

_____

_____

_____

_____

_____

_____

_____

_____

_____

_____

Part 2:   *Working With the First Sentence Stem*

Section 1: Completing the First Sentence Stem

In this exercise, you'll complete the following sentence stem with at least ten different answers. There are no right or wrong answers. It's okay to write things that are unusual, sound silly, or don't make sense. Relax and let yourself write whatever pops into your mind. At this point, ignore the yes-or-no answers at the end of each line.

"I know I'm in trouble with my recovery when ..."   **Is this a hot response?**

1-1 _____ ☐ Yes ☐ No

1-2 _____ ☐ Yes ☐ No

1-3 _____ ☐ Yes ☐ No

1-4 _____ ☐ Yes ☐ No

1-5 _____ ☐ Yes ☐ No

1-6 _____ ☐ Yes ☐ No

1-7 _____ ☐ Yes ☐ No

1-8 _____ ☐ Yes ☐ No

1-9 _____ ☐ Yes ☐ No

1-10 _____ ☐ Yes ☐ No

1-11 _____ ☐ Yes ☐ No

1-12 _____ ☐ Yes ☐ No

1-13 _____ ☐ Yes ☐ No

1-14 _____ ☐ Yes ☐ No

1-15 _____ ☐ Yes ☐ No

1-16 _____ ☐ Yes ☐ No

1-17 _____ ☐ Yes ☐ No

1-18 _____ ☐ Yes ☐ No

1-19 _____ ☐ Yes ☐ No

1-20 _____ ☐ Yes ☐ No

Section 2: Finding Hot Responses

A hot response is any answer to a sentence completion that causes you to remember an unpleasant memory, have a strong feeling, or start a private argument within yourself.

2-1   Read the list of answers that you've just written.

2-2   As you read each answer, take a deep breath and notice what you're thinking and feeling.

2-3   Decide if that answer is a hot response. In other words, does it stir up an unpleasant memory, cause a strong feeling, or cause you to start an argument within yourself?

2-4   At the end of each answer on the previous page is the question, "Is this a hot response?" followed by a place to answer "yes" or "no." Check "yes" if the statement is a hot response. Check "no" if it's not a hot response.

Section 3: Writing the First New Sentence Stem

Pick one hot response that you'd like to work with, and write a new sentence stem using that response. These examples show how to do that:

If the hot response is . . .	**The new sentence stem will be . . .**
I know I'm in trouble with my recovery when I yell at my kids.	I yell at my kids when . . .
I know I'm in trouble with my recovery when I feel angry for no reason.	I feel angry for no reason when . . .
I know I'm in trouble with my recovery when I start to work long hours.	I work long hours when . . .

3-1   The hot response I want to work with is . . .

_____

3-2   The new sentence stem is . . .

_____

Part 3:   *Working With the Second Sentence Stem*

Section 1: Completing the Second Sentence Stem

Write your new sentence stem in the space below.

_____

Complete that sentence stem with a different answer at least ten times. Again, ignore the yes-or-no questions until you've written and re-read your answers.

Is this a hot response?

1-1	_____	☐ Yes ☐ No
1-2	_____	☐ Yes ☐ No
1-3	_____	☐ Yes ☐ No
1-4	_____	☐ Yes ☐ No
1-5	_____	☐ Yes ☐ No
1-6	_____	☐ Yes ☐ No
1-7	_____	☐ Yes ☐ No
1-8	_____	☐ Yes ☐ No
1-9	_____	☐ Yes ☐ No
1-10	_____	☐ Yes ☐ No
1-11	_____	☐ Yes ☐ No
1-12	_____	☐ Yes ☐ No
1-13	_____	☐ Yes ☐ No
1-14	_____	☐ Yes ☐ No
1-15	_____	☐ Yes ☐ No
1-16	_____	☐ Yes ☐ No
1-17	_____	☐ Yes ☐ No
1-18	_____	☐ Yes ☐ No
1-19	_____	☐ Yes ☐ No
1-20	_____	☐ Yes ☐ No

Section 2: Finding Hot Responses

2-1   Read the list of answers that you've just written.

2-2   As you read each answer, take a deep breath and notice what you're thinking and feeling.

2-3   Decide if that answer is a hot response.

2-4   At the end of each answer on the previous page, answer the question, "Is this a hot response?"

Section 3: Writing the Second New Sentence Stem

Pick one hot response that you'd like to work with, and write a new sentence stem using that response.

3-1   The hot response I want to work with is . . .

_____

3-2   The new sentence stem is . . .

_____

Part 4:   *Working With the Third Sentence Stem*

Write your new sentence stem in the space below.

_____

Complete that sentence stem with a different answer at least ten times.

Is this a hot response?

1. _____ ☐ Yes ☐ No
2. _____ ☐ Yes ☐ No
3. _____ ☐ Yes ☐ No
4. _____ ☐ Yes ☐ No
5. _____ ☐ Yes ☐ No
6. _____ ☐ Yes ☐ No
7. _____ ☐ Yes ☐ No
8. _____ ☐ Yes ☐ No
9. _____ ☐ Yes ☐ No
10. _____ ☐ Yes ☐ No
11. _____ ☐ Yes ☐ No
12. _____ ☐ Yes ☐ No
13. _____ ☐ Yes ☐ No
14. _____ ☐ Yes ☐ No
15. _____ ☐ Yes ☐ No
16. _____ ☐ Yes ☐ No
17. _____ ☐ Yes ☐ No
18. _____ ☐ Yes ☐ No
19. _____ ☐ Yes ☐ No
20. _____ ☐ Yes ☐ No

Read the list of answers that you've just written. As you read each answer, take a deep breath and notice what you're thinking and feeling. Decide if that answer is a hot response. Check "yes" if the statement is a hot response. Check "no" if it's not a hot response.

Section 1: Completing the Final Sentence Stem

I'm now becoming aware that ...   **Is this a hot response?**

1-1   _____   ☐ Yes ☐ No

1-2   _____   ☐ Yes ☐ No

1-3   _____   ☐ Yes ☐ No

1-4   _____   ☐ Yes ☐ No

1-5   _____   ☐ Yes ☐ No

1-6   _____   ☐ Yes ☐ No

1-7   _____   ☐ Yes ☐ No

1-8   _____   ☐ Yes ☐ No

1-9   _____   ☐ Yes ☐ No

1-10 _____   ☐ Yes ☐ No

1-11 _____   ☐ Yes ☐ No

1-12 _____   ☐ Yes ☐ No

1-13 _____   ☐ Yes ☐ No

1-14 _____   ☐ Yes ☐ No

1-15 _____   ☐ Yes ☐ No

1-16 _____   ☐ Yes ☐ No

1-17 _____   ☐ Yes ☐ No

1-18 _____   ☐ Yes ☐ No

1-19 _____   ☐ Yes ☐ No

1-20 _____   ☐ Yes ☐ No

Section 2: Finding Hot Responses

2-1   Read the list of answers that you've just written.

2-2   As you read each answer, take a deep breath and notice what you're thinking and feeling.

2-3   Decide if that answer is a hot response.

2-4   At the end of each line, answer the question, "Is this a hot response?"

Section 3: Finding Hidden Warning Signs

Review all five sentence completion exercises. Read each answer that you marked as a hot response. Look through your warning sign cards, and see if there's a card that describes that hot response.

3-1   If there is a card describing it, go on to the next hot response

3-2   If there's no card describing that hot response, write a new warning sign card describing it. Put that card in the appropriate sequence with the other warning sign cards, and go on to the next hot response.

Overview

In this process you'll see all the work you've done in the *Warning Sign Management* phase come together. The *Final Warning Sign List* that you create won't be a series of entries on a piece of paper. It will be a series of *Warning Sign Identification Cards* like the ones you've already started. This process has two parts:

- In *Creating the Final Warning Sign List,* you'll follow a detailed set of directions for completing Side 1 of your warning sign cards, arranging the cards in the order in which they occur, combining and removing cards to eliminate duplications, and filling in any gaps in the sequence of cards.

- In *Identifying Critical Warning Signs,* you'll find the three warning signs that give you the best opportunity to stop the relapse process before it gets out of hand.

Critical warning signs are ones that happen early in the relapse process, before your feelings and behavior have gotten out of control. They're signs that aren't emotionally "loaded" for you, so you can recognize them even if you're upset or angry. And they're signs that you're willing and able to work on managing.

This process is less emotionally challenging than the last two processes you completed, *Warning Sign Analysis* and *Sentence Completion.* But it's no less important.

The stack of cards that you create, and the critical warning signs that you identify, will serve as your main reference points in the *Warning Sign Management* and *Recovery Planning* phases. You'll complete Side 2 of your critical warning sign cards in *Warning Sign Management,* and Side 2 of the rest of the cards in *Recovery Planning.* These cards will be valuable tools for you throughout your ongoing recovery efforts.

Part 1:   Creating The Final Warning Sign List

Goal of This Exercise

The goal of the following exercise is to help you to create a clear and concise list of the situations, thoughts, feelings, and actions that lead you from stable recovery back to relapse. This list will be on the warning sign cards that you started in Process 8.

You begin the final warning sign list by carefully reviewing the warning sign cards that you've started up to this point. *The goal is to reduce the total number of cards to between 12 and 15 without leaving out any of the important things that happen that lead you to relapse.* You can reduce the total number by eliminating duplications, and by finding the warning sign cards that are actually thought, feeling, urge, action, or enabling relationship statements related to other warning signs. Creating new and clearly written warning sign identification cards will help you fill in anything that was missing in your first warning sign list.

To write a clear and concise final warning sign list, complete the procedures on the following pages.

Section 1: Checking the Titles

Read your stack of *Warning Sign Identification Cards* and check to be sure that each card has a title. The title should be a word or a short phrase that's easy for you to remember and that tells you exactly what the warning sign is all about. Good titles are short, clear, and easy to remember. Correct any titles that need it.

Section 2: Checking the Descriptions

Read the warning sign cards again. This time pay special attention to each description statement. Make sure the descriptions are clear by asking yourself the following questions about each card:

2-1   Is the description a complete sentence?

2-2   Does the sentence describe you doing something or wanting to do something, either by yourself or with (or to) someone or something else?

2-3   Are you the person who's doing the action in the warning sign? (What other people do or want to do are not warning signs for you. Your warning signs are *your* feelings and reactions to what they do.)

2-4   Did you use the same words in the title and the description? It is important to try to use different words in the title and the description. Rewrite the description if you need to.

Section 3: Eliminating Duplications

Read each warning sign card and notice if there are any other warning signs that say about the same thing. Sometimes two or more warning signs can be combined easily. Many warning sign cards contain thoughts, feelings, or urges that can be merged with other cards. Remember, *your goal is to end up with a final warning sign list of between 12 and 15 warning sign cards.* As you complete the following sections, keep looking for warning signs that can be combined or eliminated.

Section 4: Completing the Front of the Cards

On the front of each card, after the title and description, is a place for you to write a thought, feeling, urge, action, and enabling relationship statement. Starting with the first card, do the following:

4-1 **Thought Statement:** Read the title and the description and ask yourself what you're usually thinking when you're experiencing that warning sign. Pick the most important thought and write it in the space next to the words, "When I experience this warning sign I tend to think ..."

Make sure the thought is written in a complete sentence. Now ask yourself these questions:

a. Does the thought statement contain any *generalities,* such as, *"Everyone is against me"* (Who is everyone?), *"Things always go wrong"* (Is there ever a time when things go right? At what specific times do things tend to go wrong?), or *"I can't do it"* (What specifically is it that you can't do?). By identifying and challenging the generalities with questions like these, you can make your thought statements more clear and concrete.

b. Does the thought statement contain any *deletions,* such as, *"I can't anymore"* (Can't what?) or *"I don't know any more"* (What is it that you don't know?)?

c. Does the thought statement contain a *distorted metaphor,* such as, *"He treated me like garbage"* or *"I was blown away when she said that"?* These types of metaphors communicate feeling, but they don't accurately describe what's happening. Translate any distorted metaphors into accurate descriptions.

4-2 **Feeling Statement:** Read the title and description again and ask yourself what you usually feel when you're experiencing this warning sign. Read your thought statement out loud several times and ask yourself "What kinds of feelings will be caused by thinking this thought?" Write a feeling statement in the correct place that completes the statement, *"When I experience this warning sign I tend to feel ..."* Use the following list of feeling words to help you describe your feelings, and note how strongly you feel them on a scale of one to ten.

☐ Strong or ☐ Weak _____	☐ Safe or ☐ Threatened _____
☐ Angry or ☐ Caring _____	☐ Fulfilled or ☐ Frustrated _____
☐ Happy or ☐ Sad _____	☐ Proud or ☐ Ashamed, guilty _____

4-3 **Urge Statement:** Read the title and the description again and ask yourself, "What do I usually have an urge to do when I experience this warning sign?" Read the thought and feeling statement several times and ask yourself, "What are those thoughts and feelings likely to cause me to want to do about it?" Write the answer in the appropriate place. Write an urge statement in the correct place that completes the statement, *"When I experience this warning sign I have an urge to ..."*

4-4 **Action Statement:** An action is an external behavior that others can actually observe. Read the title and the description again and ask yourself, "What do I actually do when I experience this warning sign?" Read the urge statement and ask yourself, "Do I usually act out the urge or do I push the urge down and force myself to do something else?" Write an urge statement in the correct place that completes the statement, *"When I experience this warning sign what I actually do is ..."*

4-5   **Enabling Relationship Statement:** Read the action statement again and ask yourself, "How are other people affected by what I do? How does my behavior invite other people to become part of my problem?" Write an enabling relationship statement in the correct place that completes the sentence, *"I tend to invite others to become part of my problem by ..."*

Section 5: Reading the Next Warning Sign Card

The next warning sign card should describe an event that follows logically from the urge and action statements. The question you should ask yourself is, "How does my reaction to the previous warning sign set me up to experience the next warning sign?" When we have an urge, either we try to ignore it or we act it out. Here's an example:

Title of Warning Sign #1: **Trapped**

> *Description:* I know I'm in trouble with my recovery when I start to believe that being clean and sober is like being in jail because I can't do what I want to do.
>
> *When I experience this warning sign I tend to think* I can't win no matter what I do.
>
> *When I experience this warning sign I tend to feel* sad and depressed.
>
> *When I experience this warning sign I have an urge to* go back into the old life in order to get my freedom back and feel excited and alive.
>
> *When I experience this warning sign what I actually do is* keep doing what I need to do to stay sober, hating every minute of it and keeping it a secret.
>
> *I tend to invite others to become part of my problem by* avoiding them and refusing to tell them what's really happening inside me.

Title of Warning Sign #2: **Old Friends**

> *Description:* I know that I'm in trouble with my recovery when I feel the urge to hang out with the people I used to drink and use drugs with.

In the example of Warning Sign #1, notice how the thought creates the feeling, the feeling creates the urge, the urge is either acted out or pushed down, and the action invites others to become part of the problem. The action coupled with the enabling response of others creates the next warning sign.

Section 6: Filling in the Gaps in the Action

Slowly read the warning sign list again, and see yourself moving through the sequence of events. Notice in your mind how you move from one warning sign to the next. Ask yourself, "Are there any gaps in the action? Do I skip a step anywhere in the process?" If you notice any gaps in the action, write new warning sign cards that will fill in those gaps.

One way of filling in the gaps in the action is to use the following method.

6-1   Identify the warning sign before and after the gap in the action.

6-2   Read the warning sign before the gap in the action and create a sentence stem that reads: *"One of the things I do after (describe the action in the warning sign before the gap) is ..."*. This should bring to the surface the next step in the action sequence.

6-3   Read the warning sign after the gap in the action and create a sentence stem that reads: *"One of the things that causes me to (describe the action in the warning sign after the gap) is ..."*. This should bring to the surface the previous step in the action sequence.

6-4   Review your answers to the sentence completion exercise in steps 6-2 and 6-3 above, and write one or more Warning Sign Cards that fill in the gap in the action.

Section 7: Backtracking to Earlier Warning Signs

We usually don't start to notice that we're in trouble until things have already started to go wrong. Look at the first warning sign card and ask yourself, "Is this really where it started? What happened that caused this first warning sign to happen?" If you can think of an earlier warning sign, write a new warning sign card that describes it. Read the new warning sign you just wrote and ask yourself, "What happened that caused this warning sign to happen?" If you can think of an earlier warning sign, write it below. Repeat this process until you can't think of any earlier warning signs.

Section 8: Thinking About Relapse

Think about exactly how you talk yourself into relapse.

8-1   Number each card in the upper right-hand corner so you can easily put them back in the order they're in, if you choose to.

8-2   Read each of your warning sign cards again and ask yourself, "Do I start to think about relapsing when I experience this warning sign?" If the answer is yes, put the letter R (standing for relapse) at the top right-hand corner of the card next to the number.

8-3   The warning signs that trigger an urge to relapse normally come near the end of the warning sign list. As an experiment, pull out each card that triggers an urge to relapse (those marked with an R) and put them at the end of the sequence, keeping them in the same order in relation to one another. In most cases this helps make the progression of warning sign cards clearer. If it doesn't work, put the cards back in the original order. If it does work, number the cards again in the upper right-hand corner.

Section 9: Reviewing the Final Warning Sign List

Read your warning sign cards one last time. You should clearly see that one warning sign causes the next one to occur. The first warning sign happens, then we think self-defeating thoughts that cause us to have unmanageable feelings, which create the urge to act out the next warning sign. Here is an example of how it works:

Warning Sign #1: Title: Got to Have it My Way

Description: I know I'm in trouble with my recovery when I believe I have to have everything go the way I want it to, whether I'm right or not.

When this happens, I tend to think: I'm right and you're wrong! I can't do anything wrong!

When I think these thoughts, I tend to feel: Powerful and strong.

When I feel this way, I have an urge to: Push other people around and tell them what to do.

When I have this urge, what I actually do is: Manipulate and threaten others to get my way.

When I do this, I invite others to become part of my problem by: Threatening them and forcing them to do it my way or leave me alone.

Warning Sign #2: Title: Pushing Others Around

Description: I know I'm in trouble with my recovery when I start to act like a bully and force people to do things my way by manipulating and threatening them.

When this happens, I tend to think: Other people are dumb and stupid and need me to tell them what to do.

When I think these thoughts, I tend to feel: Angry at others, powerful.

When I have these feelings, I have an urge to: Get away from these dumb people who make so much trouble for me.

When I have this urge, what I actually do is: Isolate myself and feel sorry for myself.

When I do this, I invite others to become part of my problem by: Refusing to talk to them.

Warning Sign #3: Being Alone

Look at how the warning signs lead from one to another. Go through your cards and identify the ways in which they do lead from one to another, and any remaining gaps in the action. Fill in the gaps with new warning signs. When you're done, you'll have a complete picture of the chain of thoughts, feelings, urges, and actions that lead from stable recovery to relapse.

Part 2:   Identifying Critical Warning Signs

Instructions

The purpose of this exercise is to help you to select the key or critical warning signs that lead you from recovery back into relapse. Once you've identified these critical warning signs, you'll learn how to manage them effectively in recovery.

Critical warning signs are warning signs that can alert you to the fact that you're moving toward relapse, and give you a chance to stop the relapse process before it gets too strong. These are signs that:

- You'll easily recognize even if you're upset or angry

- Happen early enough for you to take positive action to intervene (interrupt the process)

- You're willing to deal with in order to avoid relapse

To identify your critical warning signs, you can do the following:

1.   Review your final warning sign list and identify the warning signs that start early in the relapse process, ones that you'll be able to recognize easily and do something about.

2.   Review the warning signs that you've identified as possible critical warning signs. Pick the three that best seem to fit the description of a critical warning sign above. Write the letters CWS in the upper right-hand corner of each of the three.

3.   Check each of the three cards against the instructions in Part 1, Creating the Final Warning Sign List. Make sure each of these cards matches all of those instructions, and has very clear thought, feeling, urge, and action statements. If any of these are missing or not clear, rewrite them.

4.   Fill out Sections 1, 2, and 3 on the following pages, one section for each critical warning sign. These should include an exact version of what's on your cards, or an improved version.

5.   If Sections 1, 2, and 3 turn out to be much different from your cards, rewrite the cards so that they also contain the improved versions.

You'll be using these warning signs in the rest of the workbook, as you learn how to manage thoughts, feelings, situations, and behaviors and develop a recovery plan that meets your personal recovery needs. That is why it's so important that these cards be very clear and very honest. That will make a big difference in your success in learning to manage your relapse warning signs.

Section 1: Critical Warning Sign #1

The title of Critical Warning Sign #1 is: _____

I selected this card as a critical warning sign because ... _____

_____

_____

_____

Now write in the following spaces exactly what's on this warning sign card, or an improved version of what's on the card.

Title: _____

Description: I know I'm in trouble with my recovery when ...

_____

_____

Thought: When I experience this warning sign I tend to think ...

_____

_____

Feeling: When I experience this warning sign I tend to feel ...

_____

Urge: When I experience this warning sign I have an urge to ...

_____

Action: When I experience this warning sign what I actually do is ...

_____

Enabling Relationships: I tend to invite others to become part of my problem by ...

_____

Section 2: Critical Warning Sign #2

The title of Critical Warning Sign #2 is: _____

I selected this card as a critical warning sign because ... _____

_____

_____

_____

Now write in the following spaces exactly what's on this warning sign card, or an improved version of what's on the card.

Title: _____

Description: I know I'm in trouble with my recovery when ...

_____

_____

Thought: When I experience this warning sign I tend to think ...

_____

_____

Feeling: When I experience this warning sign I tend to feel ...

_____

Urge: When I experience this warning sign I have an urge to ...

_____

Action: When I experience this warning sign what I actually do is ...

_____

Enabling Relationships: I tend to invite others to become part of my problem by ...

_____

Section 3: Critical Warning Sign #3

The title of Critical Warning Sign #3 is: _____

I selected this card as a critical warning sign because ... _____

_____

_____

_____

_____

Now write in the following spaces exactly what's on this warning sign card, or an improved version of what's on the card.

Title: _____

Description: I know I'm in trouble with my recovery when ...

_____

_____

Thought: When I experience this warning sign I tend to think ...

_____

_____

Feeling: When I experience this warning sign I tend to feel ...

_____

Urge: When I experience this warning sign I have an urge to ...

_____

Action: When I experience this warning sign what I actually do is ...

_____

Enabling Relationships: I tend to invite others to become part of my problem by ...

_____

Phase IV: *Warning Sign Management*

What?

Developing new and more effective ways to manage the sequence of problems that leads from stable recovery to relapse

Learning to manage the thoughts, feelings, urges, and actions that drive that sequence of problems

Why?

Insight is the booby prize of life

Understanding what's wrong without having a plan to do something more effective won't stop you from relapsing

You can't solve a problem without the vision of a solution

Overview

This phase has its own overall introduction because it's arranged differently than the other phases. Without an explanation, this might get a little confusing.

There are four basic processes in *Warning Sign Management:*

- *Thought Management*—Learning to understand and manage the irrational thoughts that drive the relapse warning signs and replace those thoughts with rational, constructive ones. This is Process 11.

- *Feeling Management*—Learning to understand and manage the formerly unmanageable feelings that drive the relapse warning signs, and to think and act in ways that will produce more manageable feelings. This is Process 12.

- *Behavior and Situation Management*—Learning to understand how your self-defeating behavior and high-risk situations drive your relapse warning signs, and finding more effective ways of thinking, managing your feelings, and acting. This is Process 13.

- *Integrated TFUAR (Thought, Feeling, Urge, Actioin, Relationship) Management*—Bringing all those management skills together and making them readily available by writing key reminders on the back of your Relapse Warning Sign Cards. This is Process 14.

Often it's especially hard to identify and manage thoughts, feelings, urges, and actions because they're "automatic"—they happen without your conscious awareness. But that's all the more reason you need to learn to identify and clearly label your experiences. As long as you're not conscious of your thoughts, feelings, urges, and actions, you have little hope of managing them.

It's important to look at thought, feeling, behavior, and situation management skills separately— then together—because of two problems that often lead people into relapse: "fuzzy thinking" and "compartmental thinking."

Fuzzy thinking is a tendency to confuse thoughts, feelings, urges, actions, and relationships. For example, if someone asks you how you feel about your boss, you might say, "I feel like he's not being fair to me." But that's not really a feeling; it's a thought. Or you might have strong feelings of fear and anger and interpret them as a need to take a drink or a tranquilizer.

Compartmental thinking is a tendency to think of thoughts, feelings, urges, actions, and relationships as completely separate and unrelated—and never look at how one area might lead to another. For example, you might be having trouble with your boss (a relationship), and think that's the end of the story.

But really, you might have done things on the job that made him angry or mistrustful (actions). And you might have done those things in response to a desire to get back at him for something he said or did (an urge). That urge might have followed feelings of anger and fear (feelings), which might have been sparked by thoughts about how he didn't have a right to say what he said or act the way he acted, and how he could fire you if he wanted to (thoughts).

That's why it's so important to trace warning signs through the thoughts, feelings, urges, actions, and relationships that drive them. You need to prevent fuzzy thinking by clearly labeling and understanding your thoughts, feelings, urges, actions, and relationships. The first three processes in this phase will prepare you to do just that.

You also need to prevent compartmental thinking by looking at how your thoughts, feelings, urges, actions, and relationships lead from one to another. The *Integrated TFUAR Management* process will help you do that, and put it on a handy warning sign card that you can look at any time—for example, when you're about to go into a meeting with your boss.

In the *Warning Sign Management* phase, you're going to go through all four processes with each of the three critical warning signs you identified in the last process, the *Final Warning Sign List*. But you're *not* going to take all three warning signs through Process 11, then take them all through Process 12, then through Process 13, then through 14. If you did that, you'd miss the way all four processes fit together.

Instead, you're going to deal with one critical warning sign at a time, taking it through all four processes. For this reason, the process numbering in the *Warning Sign Management* phase is different from the numbering in the other phases:

- First you take your first critical warning sign through Process 11A (*Thought Management for the First Critical Warning Sign*), Process 12A (*Feeling Management for the First Critical Warning Sign*), Process 13A (*Behavior and Situation Management for the First Critical Warning Sign*), and Process 14A (*Integrated TFUAR Management for the First Critical Warning Sign*).

- Next you take your second critical warning sign through Process 11B (*Thought Management for the Second Critical Warning Sign*), Process 12B (*Feeling Management for the Second Critical Warning Sign*), Process 13B (*Behavior and Situation Management for the Second Critical Warning Sign*), and Process 14B (*Integrated TFUAR Management for the Second Critical Warning Sign*).

- Finally you take your third critical warning sign through Process 11C (*Thought Management for the Third Critical Warning Sign*), Process 12C (*Feeling Management for the Third Critical Warning Sign*), Process 13C (*Behavior and Situation Management for the Third Critical Warning Sign*), and Process 14C (*Integrated TFUAR Management for the Third Critical Warning Sign*).

So if you're paging through this phase and you find yourself going from 11A to 12A and wondering where 11B went, don't worry. You'll be going through all the A's, then all the B's, then all the C's. The result will be a much more effective learning process.

Thought Management
For the First Critical Warning Sign

Overview

The *Thought Management* process is divided into three parts:

- In *Identifying Mandates and Injunctions,* you'll look at the thoughts on your first critical warning sign card and find any "mandates" (beliefs that you *must* think, feel, or do something in particular) and "injunctions" (beliefs that you *must not* think, feel, or do something) hidden in those thoughts. Then you'll identify the "threatened consequences" carried by those mandates and injunctions—what you believe will happen if you don't follow them. At this point your aim is to notice and clearly identify the mandates and injunctions.

- In *Challenging Mandates and Injunctions,* you'll look at where you might have learned those beliefs; the possibility that your mandates, injunctions, and threatened consequences are incorrect; and the benefits, disadvantages, and likely outcome of holding those beliefs.

- In *Identifying New Choices,* you'll look at the thoughts you might have when you manage this warning sign more effectively. You'll compare the choices that this kind of thinking gives you with the choices you have when you cling to your old thought patterns and manage the warning sign ineffectively.

The first purpose of this process is to point out how you're imprisoned by the old beliefs that drive your thought patterns when your relapse warning signs are activated. The second purpose is to identify new thoughts and beliefs that can free you to make new choices.

Everyone has an undercurrent of old mandates and injunctions that they've picked up throughout the course of life. But people who are working for their own well-being learn to question those mandates and injunctions. They find that they're not forced to take them seriously, or to act on them. They find that they can choose to think differently—and that doing so opens up a whole world of new choices.

Thought Management
For the First Critical Warning Sign

Part 1:   *Identifying Mandates and Injunctions*

1.   Review the three critical warning signs that you identified in Process 7, Part 3, *The Initial Warning Sign List* (page 126). Choose the one that you want to work on first. Write your personal title for this warning sign below.

_____

2.   Copy the thought statement for this warning sign.

When I experience this warning sign I tend to think ..._____

_____

_____

3.   What does this way of thinking tell you that you must think, feel, or do? (This is called a "mandate.")

I must ..._____

_____

_____

4.   What do you think will happen if you *don't* do what this thought tells you that you *must* do? (This is a "threatened consequence"—*Do it or else!)*

I believe that I must do what this thoughts tells me to do, or else ..._____

_____

_____

5.   Again review the thoughts you listed under question 2. What does this way of thinking tell you that you *must not* or *can't* think, feel, or do? (This is called an "injunction.")

I must not ..._____

_____

_____

6.   What do you think will happen if you *do* what this thought tells you that you *must not* do? (This is another threatened consequence—*Don't do it or else!)*

If I do what this thought is telling me not to do, I believe the following negative thing will happpen ... _____

_____

_____

Thought Management
For the First Critical Warning Sign

Part 2:   Challenging Mandates and Injunctions

Review the mandates and injunctions you identified in Part 1 for your first critical warning sign.

1.   Who taught you that you must or must not think, feel, or act in this way?

_____

2.   Is it possible that you were taught wrong?   ❑ Yes   ❑ No   ❑ Unsure

       Please explain:

_____

_____

3.   What are the benefits of thinking about things in this way?

_____

_____

4.   What are the disadvantages of thinking about things in this way?

_____

_____

5.   If you continue to think about things in this way, what's the *best* thing that could happen?

_____

_____

6.   If you continue to think about things in this way, what's the *worst* thing that could happen?

_____

_____

7.   If you continue to think about things in this way, what's *most likely* to happen?

_____

_____

Part 3:   Identifying New Choices

1. Review the critical warning sign that you identified in Part 1. Think of a situation in which you managed this warning sign *effectively*. If you can't remember managing this warning sign effectively, imagine how you might manage it more effectively.

    When you managed this warning sign effectively (or imagined yourself doing so), what did you tend to think?

    _____

    _____

    _____

    _____

    _____

2. What choices did this way of thinking give you that you didn't have when you were managing the warning sign *ineffectively*?

    I can choose to ... _____

    _____

    _____

    _____

    _____

    _____

3. Go back and review the thoughts, mandates, and injunctions that you identified in Part 1. What is another way of thinking about this situation that can give you new and more effective choices in what you can do about it?

    _____

    _____

    _____

    _____

    _____

    _____

Overview

Not knowing how to manage feelings effectively is a major cause of relapse. When you're caught in the grip of painful or upsetting feelings, it might seem like you have only two choices: to "numb off," often through addictive behavior, or to over-react to the feelings and cause more trouble in your life. Process 12 will teach you a third choice: to manage your feelings effectively. This is an important way to lower your risk of relapse.

The process for *Feeling Management* rests on five basic principles:

1.   It's normal and natural to have feelings.

2.   Every feeling has a purpose, even painful feelings. For example, some feelings are meant to tell you that something or someone is dangerous to you. Some feelings are necessary so you can grieve and heal your losses. There are all kinds of purposes for the feelings you have.

3.   There are no "good" feelings or "bad" feelings, no matter what you might have been taught.

4.   There are only "pleasant" feelings and "unpleasant" feelings. Pleasant feelings aren't necessarily good, and unpleasant feelings aren't necessarily bad.

5.   Feelings are part of an inter-related system of thoughts, feelings, urges, actions, and relationships.

Mismanagement of Feelings

If you want to know how to manage feelings effectively, first look at how people often "mismanage" feelings:

• **They "block" their feelings**. Sometimes they stop breathing or tense up their muscles. Sometimes they start thinking about something else or doing something else—usually some compulsive behavior. This process is sometimes called "repression" of feelings, because it represses or pushes them down. In time, they learn not to notice what they feel.

• **They judge their feelings**. They decide the feelings are bad ("This is morally wrong!"), awful ("This is terrible!"), or unbearable ("I can't stand it!"). Judgments are decisions about the nature or worth of people or things. When people judge their feelings, they don't realize that they're making decisions about the nature of their feelings, but they are.

• **They judge themselves**. They decide that, because they have those feelings, they're bad ("I'm wrong or defective!"), weak ("I'm not strong; I'm a coward!"), crazy ("I have emotional problems!"), or inferior ("I'm less than other people!").

• **They mandate their feelings** ("I *must* feel this way ... or I'll be no good!" "... or something awful will happen!" "... or I'll die!").

• **They forbid their feelings**, or form injunctions against them ("I *must not* feel this way ... or I'll be no good!" "... or something awful will happen!" "... or I'll die!").

These feeling mismanagement strategies do a lot of damage.

- Sometimes they repress the feelings, or block them from awareness.

- Sometimes these strategies exaggerate painful or upsetting feelings. They *magnify* the feelings—blow them up bigger than they really are. They *amplify* the feelings, so the feelings are practically deafening. Or they *intensify* the feelings, so they feel unbearable.

- And sometimes they distort the feelings. For example, mismanagement of anger can turn it into hatred or resentment. Mismanagement of normal sadness can turn it into depression.

Effective Feeling Management Strategies

Effective feeling management works much differently. There are five major strategies of effective feeling management:

1. **Recognize the feeling:** Take a deep breath and notice any feelings in your body. Notice any images that you have, any memories or fantasies. Let yourself feel what you feel.

2. **Label the feeling:** Put a word-label on your feeling. If you're not sure what to call it, look at the feeling list. Use a sentence completion exercise that begins, "Right now I feel ..." Keep trying different feeling words until you've got it right.

3. **Affirm the feeling:** Say to yourself, "I'm feeling _____, and it's okay to have this feeling."

4. **Communicate the feeling:** Find someone who's safe to confide in—someone who won't make fun of you, won't insult you, won't use the information against you, and won't tell anyone else what you've said. Tell that person what you're feeling, the thoughts that are related to that feeling, the urges that you're having as a result of the feeling, and the actions that those urges tell you to take.

5. **Resolve the feeling:** Identify and talk about your current triggers for the feeling, any unfinished business—from childhood or adulthood—that's making the feeling more intense, and the consequences of acting out the feeling.

If you're having trouble putting a name to your feelings, you can use the feeling chart below to identify your feelings and rate their strength on a scale of one to ten.

☐ Strong or ☐ Weak _____	☐ Safe or ☐ Threatened _____
☐ Angry or ☐ Caring _____	☐ Fulfilled or ☐ Frustrated _____
☐ Happy or ☐ Sad _____	☐ Proud or ☐ Ashamed, guilty _____

Appendix 8 (page 296) contains a more detailed list of effective feeling management skills. And Part 3 of this process gives you an opportunity to apply those skills to your critical warning sign.

The Feeling Management Process

The *Feeling Management* process has two parts:

- In *Identifying Ineffective Feeling Management Strategies,* you'll look at the feelings you tend to have when you manage this warning sign ineffectively or "mismanage" it, and the thoughts and actions connected with those feelings.

- In *Learning New Feeling Management Skills,* you'll apply 16 basic skills to a typical situation in which this warning sign has been turned on.

As you go through this process for your first critical warning sign, concentrate on simply noticing your feelings and building your emotional vocabulary. Sit in a comfortable position, take deep and slow breaths, and notice what you're feeling. Use the feeling chart to help you put word labels on your feelings and rate their intensity. Awareness of feelings is an all-important first step in learning the skills of feeling management.

Feeling Management
For the First Critical Warning Sign

Part 1:   *Identifying Ineffective Feeling Management Strategies*

1.   Choose the same critical warning sign that you worked with in Process 11A (page 176). Again, write your personalized title for that warning sign below.

_____

2.   In Process 7, Part 3, *The Initial Warning Sign List* (126), find the feeling statement that you wrote for that critical warning sign, and write it below. When I experience this warning sign I tend to feel ...

_____

_____

3.   Use the feeling chart to describe how you tend to feel when this warning sign is turned on, and how strongly you feel this way.

☐ Strong or ☐ Weak _____	☐ Safe or ☐ Threatened _____
☐ Angry or ☐ Caring _____	☐ Fulfilled or ☐ Frustrated _____
☐ Happy or ☐ Sad _____	☐ Proud or ☐ Ashamed, guilty _____

4.   What are some of the thoughts that cause you to feel this way?

_____

_____

5.   What are you usually doing that causes you to feel this way?

_____

_____

6.   What do you usually do to try to manage these feelings?

_____

_____

7.   Does the way you choose to think and act make you feel better or worse?

❑ Makes me feel better.   ❑ Makes me feel worse.   ❑ Doesn't change how I feel.

Why do you say that? _____

_____

_____

_____

Feeling Management
For the First Critical Warning Sign

Part 2:   Learning New Feeling Management Skills

This exercise will help you examine some possible ways to improve your feeling-management skills when your warning signs are turned on. They follow the Guidelines for Effective Feeling Management listed in Appendix 8. Answer these questions for the critical warning sign that you're working on.

1.   How can you anticipate and prepare for situations that can trigger the kinds of strong feelings or emotions that this warning sign raises?

_____

_____

_____

_____

2.   How can you recognize when you start to have these strong feelings or emotions?

_____

_____

3.   How can you stop yourself from automatically responding to the feelings before you've had a chance to think them through (for example, taking a few slow, deep breaths and noticing what you're feeling; calling a "time out"; getting away from the situation; or using an immediate relaxation technique to bring down the intensity of your feelings)?

_____

_____

_____

_____

4.   How can you find words to describe what you're feeling and how strong the feelings are? (What words might you check if you used the feeling list? How would you rate the intensity of your feeling using a ten-point scale? Can you consciously acknowledge the feeling and its intensity by saying to yourself, "Right now I'm feeling _____ and it's okay to be feeling this way"?)

☐ Strong or ☐ Weak _____	☐ Safe or ☐ Threatened _____
☐ Angry or ☐ Caring _____	☐ Fulfilled or ☐ Frustrated _____
☐ Happy or ☐ Sad _____	☐ Proud or ☐ Ashamed, guilty _____

5.   How can you identify what you're thinking that makes you feel this way?

_____

_____

6. How can you change what you're thinking in a way that will let you feel better?

    _____

    _____

7. How can you identify what you're doing that makes you feel this way?

    _____

    _____

8. How can you change what you're doing in a way that will let you feel better?

    _____

    _____

9. How can you recognize and resist your urges to create problems, hurt yourself, or hurt other people?

    _____

    _____

10. How can you recognize your resistance to doing things that will help you or your situation, and force yourself to do those things in spite of the resistance?

    _____

    _____

11. How can you get outside of yourself and recognize and respond to what other people are feeling?

    _____

    _____

12. Do you have a safe person you can talk to about what you're feeling? Who is that person, and what would be the best way to contact him or her?

    _____

    _____

Behavior and Situation Management
For the First Critical Warning Sign

Overview

The *Behavior and Situation Management* process adds another dimension to the work begun in thought and feeling management. Its aim is to look at high-risk situations that you've handled ineffectively in the past, and find "intervention points."

Intervention points are opportunities within the situation where you could have done things differently—thought differently, managed your feelings or emotions differently, acted differently, or treated other people differently—to produce a better outcome.

To find these intervention points, you'll start with a situation map like the one you completed in Process 8, *Warning Sign Analysis*. Then you'll look for likely intervention points near the beginning of the situation, near the middle of the situation, and near the end of the situation. You'll be asked to write how you could have done things differently at these times, and how it would have changed the outcome.

The final step of this process is to look at a high-risk situation coming up in the near future that might trigger this warning sign, and to look at how you might apply what you've learned in this exercise to other situations.

As you go through this process, work at identifying two kinds of things:

1.   The high-risk situations you tend to get into when this warning sign is turned on, and the high-risk situations you're likely to get into in the future.

2.   The self-defeating behaviors that you tend to act out in this situation. These are behaviors that might feel good or satisfying now, but they usually work against your long-term well being and bring problems or discomfort in the end.

Many people keep returning to high-risk situations and acting out self-defeating behaviors simply because they've never thought of them as such. Putting these kinds of labels on situations and behaviors will give you a head start on managing them effectively.

Behavior and Situation Management
For the First Critical Warning Sign

Think of the critical warning sign you've been working on. Now think of a specific past situation in which you experienced this warning sign while in recovery and *managed it poorly or ineffectively*. Tell the experience as if it were a story with a beginning, a middle, and an ending.

Sequencing Statements	Clarifying Questions
1. The warning sign was triggered when ...	1. Who were you with and what were they doing?
2. The first thing I did was ...	2. What were you doing?
3. The next thing I did was ...	3. What was going on around you?
4. The next thing I did was ...	4. Where did this happen?
5. What finally happened was ...	5. When did this happen? (Month, day, time)

The warning sign was triggered when ... _____

_____

_____

_____

_____

_____

_____

_____

_____

_____

_____

_____

_____

_____

_____

_____

_____

_____

_____

1. **Intervention Point #1**: What could you have done differently near the beginning of the situation to produce a better outcome? (How could you have thought differently? Managed your feelings and emotions differently? Acted differently? Treated other people differently?)

    _____

    _____

    _____

    _____

    _____

    • If you had done these things, how would it have changed the outcome?

    _____

    _____

    _____

2. **Intervention Point #2**: What could you have done differently near the middle of the situation to produce a better outcome? (How could you have thought differently? Managed your feelings and emotions differently? Acted differently? Treated other people differently?)

    _____

    _____

    _____

    _____

    _____

    • If you had done these things, how would it have changed the outcome?

    _____

    _____

    _____

3. **Intervention Point #3**: What could you have done differently near the end of the situation to produce a better outcome? (How could you have thought differently? Managed your feelings and emotions differently? Acted differently? Treated other people differently?)

    _____

    _____

    _____

    _____

    _____

• If you had done these things, how would it have changed the outcome?

_____

_____

_____

4.   **Most Important Thing Learned**: What is the most important thing that you learned by completing this exercise?

_____

_____

_____

5.   **Future High-Risk Situation**: Is there a situation coming up in the near future that will put you at risk of experiencing this critical warning sign?   ❏ Yes   ❏ No   ❏ Unsure

Please describe how this might happen.   _____

_____

_____

_____

6.   **Application to Other High-Risk Situations**: How can you apply what you learned in this situation to other high-risk situations in your life?

_____

_____

_____

Overview

"TFUAR" stands for thoughts, feelings, urges, actions, and relationships. You've looked at these elements separately in the first three processes of this phase. Now it's time to look at how they all fit together.

The *Integrated TFUAR Management* process brings home all the work you've done in *Thought Management, Feeling Management,* and *Behavior and Situation Management*, and puts it in a practical, portable, easy-to-use form: Side 2 of your Warning Sign Identification Card.

Now that you've taken your first critical warning sign through the first three management processes, you're in the best position to start filling in Side 2. This side is designed to hold the solutions to the problems you identified on Side 1.

Please note that this process doesn't cover the first item on Side 2, "Recovery Activities." Recovery activities are the main focus of Phase V, *Recovery Planning.* You might choose to wait and fill in this line of Side 2 when you get to that final phase. If you'd like to give it a try now, go ahead. But understand that your answers may well change when you do your *Recovery Planning* work.

The *TFUAR Management* process is a simple one, but it will require a lot of thought. It will be helpful to look back through all the management strategies you've been working on in the first three processes and choose the ones that seem most effective for this critical warning sign.

Part 1:   Managing Thoughts

Write the title of your first critical warning sign:

_____

1.   Look at Side 1 of your first critical warning sign card, and write the "thought" statement below.

      When I experience this warning sign I tend to think ...

      _____

      _____

2.   What are some of the ways of thinking that make it harder to manage this warning sign? (Refer to Process 11A, Part 1.) Remember your mandates ("I *must* or else...") and injunctions ("I'd *better not*, or else...").

      _____

      _____

      _____

      _____

3.   What's another way of thinking about this that might give you better choices? (Refer to Process 11A, Part 3.) How could those new choices promote healthy recovery?

      _____

      _____

      _____

      _____

4.   How can you change your way of thinking so you can feel better? (Refer to Process 12A, Part 2.)

      _____

      _____

      _____

      _____

5.   What kinds of more helpful thoughts can you have at important intervention points in this warning sign? (Refer to Process 13A.)   (An "intervention point" is a point where making a different choice might make the situation come out differently.)

_____

_____

_____

6.   Breathe deeply and imagine yourself in a situation in which this critical warning sign is turned on. What are the thoughts that seem most likely to strengthen your recovery and prevent relapse?

_____

_____

7.   Turn to Side 2 of your first critical warning sign card. Under "Managing Thoughts," copy the thoughts that you wrote in answer to question 6, above.

Part 2:   *Managing Feelings*

Write the title of your first critical warning sign:

_____

1.   Look at Side 1 of your first critical warning sign card, and write the "Feeling" statement below.

When I experience this warning sign I tend to feel ...

_____

2.   What are some of the ineffective feeling management strategies that you use most often when this warning sign is turned on? (Refer to Process 12A, Part 1.) How do they make you feel?

_____

_____

_____

_____

3.   What are some other ways of managing your feelings that would be more helpful to you? (Refer to Process 12A, Part 3.)

_____

_____

_____

_____

4.   Which feeling management skills would be most effective at important intervention points in this warning sign? (Refer to Process 13A.)

_____

_____

_____

_____

5. Breathe deeply and imagine yourself in a situation in which this critical warning sign is turned on. Which ways of managing your feelings seem most likely to strengthen your recovery and prevent relapse?

_____

6. Turn to Side 2 of your first critical warning sign card. Under "Managing Feelings," copy the thoughts that you wrote in answer to question 5, above.

Part 3:   *Managing Urges*

Write the title of your first critical warning sign:

_____

1.   Look at Side 1 of your first critical warning sign card, and write the "Urge" statement below.

     When I experience this warning sign I have an urge to ...

     _____

2.   Think about the mandates and injunctions you have when this warning sign is turned on. (Refer to Process 11A, Part 1.) What are some of the urges that those mandates and injunctions tend to create?

     _____

     _____

     _____

     _____

3.   Think again about **new** ways of thinking in this situation, and the new choices that those ways of thinking give you. (Refer to Process 11A, Part 3.) How can these choices help you manage your urges?

     _____

     _____

     _____

     _____

4.   When you manage your feelings in ineffective ways, what kinds of urges do you tend to have? (Refer to Process 12A, Part 1.)

     _____

     _____

     _____

     _____

5.   How can you manage your urges more effectively if you use more effective feeling management skills? (Refer to Process 12A, Part 2.)

_____

_____

_____

_____

6.   Picture yourself making better use of the important intervention points in this situation. (Refer to Process 13A.) What can you do to manage your urges at those intervention points?

_____

_____

_____

_____

7.   Breathe deeply and imagine yourself in a situation in which this critical warning sign is turned on. Which urge management skills seem most likely to strengthen your recovery and prevent relapse?

_____

_____

8.   Turn to Side 2 of your first critical warning sign card. Under "Managing Urges," copy the thoughts that you wrote in answer to question 7, above.

Integrated TFUAR Management
For the First Critical Warning Sign

Part 4:   Changing Actions

Write the title of your first critical warning sign:

_____

1.   Look at Side 1 of your first critical warning sign card, and write the "Action" statement below.

      When I experience this warning sign what I actually do is ...

      _____

2.   When you have the mandates and injunctions activated by this situation, and the resulting urges, what do you tend to do? (Refer to Process 11A, Part 1.)

      _____

      _____

      _____

      _____

3.   What is most likely to happen if you keep acting the way those mandates and injunctions tell you to act? (Refer to Process 11A, Part 2.) What actions could you take to keep that from happening?

      _____

      _____

      _____

      _____

4.   Think about the better choices that your new ways of thinking can give you. (Refer to Process 11A, Part 3.) If you let yourself believe in those new choices, what kinds of actions will be possible for you?

      _____

      _____

      _____

      _____

Think about how you can prepare for difficult situations that are coming up. How can you act differently in those situations? (Refer to Process 12A, Part 2.) How will this affect your ability to manage this warning sign?

_____

_____

_____

_____

6. Which actions seem most helpful at the important intervention points in these situations?
    (Refer to Process 13A.)

_____

_____

_____

_____

7. Breathe deeply and imagine yourself in a situation in which this critical warning sign is turned on. Which actions seem most likely to promote ongoing recovery and prevent relapse.

_____

8. Turn to Side 2 of your first critical warning sign card. Under "Changing Actions," copy the thoughts that you wrote in answer to question 7, above.

Part 5:   *Changing Enabling Relationships*

Write the title of your first critical warning sign:

_____

1.   Look at Side 1 of your first critical warning sign card, and write the "Enabling Relationship" statement below.

I tend to invite others to become part of my problem by ...

_____

2.   When you're operating under the mandates and injunctions that this warning sign turns on, how does it affect your relationships? (Refer to Process 11A, Part 1.)

_____

_____

_____

_____

3.   Think about different ways of thinking, and the choices that these new thoughts can give you. (Refer to Process 11A, Part 3.)   If you let yourself believe in those choices, how will it affect your relationships?

_____

_____

_____

_____

4.   When you're managing your feelings in the old ways that this warning sign activates, how does it tend to affect your relationships? (Refer to Process 12A, Part 1.)

_____

_____

_____

_____

5. If you use your new, more effective feeling management skills in this situation, how is it likely to affect your relationships? (Refer to Process 12A, Part 2.)

_____

_____

_____

_____

6. Think about ways of treating other people differently at the intervention points in this situation. (Refer to Process 13A.) Which ways seem most helpful?

_____

_____

_____

_____

7. Breathe deeply and imagine yourself in a situation in which this critical warning sign is turned on. Which ways of relating to people seem most likely to strengthen your recovery and prevent relapse?

_____

8. Turn to Side 2 of your first critical warning sign card. Under "Changing Enabling Relationships," copy the thoughts that you wrote in answer to question 7, above.

Thought Management
For the Second Critical Warning Sign

Overview

This process begins the cycle of *Thought Management, Feeling Management, Behavior and Situation Management*, and *TFUAR Management* for the second critical warning sign. As it was in Process 11A, *Thought Management* is divided into three parts:

- In *Identifying Mandates and Injunctions,* you'll look at the thoughts on your second critical warning sign card and find any mandates and injunctions hidden in those thoughts. Then you'll identify the threatened consequences carried by those mandates and injunctions.

- In *Challenging Mandates and Injunctions,* you'll look at where you might have learned those beliefs; the possibility that your mandates, injunctions, and threatened consequences are incorrect; and the benefits, disadvantages, and likely outcome of holding those beliefs.

- In *Identifying New Choices,* you'll look at the thoughts you might have when you manage this warning sign more effectively. You compare the choices that this kind of thinking gives you with the choices you have when you cling to your old thought patterns and manage the warning sign ineffectively.

It will be interesting to see how much better you understand *Thought Management* now that you've taken one warning sign through all four management processes.

This time, as you identify your thoughts, also look for the judgments that you tend to make when you have those thoughts. These might be judgments about yourself—about your worth or effectiveness as a person, whether you're a "good person" or a "bad person," whether you're safe or in danger, etc. Or they might be similar judgments about other people. Often these take the form of "self-talk," the bits and pieces of conversation that go on in your head.

Some automatic thoughts are connected to judgments that promote comfortable recovery. Others are connected to judgments that take you closer to relapse. For example, when you tell yourself, "You blew it again, stupid!" that automatic thought might be connected to the judgment that you're stupid, worthless, or bad. And you're more likely to relapse if you judge yourself as a stupid, worthless, bad person than you are if you judge yourself as a capable, worthwhile, good person.

Identifying the judgments connected with your thoughts will make you much better at thought management. When you become more aware of your judgments, you can begin to work on choosing thoughts that are connected with judgments that promote recovery.

This doesn't mean you'll deny or ignore the truth about yourself, others, or the situations you're in. It actually means you'll be more honest, because you'll be looking at more possibilities than you're used to looking at.

For example, the automatic self-talk that says, "You blew it again, stupid!" might be replaced by the message, "I made a mistake. Everybody makes mistakes. Now I need to look at what I can do to correct it. Then I need to look at what I can do to keep it from happening again." This message is connected to the judgment that you're no better or worse than anyone else, that you're responsible for your actions, and that you're capable of correcting and learning from your mistakes.

When you make that kind of judgment about yourself, you have the best possible chance at successful, lasting recovery.

Thought Management
For the Second Critical Warning Sign

Part 1:   Identifying Mandates and Injunctions

1.   Review the three critical warning signs that you identified in Process 7, Part 3, *The Initial Warning Sign List* (page 126). Choose the second one that you want to work on. Write your personal title for this warning sign below.

_____

2.   Copy the thought statement for this warning sign.

When I experience this warning sign I tend to think ...

_____

_____

3. What does this way of thinking tell you that you must think, feel, or do? (This is called a "mandate.")

I must ...   _____

_____

_____

4.   What do you think will happen if you *don't* do what this thought tells you that you *must* do? (This is a "threatened consequence"—*Do it or else!*)

I believe that I must do what this thoughts tells me to do, or else ... _____

_____

_____

5.   Again review the thoughts you listed under question 2. What does this way of thinking tell you that you *must not* or *can't* think, feel, or do? (This is called an "injunction.")
I must not ...   _____

_____

_____

6.   What do you think will happen if you *do* what this thought tells you that you *must not* do? (This is another threatened consequence—*Don't do it or else!*)

If I do what this thought is telling me not to do, I believe the following negative thing will happpen ...

_____

_____

Part 2: *Challenging Mandates and Injunctions*

1. Who taught you that you must or must not think, feel, or act in this way?

   _____

2. Is it possible that you were taught wrong? ☐ Yes ☐ No ☐ Unsure
   Please explain:

   _____

   _____

3. What are the benefits of thinking about things in this way?

   _____

   _____

4. What are the disadvantages of thinking about things in this way?

   _____

   _____

5. If you continue to think about things in this way, what's the *best* thing that could happen?

   _____

   _____

6. If you continue to think about things in this way, what's the *worst* thing that could happen?

   _____

   _____

7. If you continue to think about things in this way, what's *most likely* to happen?

   _____

   _____

Thought Management
For the Second Critical Warning Sign

Part 3:   *Identifying New Choices*

1.   Review the critical warning sign that you identified in Part 1. Think of a situation in which you managed this warning sign *effectively*. If you can't remember managing this warning sign effectively, imagine how you might manage it more effectively.

When you managed this warning sign effectively (or imagined yourself doing so), what did you tend to think?

_____

_____

_____

_____

_____

2.   What choices did this way of thinking give you that you didn't have when you were managing the warning sign *ineffectively*?

I can choose to ... _____

_____

_____

_____

_____

3.   Go back and review the thoughts, mandates, and injunctions that you identified in Part 1. What is another way of thinking about this situation that can give you new and more effective choices in what you can do about it?

_____

_____

_____

_____

_____

Overview

Process 12B works very much like Process 12A, *Feeling Management for the First Critical Warning Sign.* But as you go through the process this time, take a look at how you might be judging your feelings at different times—in general, right now, when this warning sign is activated, and when you're managing the warning sign effectively.

As mentioned in the earlier process, effective feeling management rests on five basic principles:

1.   It's normal and natural to have feelings.

2.   Every feeling has a purpose.

3.   There are no "good" feelings or "bad" feelings.

4.   There are only "pleasant" feelings and "unpleasant" feelings.

5.   Feelings are part of an inter-related system of thoughts, feelings, urges, actions, and relationships.

If you want to know how to manage feelings effectively, first look at how people often "mismanage" feelings:

• They "block" their feelings.

• They judge their feelings.

• They judge themselves.

• They mandate their feelings.

• They forbid their feelings.

These feeling mismanagement strategies do a lot of damage. Sometimes they repress the feelings, or block them from awareness. Sometimes these strategies exaggerate painful or upsetting feelings. And sometimes they distort the feelings.

Effective feeling management works much differently. There are five major strategies of effective feeling management:

1.   Recognize the feeling

2.   Label the feeling

3.   Affirm the feeling

4.   Communicate the feeling

5.   Resolve the feeling

If you're having trouble putting a name to your feelings, you can use the feeling chart to identify your feelings and rate their strength on a scale of one to ten.

As it did in Process 12A, *Feeling Management* has two parts:

- In *Identifying Ineffective Feeling Management Strategies,* you'll look at the feelings you tend to have when you manage this warning sign ineffectively or "mismanage" it, and the thoughts and actions connected with those feelings.

- In *Learning New Feeling Management Skills,* you'll apply 16 basic feeling management skills to a typical situation in which this warning sign has been turned on.

Remember, as you go through these exercises this time, look for judgments. Your judgments of your feelings might provide an important clue to the problems you've been having with feeling management.

Feeling Management
For the Second Critical Warning Sign

Process 12B

Part 1:   Identifying Ineffective Feeling Management Strategies

1.   Choose the same critical warning sign that you worked with in Process 11B (page 199). Again, write your personalized title for that warning sign below.

_____

2.   In Process 7, Part 3, *The Initial Warning Sign List,* find the feeling statement that you wrote for that critical warning sign, and write it below. When I experience this warning sign I tend to feel ...

_____

_____

3.   Use the feeling chart to describe how you tend to feel when this warning sign is turned on, and how strongly you feel this way.

☐ Strong or ☐ Weak _____	☐ Safe or ☐ Threatened _____
☐ Angry or ☐ Caring _____	☐ Fulfilled or ☐ Frustrated _____
☐ Happy or ☐ Sad _____	☐ Proud or ☐ Ashamed, guilty _____

4.   What are some of the thoughts that cause you to feel this way?

_____

_____

5.   What are you usually doing that causes you to feel this way?

_____

_____

6.   What do you usually do to try to manage these feelings?

_____

_____

7.   Does the way you choose to think and act make you feel better or worse?

   ❑ Makes me feel better.   ❑ Makes me feel worse.   ❑ Doesn't change how I feel.

   Why do you say that? _____

_____

_____

_____

Feeling Management
For the Second Critical Warning Sign

Process 12B

Part 2:   Learning New Feeling Management Skills

This exercise will help you examine some possible ways to improve your feeling-management skills when your warning signs are turned on. They follow the Guidelines for Effective Feeling Management listed in Appendix 8. Answer these questions for the critical warning sign that you're working on.

1. How can you anticipate and prepare for situations that can trigger the kinds of strong feelings or emotions that this warning sign raises?

    _____

    _____

    _____

    _____

2. How can you recognize when you start to have these strong feelings or emotions?

    _____

    _____

3. How can you stop yourself from automatically responding to the feelings before you've had a chance to think them through (for example, taking a few slow, deep breaths and noticing what you're feeling; calling a "time out"; getting away from the situation; or using an immediate relaxation technique to bring down the intensity of your feelings)?

    _____

    _____

    _____

4. How can you find words to describe what you're feeling and how strong the feelings are? (What words might you check if you used the feeling list? How would you rate the intensity of your feeling using a ten-point scale? Can you consciously acknowledge the feeling and its intensity by saying to yourself, "Right now I'm feeling _____ and it's okay to be feeling this way"?)

☐ Strong or ☐ Weak _____	☐ Safe or ☐ Threatened _____
☐ Angry or ☐ Caring _____	☐ Fulfilled or ☐ Frustrated _____
☐ Happy or ☐ Sad _____	☐ Proud or ☐ Ashamed, guilty _____

5. How can you identify what you're thinking that makes you feel that way?

    _____

    _____

6. How can you change what you're thinking in a way that will let you feel better?

_____

_____

7. How can you identify what you're doing that makes you feel that way?

_____

_____

8. How can you change what you're doing in a way that will let you feel better?

_____

_____

9. How can you recognize and resist your urges to create problems, hurt yourself, or hurt other people?

_____

_____

10. How can you recognize your resistance to doing things that will help you or your situation, and force yourself to do those things in spite of the resistance?

_____

_____

11. How can you get outside of yourself and recognize and respond to what other people are feeling?

_____

_____

12. Do you have a safe person you can talk to about what you're feeling? Who is that person, and what would be the best way to contact him or her?

_____

_____

Overview

As it was in Process 13A, *Behavior and Situation Management* is designed to find intervention points in high-risk situations that you've handled ineffectively in the past. Once again you'll start with a situation map and look for likely intervention points near the beginning of the situation, near the middle of the situation, and near the end of the situation.

As you go through *Behavior and Situation Management* for your second critical warning sign, look for the judgments you make in your high-risk situations, and how your judgments might be connected to your actions. For example, what judgments do you make that lead you into high-risk situations? When you're in those situations, what judgments do you make about yourself and others? What judgments tend to lead to your self-defeating behavior, and what judgments do you make when you're feeling the effects of that behavior?

When you find your intervention points, think about the judgments that would be connected to effective intervention in this critical warning sign.

As you identify these and other judgments, also look at how they relate to the judgments you identified in Process 11B, *Thought Management for the Second Critical Warning Sign;* and Process 12B, *Feeling Management For the Second Critical Warning Sign.* You'll begin to get a clearer picture of how your judgments link your thoughts, feelings, and actions.

Behavior and Situation Management
For the Second Critical Warning Sign

Think of the critical warning sign you've been working on. Now think of a specific past situation in which you experienced this warning sign while in recovery and *managed it poorly or ineffectively*. Tell the experience as if it were a story with a beginning, a middle, and an ending.

Sequencing Statements	Clarifying Questions
1. The warning sign was triggered when ...	1. Who were you with and what were they doing?
2. The first thing I did was ...	2. What were you doing?
3. The next thing I did was ...	3. What was going on around you?
4. The next thing I did was ...	4. Where did this happen?
5. What finally happened was ...	5. When did this happen? (Month, day, time)

This critical warning sign was triggered when ... _____

_____

_____

_____

_____

_____

_____

_____

_____

_____

_____

_____

_____

_____

_____

_____

_____

_____

_____

_____

_____

1. **Intervention Point #1:** What could you have done differently near the beginning of the situation to produce a better outcome? (How could you have thought differently? Managed your feelings and emotions differently? Acted differently? Treated other people differently?)

   _____

   _____

   _____

   _____

   _____

   • If you had done these things, how would it have changed the outcome?

   _____

   _____

2. **Intervention Point #2:** What could you have done differently near the middle of the situation to produce a better outcome? (How could you have thought differently? Managed your feelings and emotions differently? Acted differently? Treated other people differently?)

   _____

   _____

   _____

   _____

   • If you had done these things, how would it have changed the outcome?

   _____

   _____

3. **Intervention Point #3:** What could you have done differently near the end of the situation to produce a better outcome? (How could you have thought differently? Managed your feelings and emotions differently? Acted differently? Treated other people differently?)

   _____

   _____

   _____

   _____

   _____

• If you had done these things, how would it have changed the outcome?

_____

_____

_____

4.   **Most Important Thing Learned**: What is the most important thing that you learned by completing this exercise?

_____

_____

_____

_____

5.   **Future High-Risk Situation**: Is there a situation coming up in the near future that will put you at risk of experiencing this critical warning sign? ❑ Yes   ❑ No   ❑ Unsure

Please describe how this might happen.   _____

_____

_____

_____

_____

6.   **Application to Other High-Risk Situations**: How can you apply what you learned in this situation to other high-risk situations in your life?

_____

_____

_____

Overview

As you well remember by now, "TFUAR" stands for thoughts, feelings, urges, actions, and relationships. Once again, the *TFUAR Management* process brings home all the work you've done in *Thought Management, Feeling Management,* and *Behavior and Situation Management,* and puts it on the "solution side" of your Warning Sign Identification Card.

This time around, pay special attention to the role your judgments play in the way your thoughts, feelings, urges, actions, and relationships lead from one to another. How do your judgments form the "glue" that holds your relapse process together? How can you make better judgment decisions that will promote lasting recovery and prevent relapse?

Remember, you'll have the rest of your life to change and improve what's written on your cards. But the process of sifting through this material and choosing what seems most helpful will be valuable, even if you change your card many times in the future. And even a card that isn't perfect can save your life, if you look at it when you need it.

Integrated TFUAR Management
For the Second Critical Warning Sign

Process 14B

Part 1: *Managing Thoughts*

Write the title of your second critical warning sign:

_____

1. Look at Side 1 of your second critical warning sign card, and write the "thought" statement below.

   When I experience this warning sign I tend to think ...

   _____

   _____

2. What are some of the ways of thinking that make it harder to manage this warning sign? (Refer to Process 11B, Part 1.) Remember your mandates ("I *must* or else...") and injunctions ("I'd *better not*, or else...").

   _____

   _____

   _____

   _____

3. What's another way of thinking about this that might give you better choices? (Refer to Process 11B, Part 3.) How could those new choices promote healthy recovery?

   _____

   _____

   _____

4. How can you change your way of thinking so you can feel better? (Refer to Process 12B, Part 2.)

   _____

   _____

   _____

   _____

5. What kinds of more helpful thoughts can you have at important intervention points in this warning sign? (Refer to Process 13B.) (An "intervention point" is a point where making a different choice might make the situation come out differently.)

    _____

    _____

    _____

    _____

6. Breathe deeply and imagine yourself in a situation in which this critical warning sign is turned on. What are the thoughts that seem most likely to strengthen your recovery and prevent relapse?

    _____

    _____

7. Turn to Side 2 of your second critical warning sign card. Under "Managing Thoughts," copy the thoughts that you wrote in answer to question 6, above.

Part 2:   Managing Feelings

Write the title of your second critical warning sign:

_____

1.   Look at Side 1 of your second critical warning sign card, and write the "Feeling" statement below.

When I experience this warning sign I tend to feel ...

_____

2.   What are some of the ineffective feeling management strategies that you use most often when this warning sign is turned on? (Refer to Process 12B, Part 1.) How do they make you feel?

_____

_____

_____

_____

3.   What are some other ways of managing your feelings that would be more helpful to you? (Refer to Process 12B, Part 3.)

_____

_____

_____

_____

4.   Which feeling management skills would be most effective at important intervention points in this warning sign? (Refer to Process 13B.)

_____

_____

_____

_____

5. Breathe deeply and imagine yourself in a situation in which this critical warning sign is turned on. Which ways of managing your feelings seem most likely to strengthen your recovery and prevent relapse?

   _____

6. Turn to Side 2 of your second critical warning sign card. Under "Managing Feelings," copy the thoughts that you wrote in answer to question 5, above.

Part 3:   *Managing Urges*

Write the title of your second critical warning sign:

_____

1.   Look at Side 1 of your second critical warning sign card, and write the "Urge" statement below.

      When I experience this warning sign I have an urge to ...

      _____

2.   Think about the mandates and injunctions you have when this warning sign is turned on. (Refer to Process 11B, Part 1.) What are some of the urges that those mandates and injunctions tend to create?

      _____

      _____

      _____

      _____

3.   Think again about **new** ways of thinking in this situation, and the new choices that those ways of thinking give you. (Refer to Process 11B, Part 3.) How can these choices help you manage your urges?

      _____

      _____

      _____

      _____

4.   When you manage your feelings in ineffective ways, what kinds of urges do you tend to have? (Refer to Process 12B, Part 1.)

      _____

      _____

      _____

      _____

5.   How can you manage your urges more effectively if you use more effective feeling management skills? (Refer to Process 12B, Part 2.)

_____

_____

_____

_____

6.   Picture yourself making better use of the important intervention points in this situation. (Refer to Process 13B.) What can you do to manage your urges at those intervention points?

_____

_____

_____

_____

7.   Breathe deeply and imagine yourself in a situation in which this critical warning sign is turned on. Which urge management skills seem most likely to strengthen your recovery and prevent relapse?

_____

8.   Turn to Side 2 of your second critical warning sign card. Under "Managing Urges," copy the thoughts that you wrote in answer to question 7, above.

Part 4:   *Changing Actions*

Write the title of your second critical warning sign:

_____

1.   Look at Side 1 of your second critical warning sign card, and write the "Action" state-
      ment below.

      When I experience this warning sign what I actually do is ...

      _____

2.   When you have the mandates and injunctions activated by this situation, and the resulting
      urges, what do you tend to do? (Refer to Process 11B, Part 1.)

      _____

      _____

      _____

      _____

3.   What is most likely to happen if you keep acting the way those mandates and injunctions
      tell you to act? (Refer to Process 11B, Part 2.) What actions could you take to keep that
      from happening?

      _____

      _____

      _____

4.   Think about the better choices that your new ways of thinking can give you. (Refer to
      Process 11B, Part 3.) If you let yourself believe in those new choices, what kinds of
      actions will be possible for you?

      _____

      _____

      _____

      _____

5. Think about how you can prepare for difficult situations that are coming up. How can you act differently in those situations? (Refer to Process 12B, Part 2.) How will this affect your ability to manage this warning sign?

_____

_____

_____

_____

6. Which actions seem most helpful at the important intervention points in these situations? (Refer to Process 13B.)

_____

_____

_____

_____

7. Breathe deeply and imagine yourself in a situation in which this critical warning sign is turned on. Which actions seem most likely to promote ongoing recovery and prevent relapse.

_____

8. Turn to Side 2 of your second critical warning sign card. Under "Changing Actions," copy the thoughts that you wrote in answer to question 7, above.

Part 5:   *Changing Enabling Relationships*

Write the title of your second critical warning sign:

_____

1.   Look at Side 1 of your second critical warning sign card, and write the "Enabling Relationship" statement below.

I tend to invite others to become part of my problem by ...

_____

2.   When you're operating under the mandates and injunctions that this warning sign turns on, how does it affect your relationships? (Refer to Process 11B, Part 1.)

_____

_____

_____

_____

3.   Think about different ways of thinking, and the choices that these new thoughts can give you. (Refer to Process 11B, Part 3.) If you let yourself believe in those choices, how will it affect your relationships?

_____

_____

_____

_____

4.   When you're managing your feelings in the old ways that this warning sign activates, how does it tend to affect your relationships? (Refer to Process 12B, Part 1.)

_____

_____

_____

_____

5. If you use your new, more effective feeling management skills in this situation, how is it likely to affect your relationships? (Refer to Process 12B, Part 2.)

_____

_____

_____

_____

6. Think about ways of treating other people differently at the intervention points in this situation. (Refer to Process 13B.) Which ways seem most helpful?

_____

_____

_____

_____

7. Breathe deeply and imagine yourself in a situation in which this critical warning sign is turned on. Which ways of relating to people seem most likely to strengthen your recovery and prevent relapse?

_____

8. Turn to Side 2 of your second critical warning sign card. Under "Changing Enabling Relationships," copy the thoughts that you wrote in answer to question 7, above.

Overview

As you go through the *Thought Management* exercises this final time, look for patterns. These might be similarities or differences among the thoughts, judgments, mandates, injunctions, threatened consequences, and choices for all three critical warning signs. They might be core thinking problems that repeatedly lead toward relapse, or general alternative ways of thinking that tend to give you more options and strengthen your recovery.

It's important to identify any patterns that exist in the thoughts that drive your critical warning signs. These often provide the keys to far better understanding of the warning signs and of the work needed for ongoing recovery.

Part 1:   Identifying Mandates and Injunctions

1. Look again at the three critical warning signs that you identified in Process 7, Part 3, *The Initial Warning Sign List* (page 126). Write your personal title for the remaining warning sign below.

    _____

2. Copy the thought statement for this warning sign.
    When I experience this warning sign I tend to think ...

    _____

    _____

3. What does this way of thinking tell you that you must think, feel, or do? (A mandate.)
    I must ... _____

    _____

    _____

4. What do you think will happen if you don't do what this thought tells you that you must do? (A threatened consequence—*Do it or else!*)

    I believe that I must do what this thoughts tells me to do, or else ..._____

    _____

    _____

5. Again review the thoughts you listed under question 2. What does this way of thinking tell you that you *must not* or *can't* think, feel, or do? (An injunction.)

    I must not ...   _____

    _____

    _____

6. What do you think will happen if you *do* what this thought tells you that you *must not* do? (Another threatened consequence—*Don't do it or else!*)

    If I do what this thought is telling me not to do, I believe the following negative thing will happpen ...

    _____

    _____

Part 2:   *Challenging Mandates and Injunctions*

1.   Who taught you that you must or must not think, feel, or act in this way?

_____

2.   Is it possible that you were taught wrong?   ❑ Yes   ❑ No   ❑ Unsure
       Please explain:

_____

_____

3.   What are the benefits of thinking about things in this way?

_____

_____

4.   What are the disadvantages of thinking about things in this way?

_____

_____

5.   If you continue to think about things in this way, what's the *best* thing that could happen?

_____

_____

6.   If you continue to think about things in this way, what's the *worst* thing that could happen?

_____

_____

7.   If you continue to think about things in this way, what's *most likely* to happen?

_____

_____

Part 3:   Identifying New Choices

1.   Review the critical warning sign that you identified in Part 1. Think of a situation in which you managed this warning sign *effectively*. If you can't remember managing this warning sign effectively, imagine how you might manage it more effectively.

When you managed this warning sign effectively (or imagined yourself doing so), what did you tend to think?

_____

_____

_____

_____

_____

2.   What choices did this way of thinking give you that you didn't have when you were managing the warning sign *ineffectively*?

I can choose to ... _____

_____

_____

_____

_____

3.   Go back and review the thoughts, mandates, and injunctions that you identified in Part 1. What is another way of thinking about this situation that can give you new and more effective choices in what you can do about it?

_____

_____

_____

_____

_____

_____

Feeling Management
For the Third Critical Warning Sign

Overview

As you go through Process 12C, *Feeling Management for the Third Critical Warning Sign,* look for patterns in the feelings that you have when you're managing this warning sign effectively vs. ineffectively. How are your feelings generally different? How are they similar?

Also look for patterns in:

- The types of feeling management strategies that work best for you

- The types of mismanagement that cause you the most trouble

- The results of different feeling management strategies

Pay special attention to any patterns in the types of feelings that seem to lead to relapse vs. the types of feelings that lead to healthy recovery. Once you've identified these feelings, they can become important signals that your critical warning signs are being activated.

Feeling Management
For the Third Critical Warning Sign

Process 12C

Part 1:   Identifying Ineffective Feeling Management Strategies

1.   Choose the same critical warning sign that you worked with in Process 11C (page 224).
     Again, write your personalized title for that warning sign below.

     _____

2.   In Process 7, Part 3, *The Initial Warning Sign List,* find the feeling statement that you
     wrote for that critical warning sign, and write it below. When I experience this warning
     sign I tend to feel ...

     _____

     _____

3.   Use the feeling chart to describe how you tend to feel when this warning sign is turned
     on, and how strongly you feel this way.

☐ Strong or ☐ Weak _____	☐ Safe or ☐ Threatened _____
☐ Angry or ☐ Caring _____	☐ Fulfilled or ☐ Frustrated _____
☐ Happy or ☐ Sad _____	☐ Proud or ☐ Ashamed, guilty _____

4.   What are some of the thoughts that cause you to feel this way?

     _____

     _____

5.   What are you usually doing that causes you to feel this way?

     _____

     _____

6.   What do you usually do to try to manage these feelings?

     _____

     _____

7.   Does the way you choose to think and act make you feel better or worse?
     ☐ Makes me feel better.   ☐ Makes me feel worse.   ☐ Doesn't change how I feel.

     Why do you say that? _____

     _____

     _____

     _____

Feeling Management
For the Third Critical Warning Sign

Part 2:   Learning New Feeling Management Skills

This exercise will help you examine some possible ways to improve your feeling-management skills when your warning signs are turned on. They follow the Guidelines for Effective Feeling Management listed in Appendix 8. Answer these questions for the critical warning sign that you're working on.

1.   How can you anticipate and prepare for situations that can trigger the kinds of strong feelings or emotions that this warning sign raises?

_____

_____

_____

_____

2.   How can you recognize when you start to have these strong feelings or emotions?

_____

_____

3.   How can you stop yourself from automatically responding to the feelings before you've had a chance to think them through (for example, taking a few slow, deep breaths and noticing what you're feeling; calling a "time out"; getting away from the situation; or using an immediate relaxation technique to bring down the intensity of your feelings)?

_____

_____

_____

_____

4.   How can you find words to describe what you're feeling and how strong the feelings are? (What words might you check if you used the feeling list? How would you rate the intensity of your feeling using a ten-point scale? Can you consciously acknowledge the feeling and its intensity by saying to yourself, "Right now I'm feeling _____ and it's okay to be feeling this way"?)

☐ Strong or ☐ Weak _____	☐ Safe or ☐ Threatened _____
☐ Angry or ☐ Caring _____	☐ Fulfilled or ☐ Frustrated _____
☐ Happy or ☐ Sad _____	☐ Proud or ☐ Ashamed, guilty _____

5.   How can you identify what you're thinking that makes you feel this way?

_____

_____

6. How can you change what you're thinking in a way that will let you feel better?

_____

_____

7. How can you identify what you're doing that makes you feel this way?

_____

_____

8. How can you change what you're doing in a way that will let you feel better?

_____

_____

9. How can you recognize and resist your urges to create problems, hurt yourself, or hurt other people?

_____

_____

10. How can you recognize your resistance to doing things that will help you or your situation, and force yourself to do those things in spite of the resistance?

_____

_____

11. How can you get outside of yourself and recognize and respond to what other people are feeling?

_____

_____

12. Do you have a safe person you can talk to about what you're feeling? Who is that person, and what would be the best way to contact him or her?

_____

_____

Overview

As you go through *Behavior and Situation Management* for your third critical warning sign, look for common patterns in the high-risk situations and self-defeating behavior you've identified. What are some of the most common mistakes you make? Where are your biggest "danger zones," and when are you most likely to go there?

Also look for common patterns in your intervention points. For example, are there certain points in situations where it's easier to intervene than at other points? Are there certain actions that tend to form your best interventions? Are there certain management strategies that hold the most promise for you?

If you identify these patterns carefully, they can give you a "shortcut" to effective intervention in many situations—even ones you've never considered before.

Think of the critical warning sign you've been working on. Now think of a specific past situation in which you experienced this warning sign while in recovery and *managed it poorly or ineffectively*. Tell the experience as if it were a story with a beginning, a middle, and an ending.

Sequencing Statements	Clarifying Questions
1. The warning sign was triggered when ...	1. Who were you with and what were they doing?
2. The first thing I did was ...	2. What were you doing?
3. The next thing I did was ...	3. What was going on around you?
4. The next thing I did was ...	4. Where did this happen?
5. What finally happened was ...	5. When did this happen? (Month, day, time)

This critical warning sign was triggered when ... _____

_____

_____

_____

_____

_____

_____

_____

_____

_____

_____

_____

_____

_____

_____

_____

_____

_____

_____

_____

_____

_____

_____

1. **Intervention Point #1**: What could you have done differently near the beginning of the situation to produce a better outcome? (How could you have thought differently? Managed your feelings and emotions differently? Acted differently? Treated other people differently?)

   _____
   _____
   _____
   _____
   _____

   • If you had done these things, how would it have changed the outcome?

   _____
   _____
   _____

2. **Intervention Point #2**: What could you have done differently near the middle of the situation to produce a better outcome? (How could you have thought differently? Managed your feelings and emotions differently? Acted differently? Treated other people differently?)

   _____
   _____
   _____
   _____
   _____

   • If you had done these things, how would it have changed the outcome?

   _____
   _____
   _____

3. **Intervention Point #3**: What could you have done differently near the end of the situation to produce a better outcome? (How could you have thought differently? Managed your feelings and emotions differently? Acted differently? Treated other people differently?)

   _____
   _____
   _____
   _____
   _____

• If you had done these things, how would it have changed the outcome?

_____

_____

_____

4. **Most Important Thing Learned**: What is the most important thing that you learned by completing this exercise?

_____

_____

_____

_____

5. **Future High-Risk Situation**: Is there a situation coming up in the near future that will put you at risk of experiencing this critical warning sign? ❑ Yes ❑ No ❑ Unsure

Please describe how this might happen. _____

_____

_____

_____

_____

6. **Application to Other High-Risk Situations**: How can you apply what you learned in this situation to other high-risk situations in your life?

_____

_____

_____

Overview

This is the final process in the *Warning Sign Management* phase. Of course, you'll be using these processes again and again throughout your recovery. You might even choose to go through all of the Relapse Prevention Planning phases again in the future, as a sort of "refresher course."

As you take your third critical warning sign through the *Integrated TFUAR Management* process, look for the big picture—overall patterns that affect your thought, feeling, urge, action, and relationship management. It's quite likely that you've discovered common patterns as you've mapped out your first two warning signs. Now is your opportunity to flag the most important patterns and bring them to your therapist's attention.

Once you've completed this process, you'll be in the best possible position to create a structured recovery program that supports your ongoing warning sign identification and management. At this point you might feel as if you never want to see another warning sign card in your life, but you'll change your mind once you've had a little rest.

These cards that now seem like a task will soon look like the lifelines that they are. Stress usually comes without warning. So do loss, and romance, and bad luck, and good luck, and failure, and success, and all kinds of trouble. Before, when you hit "emotional overload," you had nothing to fall back on that could effectively help you stop relapse. Now you do, and it fits in your pocket or purse.

It's worth the time and effort you're putting in. Your recovery is worth it. You're worth it.

Part 1:   *Managing Thoughts*

Write the title of your third critical warning sign:

_____

1.   Look at Side 1 of your third critical warning sign card, and write the "thought" statement below.

When I experience this warning sign I tend to think ...

_____

_____

2.   What are some of the ways of thinking that make it harder to manage this warning sign? (Refer to Process 11C, Part 1.) Remember your mandates ("I *must* or else...") and injunctions ("I'd *better not*, or else...").

_____

_____

_____

_____

3.   What's another way of thinking about this that might give you better choices? (Refer to Process 11C, Part 3.) How could those new choices promote healthy recovery?

_____

_____

_____

_____

4.   How can you change your way of thinking so you can feel better? (Refer to Process 12C, Part 2.)

_____

_____

_____

_____

5. What kinds of more helpful thoughts can you have at important intervention points in this warning sign? (Refer to Process 13C.) (An "intervention point" is a point where making a different choice might make the situation come out differently.)

    _____

    _____

    _____

    _____

6. Breathe deeply and imagine yourself in a situation in which this critical warning sign is turned on. What are the thoughts that seem most likely to strengthen your recovery and prevent relapse?

    _____

    _____

7. Turn to Side 2 of your third critical warning sign card. Under "Managing Thoughts," copy the thoughts that you wrote in answer to question 6, above.

Part 2:   *Managing Feelings*

Write the title of your third critical warning sign:

_____

1.   Look at Side 1 of your third critical warning sign card and write the "Feeling" statement below.

         When I experience this warning sign I tend to feel ...

         _____

2.   What are some of the ineffective feeling management strategies that you use most often when this warning sign is turned on? (Refer to Process 12C, Part 1.) How do they make you feel?

         _____

         _____

         _____

         _____

3.   What are some other ways of managing your feelings that would be more helpful to you? (Refer to Process 12C, Part 3.)

         _____

         _____

         _____

         _____

4.   Which feeling management skills would be most effective at important intervention points in this warning sign? (Refer to Process 13C.)

         _____

         _____

         _____

         _____

5.   Breathe deeply and imagine yourself in a situation in which this critical warning sign is turned on. Which ways of managing your feelings seem most likely to strengthen your recovery and prevent relapse?

_____

6.   Turn to Side 2 of your third critical warning sign card. Under "Managing Feelings," copy the thoughts that you wrote in answer to question 5, above.

Part 3:   *Managing Urges*

Write the title of your third critical warning sign:

_____

1.   Look at Side 1 of your third critical warning sign card and write the "Urge" statement below.

   When I experience this warning sign I have an urge to ...

   _____

2.   Think about the mandates and injunctions you have when this warning sign is turned on. (Refer to Process 11C, Part 1.) What are some of the urges that those mandates and injunctions tend to create?

   _____

   _____

   _____

   _____

3.   Think again about **new** ways of thinking in this situation, and the new choices that those ways of thinking give you. (Refer to Process 11C, Part 3.) How can these choices help you manage your urges?

   _____

   _____

   _____

   _____

4.   When you manage your feelings in ineffective ways, what kinds of urges do you tend to have? (Refer to Process 12C, Part 1.)

   _____

   _____

   _____

   _____

5. How can you manage your urges more effectively if you use more effective feeling management skills? (Refer to Process 12C, Part 2.)

_____

_____

_____

_____

6. Picture yourself making better use of the important intervention points in this situation. (Refer to Process 13C.) What can you do to manage your urges at those intervention points?

_____

_____

_____

_____

7. Breathe deeply and imagine yourself in a situation in which this critical warning sign is turned on. Which urge management skills seem most likely to strengthen your recovery and prevent relapse?

_____

8. Turn to Side 2 of your third critical warning sign card. Under "Managing Urges," copy the thoughts that you wrote in answer to question 7, above.

Part 4:   Changing Actions

Write the title of your third critical warning sign:

_____

1.   Look at Side 1 of your third critical warning sign card, and write the "Action" statement below.

When I experience this warning sign what I actually do is ...

_____

2.   When you have the mandates and injunctions activated by this situation, and the resulting urges, what do you tend to do? (Refer to Process 11C, Part 1.)

_____

_____

_____

_____

3.   What is most likely to happen if you keep acting the way those mandates and injunctions tell you to act? (Refer to Process 11C, Part 2.) What actions could you take to keep that from happening?

_____

_____

_____

_____

4.   Think about the better choices that your new ways of thinking can give you. (Refer to Process 11C, Part 3.) If you let yourself believe in those new choices, what kinds of actions will be possible for you?

_____

_____

_____

_____

5. Think about how you can prepare for difficult situations that are coming up. How can you act differently in those situations? (Refer to Process 12C, Part 2.) How will this affect your ability to manage this warning sign?

    _____

    _____

    _____

    _____

6. Which actions seem most helpful at the important intervention points in these situations? (Refer to Process 13C.)

    _____

    _____

    _____

    _____

7. Breathe deeply and imagine yourself in a situation in which this critical warning sign is turned on. Which actions seem most likely to promote ongoing recovery and prevent relapse?

    _____

8. Turn to Side 2 of your third critical warning sign card. Under "Changing Actions," copy the thoughts that you wrote in answer to question 7, above.

Part 5:   *Changing Enabling Relationships*

Write the title of your third critical warning sign:

_____

1.   Look at Side 1 of your third critical warning sign card, and write the "Enabling Relationship" statement below.

   I tend to invite others to become part of my problem by ...

   _____

2.   When you're operating under the mandates and injunctions that this warning sign turns on, how does it affect your relationships? (Refer to Process 11C, Part 1.)

   _____

   _____

   _____

   _____

3.   Think about different ways of thinking, and the choices that these new thoughts can give you. (Refer to Process 11C, Part 3.) If you let yourself believe in those choices, how will it affect your relationships?

   _____

   _____

   _____

   _____

4.   When you're managing your feelings in the old ways that this warning sign activates, how does it tend to affect your relationships? (Refer to Process 12C, Part 1.)

   _____

   _____

   _____

   _____

5.   If you use your new, more effective feeling management skills in this situation, how is it likely to affect your relationships? (Refer to Process 12C, Part 2.)

_____

_____

_____

_____

6.   Think about ways of treating other people differently at the intervention points in this situation. (Refer to Process 13C.) Which ways seem most helpful?

_____

_____

_____

_____

7.   Breathe deeply and imagine yourself in a situation in which this critical warning sign is turned on. Which ways of relating to people seem most likely to strengthen your recovery and prevent relapse?

_____

8.   Turn to Side 2 of your third critical warning sign card. Under "Changing Enabling Relationships," copy the thoughts that you wrote in answer to question 7, above.

Phase V: Recovery Planning

What?   Developing a schedule of recovery activities that will support the ongoing identification and management of relapse warning signs

Why?   Relapse begins in the privacy of our own minds

We need to make a conscious commitment to follow a schedule of activities that will support new ways of thinking, feeling, and acting

If we don't, we'll fall back into our old ways

Overview

Now that you've learned and practiced the skills for identifying and managing your relapse warning signs, you'll need to build a recovery program that will help and support you as you continue this work. The addictive process doesn't stop just because you've stopped addictive use. It often gets more intense, now that you're facing life's discomforts instead of running away from them. We all need ongoing help in facing those discomforts and growing through them.

An effective recovery program is much more than a general commitment to go to recovery meetings and read recovery materials. It's a structured program that helps you keep firm commitments to health in all major areas of your life—physical, psychological, social, occupational, and spiritual. It gives you daily contact with people, ideas, and activities that support your ongoing growth and warning sign identification and management. Without this support, you'll have little defense when the stress of everyday life triggers your cravings and addictive thinking.

Effective recovery programs form a structure that protects and strengthens you while you grow and change. These programs are made up of "recovery activities" that are maintained on a regular schedule. If you can't write it down on a calendar or planner, it isn't a recovery activity. If you make a commitment to your recovery, you're making a commitment to all of your scheduled activities.

The *Recovery Planning* process has seven parts:

- The *Recovery Goals Worksheet* asks you to set personal, occupational, family, social, and recovery goals directed at your major problems in these areas. Clear goals will help you stay on track and measure your progress.

- In *Selecting Recovery Activities,* you'll review the seven major categories of recovery activities and some of the options available in each area. Then you'll evaluate your need to cover these areas, the recovery goals they would address, the obstacles that might get in your way, and how you might overcome those obstacles. Finally you'll decide whether or not you can make a commitment to each of these areas.

- In *Scheduling Recovery Activities,* you'll create a weekly schedule of recovery activities that would be helpful to you, using the CENAPS® Weekly Planner.

- In *Testing the Schedule of Recovery Activities,* you'll use your critical warning signs to find out if your schedule will meet your ongoing relapse prevention needs. For each critical warning sign, first you'll look at each of your recovery activities to see if it can help you identify and manage that warning sign, then you'll decide which activities are most useful for ongoing identification and management. When you've done that, you'll write those activities on Side 2 of your critical warning sign card.

- *The Final Schedule of Recovery Activities* gives you another copy of the CENAPS® Weekly Planner, so you can include the changes and additions you made when you tested your initial schedule.

- The *Morning Planning Inventory* gives you a form for setting major goals for the day, recovery tasks, and daily tasks and schedules. Thinking constructively about the day in advance can help you stay on track all day long.

- The *Evening Review Inventory* helps you assess your daily progress on the personal and professional goals you set when you completed your *Recovery Goals Worksheet*. It also asks you about any warning signs that might have been activated during the day, and about your need for outside help.

When it's been a while since the last relapse, and life is starting to feel a little better, many relapse-prone people get into a trap called "complacency." Complacency is the attitude that says, "It's okay now. You're getting better. You don't have to put so much effort into your recovery program. Besides, you've got all that other stuff you have to do!"

There's a saying in A.A.: If you put something ahead of your recovery program, it will be the second thing you lose. The first thing you lose will be your recovery. The success of everything you are and everything you do will depend first and foremost on your ability to stay in recovery and avoid relapse. It's worth taking the time to create and thoroughly test a structured recovery program that will work for you.

People who have relapsed can often name excellent reasons why they weren't able to carry out the recovery activities they'd planned or promised to do. Their reasons are usually good ones: Life is stressful. But the fact remains that their failure to keep their recovery commitments was often a big factor in their relapse patterns. You need to know that, any time you make a decision to skip even one of your scheduled recovery activities—for **any** reason—you're acting out one or more warning signs.

With the final recovery plan you make a firm commitment to take full responsibility for your recovery and relapse prevention. That certainly doesn't mean you'll do it without help. But it does mean you won't expect others to remind you about the steps you need to take to stay in recovery. You'll take the initiative to get the help you need in order to fulfill your commitment to your own health and well-being.

As you grow and change, and your life circumstances change, your warning signs will change too. Your understanding of these signs—and of the thoughts, feelings, urges, and actions that drive them—will also deepen and change over the years. A strong ongoing recovery plan will help you keep up with these changes, identify and manage new warning signs, and cope with the discomfort that they sometimes cause.

Life can get a lot happier in ongoing recovery, but life will never be free of problems. People who are truly recovering are said to be "trading in one set of problems for a better set of problems." There will always be periods of uncomfortable personal growth followed by periods of contentment, followed by more growth and more contentment.

Keeping all your commitments to recovery will help you grow through times of pain and avoid complacency in times of contentment. Not only will you **not** have to go through the agony of relapse, but you'll also have a fuller and richer life.

Part 1:   *Recovery Goals Worksheet*

1.   **Personal Goals:** Please identify three personal characteristics that need to be changed if you're going to avoid relapse.

     a. _____

     _____

     _____

     _____

     b. _____

     _____

     _____

     _____

     c. _____

     _____

     _____

     _____

2.   **Occupational Goals:** Please identify three major work-related problems that will need to be resolved if you are to avoid relapse.

     a. _____

     _____

     _____

     _____

     b. _____

     _____

     _____

     c. _____

     _____

     _____

     _____

3. **Family Goals:** Please identify three major family problems that will need to be resolved if you are to avoid relapse.

a. _____
_____
_____

b. _____
_____
_____

c. _____
_____
_____

4. **Social Goals:** Please identify three major social problems that will need to be resolved if you are to avoid relapse.

a. _____
_____
_____

b. _____
_____
_____

c. _____
_____
_____

5. **Recovery Program Goals:** Please identify three major problems you've had in working your recovery program that will need to be resolved if you are to avoid relapse.

a. _____
_____
_____

b. _____
_____
_____

c. _____
_____
_____

Part 2:   Selecting Recovery Activities

The Need for a Recovery Plan

Having a plan for each day will help you recover. People who recover successfully tend to do certain basic things. These recovery activities have been tested over and over again and proven to help people stay clean and sober. In A.A., there's such a strong belief that they work that many people with solid recovery will say, "If you want what we have, do what we did!" and, "It works if you work it!"

However, not everyone in recovery does exactly the same things. For example, different people go to different kinds of recovery meetings, or choose different ways of developing their spirituality. Once you understand yourself and the basic principles of recovery and relapse prevention, you can build a personal recovery program that will work for you. First you need to look at all the types of recovery activities that make up a balanced, stable recovery program.

When people first read the following list, they tend to get defensive. "I can't do all of those things!" they say to themselves. I invite you to think about your recovery as if you were hiking in the grand canyon and had to jump across a ravine that's about three feet wide and 100 feet deep. It's better to jump three feet too far than to risk jumping one inch too short. The same is true of recovery. It's better to plan to do a little bit more than you need to do than to risk not doing enough. As they say in A.A., "Half measures availed us nothing!"

The seven basic recovery activities described below are actually habits of good, healthy living. Anyone who wants to live a responsible, healthy, and fulfilling life will get in the habit of regularly doing these things. For people in recovery, these activities are essential. A regular schedule of these activities, designed to match your own individual recovery needs and relapse warning signs, is necessary for your brain to heal from the damage caused by addiction.

Instructions

Read the list of recovery activities on the next few pages. For each one, identify:

1.   Activities that you think will be helpful in your recovery

2.   The recovery goals that these activities might address, and how they might address these goals

3.   The obstacles you face in doing them on a regular basis

4.   Possible ways of overcoming those obstacles

5.   Your willingness to put these activities on your recovery plan

Section 1: Professional Counseling

The success of your recovery will depend on regular attendance at recovery education sessions, group therapy sessions, and individual therapy sessions. The scientific literature on treatment effectiveness clearly shows that, the more time that you invest in professional counseling and therapy during the first two years of recovery, the more likely you are to stay in recovery.

1-1   Do I believe I need to do this?   ❑ Yes   ❑ No   ❑ Unsure

1-2   What recovery goals would this address, and how would it address them?

_____

_____

_____

1-3   The obstacles that might prevent me from doing it are:

_____

_____

_____

1-4   Possible ways of overcoming these obstacles are:

_____

_____

_____

1-5   Will I put this on my recovery plan?   ❑ Yes   ❑ No   ❑ Unsure

Section 2: Self-Help Programs

There are a number of self-help programs such as Alcoholics Anonymous (A.A.), Narcotics Anonymous (N.A.), Rational Recovery, and Women For Sobriety that can support you in your efforts to live a sober and responsible life. These programs all have several things in common:

a) they ask you to abstain from alcohol and drugs and live a responsible life;

b) they encourage you to regularly attend meetings, so you can meet and develop relationships with other people living sober and responsible lives;

c) they ask you to meet regularly with an established member of the group (usually called a sponsor) who will help you learn about the organization and get through the rough spots; and

d) they promote a program of recovery (often in the form of steps or structured exercises that you work on outside of meetings) that focuses on techniques for changing your thinking, feeling management, urge management, and behavior.

Scientific research shows that, the more committed and actively involved you are in self-help groups during the first two years of recovery, the greater your ability to avoid relapse.

2-1   Do I believe I need to do this? ❑ Yes ❑ No ❑ Unsure

2-2   What recovery goals would this address, and how would it address them?

_____

_____

_____

2-3   The obstacles that might prevent me from doing it are:

_____

_____

_____

2-4   Possible ways of overcoming these obstacles are:

_____

_____

_____

2-5   Will I put this on my recovery plan? ❑ Yes ❑ No ❑ Unsure

Section 3: Proper Diet

What you eat can affect how you think, feel, and act. Many chemically dependent people find that they feel better if they:

a) eat three well balanced meals a day,

b) use vitamin and amino acid supplements,

c) avoid eating sugar and foods made with white flour, and

d) cut back or stop smoking cigarettes and drinking beverages containing caffeine, such as coffee and colas.

Recovering people who don't follow these simple principles of healthy diet and meal planning tend to feel anxious and depressed, have strong and violent mood swings, feel constantly angry and resentful, and periodically experience powerful cravings. They're more likely to relapse. Those who follow a proper diet tend to feel better and have lower relapse rates.

3-1   Do I believe I need to do this?   ❑ Yes   ❑ No   ❑ Unsure

3-2   What recovery goals would this address, and how would it address them?

_____

_____

_____

3-3   The obstacles that might prevent me from doing it are:

_____

_____

_____

3-4   Possible ways of overcoming these obstacles are:

_____

_____

_____

3-5   Will I put this on my recovery plan?   ❑ Yes   ❑ No   ❑ Unsure

Section 4: Exercise Program

Doing thirty minutes of aerobic exercise each day will help your brain recover and help you feel better about yourself. Fast walking, jogging, swimming, and aerobics classes are all helpful. It's also helpful to do strength-building exercises (such as weight lifting) and flexibility exercises (such as stretching) in addition to the aerobic exercise.

4-1   Do I believe I need to do this? ❑ Yes ❑ No ❑ Unsure

4-2   What recovery goals would this address, and how would it address them?

_____

_____

_____

4-3   The obstacles that might prevent me from doing it are:

_____

_____

_____

4-4   Possible ways of overcoming these obstacles are:

_____

_____

_____

4-5   Will I put this on my recovery plan? ❑ Yes ❑ No ❑ Unsure

Section 5: Stress Management Program

Stress is a major cause of relapse. Recovering people who learn how to manage stress without using self-defeating behaviors tend to stay in recovery. Those who don't learn to manage stress tend to relapse. Stress management involves learning relaxation exercises and taking quiet time on a daily basis to relax. It also involves avoiding long hours of working, and taking time for recreation and relaxation.

5-1   Do I believe I need to do this?   ❑ Yes   ❑ No   ❑ Unsure

5-2   What recovery goals would this address, and how would it address them?

_____

_____

_____

5-3   The obstacles that might prevent me from doing it are:

_____

_____

_____

5-4   Possible ways of overcoming these obstacles are:

_____

_____

_____

5-5   Will I put this on my recovery plan?   ❑ Yes   ❑ No   ❑ Unsure

Section 6: Spiritual Development Program

Human beings have both a physical self (based on the health of our brains and bodies) and a non-physical self (based on the health of our value systems and spiritual lives). Most recovering people find that they need to invest regular time in developing themselves spiritually (in other words, exercising the non-physical aspects of who they are). Twelve-Step programs such as A.A. provide an excellent program for spiritual recovery, as do many communities of faith and other spiritual programs. At the heart of any spiritual program are three activities: (1) fellowship, during which you spend time talking with other people who use similar methods; (2) private prayer and meditation, during which you take time alone to pray and meditate and to consciously put yourself in the presence of your higher power or consciously reflect upon your spiritual self; and (3) group prayer or worship, during which you pray and meditate with other people who share a similar spiritual philosophy.

6-1   Do I believe I need to do this?   ❑ Yes   ❑ No   ❑ Unsure

6-2   What recovery goals would this address, and how would it address them?

_____

_____

_____

6-3   The obstacles that might prevent me from doing it are:

_____

_____

_____

6-4   Possible ways of overcoming these obstacles are:

_____

_____

_____

6-5   Will I put this on my recovery plan?   ❑ Yes   ❑ No   ❑ Unsure

Section 7: Morning and Evening Inventories

People who avoid relapse and successfully recover learn how to break free of automatic and unconscious self-defeating responses. They learn to live consciously each day, being aware of what they're doing and taking responsibility for what they do and its consequences. To stay consciously aware, they take time each morning to plan their day (a morning planning inventory) and they take time each evening to review their progress and problems (an evening review inventory). They discuss what they learn about themselves with other people who are involved in their recovery program.

7-1   Do I believe I need to do this?   ❑ Yes   ❑ No   ❑ Unsure

7-2   What recovery goals would this address, and how would it address them?

_____

_____

_____

7-3   The obstacles that might prevent me from doing it are:

_____

_____

_____

7-4   Possible ways of overcoming these obstacles are:

_____

_____

_____

7-5   Will I put this on my recovery plan?   ❑ Yes   ❑ No   ❑ Unsure

Part 3: *Scheduling Recovery Activities*

Instructions

On the next page is a planner that will allow you to create a weekly schedule of recovery activities. Think of a typical week and enter the recovery activities that you plan to routinely schedule in the correct time slot for each day. A *recovery activity* is a specific thing that you do at a scheduled time on a certain day. If you can't enter the activity onto a daily planner at a specific time, it's not a recovery activity. Most people find it helpful to have more than one scheduled recovery activity for each day.

CENAPS® Weekly Planner

	Sunday	Monday	Tuesday	Wednesday	Thursday	Friday	Saturday
6:00 AM							
6:30 AM							
7:00 AM							
7:30 AM							
8:00 AM							
8:30 AM							
9:00 AM							
9:30 AM							
10:00 AM							
10:30 AM							
11:00 AM							
11:30 AM							
12:00 Noon							
12:30 PM							
1:00 PM							
1:30 PM							
2:00 PM							
2:30 PM							
3:00 PM							
3:30 PM							
4:00 PM							
4:30 PM							
5:00 PM							
5:30 PM							
6:00 PM							
6:30 PM							
7:00 PM							
7:30 PM							
8:00 PM							
8:30 PM							
9:00 PM							
9:30 PM							
10:00 PM							
10:30 PM							

Part 4: *Testing the Schedule of Recovery Activities*

Section 1: Testing the Schedule With Critical Warning Sign #1

1-1   Go back to the *Warning Sign Analysis* and *Warning Sign Management* processes and review the first critical warning sign that you want your recovery program to help you identify and manage: Read the personal title and description, and the thought, feeling, urge, and action statements carefully. What are the title and description of this warning sign?

Title: _____

Description: *I know I'm in trouble with my recovery when ...*

_____

_____

_____

1-2   Review your CENAPS® Weekly Planner. What's the most important recovery activity that will help you manage this warning sign?

_____

a.   How can you use this recovery activity to help you identify this relapse warning sign if it is activated? (Remember, most warning signs are acted out in automatic and unconscious ways. A trigger is activated and we start using the old ways of thinking and acting without being consciously aware of what we're doing. To prevent relapse, it's helpful to regularly schedule recovery activities that will encourage us to talk about how we're thinking, feeling, and acting, and then receive feedback if our warning signs seem to be activated.)

_____

_____

_____

b.   If you start to experience this warning sign again, how can you use this recovery activity to manage it? (Remember, managing a warning sign means changing how you think, feel, and act. How can this recovery activity help you stop thinking and doing things that make you feel like relapsing? How can it help you start thinking and doing things that make you want to get back into recovery?)

_____

_____

_____

_____

1-3   Review your CENAPS® Weekly Planner again. What's the second most important recovery activity that will help you manage this warning sign?

_____

    a.   How can you use this recovery activity to help you identify this relapse warning sign if it is activated?

_____

_____

_____

    b.   If you start to experience this warning sign again, how can you use this recovery activity to manage it?

_____

_____

_____

1-4   Review your CENAPS® Weekly Planner again. What's the third most important recovery activity that will help you manage this warning sign?

_____

    a.   How can you use this recovery activity to help you identify this relapse warning sign if it is activated?

_____

_____

_____

    b.   If you start to experience this warning sign again, how can you use this recovery activity to manage it?

_____

_____

_____

1-5   What other recovery activities can you think of that might be more effective in helping you identify and manage this warning sign if it is activated?

_____

_____

_____

_____

Add these activities to your CENAPS® Weekly Planner.

1-6   Turn to Side 2 of your identification card for this critical warning sign. Of the recovery activities you've listed above, select the ones that would be most useful for you in managing this warning sign. Write these activities, and any important information about how you might use them, under "Recovery Activities" on your warning sign card.

Section 2: Testing the Schedule With Critical Warning Sign #2

2-1   Go back to the *Warning Sign Analysis* and *Warning Sign Management* processes and review the second critical warning sign that you want your recovery program to help you identify and manage: Read the personal title and description, and the thought, feeling, urge, and action statements carefully. What are the title and description of this warning sign?

Title: _____

Description: *I know I'm in trouble with my recovery when ...*

_____

_____

_____

2-2   Review your CENAPS® Weekly Planner. What's the most important recovery activity that will help you manage this warning sign?

_____

a.   How can you use this recovery activity to help you identify this relapse warning sign if it is activated? (Remember, most warning signs are acted out in automatic and unconscious ways. A trigger is activated and we start using the old ways of thinking and acting without being consciously aware of what we're doing. To prevent relapse, it's helpful to regularly schedule recovery activities that will encourage us to talk about how we're thinking, feeling, and acting, and then receive feedback if our warning signs seem to be activated.)

_____

_____

_____

_____

b.   If you start to experience this warning sign again, how can you use this recovery activity to manage it? (Remember, managing a warning sign means changing how you think, feel, and act. How can this recovery activity help you stop thinking and doing things that make you feel like relapsing? How can it help you start thinking and doing things that make you want to get you back into recovery?)

_____

_____

_____

_____

2-3   Review your CENAPS® Weekly Planner again. What's the second most important recovery activity that will help you manage this warning sign?

_____

a. How can you use this recovery activity to help you identify this relapse warning sign if it is activated?

_____

_____

_____

b. If you start to experience this warning sign again, how can you use this recovery activity to manage it?

_____

_____

_____

2-4 Review your CENAPS® Weekly Planner again. What's the third most important recovery activity that will help you manage this warning sign?

_____

a. How can you use this recovery activity to help you identify this relapse warning sign if it is activated?

_____

_____

_____

b. If you start to experience this warning sign again, how can you use this recovery activity to manage it?

_____

_____

_____

2-5 What other recovery activities can you think of that might be more effective in helping you identify and manage this warning sign if it is activated?

_____

_____

_____

_____

Add these activities to your CENAPS® Weekly Planner.

2-6 Turn to Side 2 of your identification card for this critical warning sign. Of the recovery activities you've listed above, select the ones that would be most useful for you in managing this warning sign. Write these activities, and any important information about how you might use them, under "Recovery Activities" on your warning sign card.

Section 3: Testing the Schedule With Critical Warning Sign #3

3-1   Go back to the *Warning Sign Analysis* and *Warning Sign Management* processes and review the third critical warning sign that you want your recovery program to help you identify and manage: Read the personal title and description, and the thought, feeling, urge, and action statements carefully. What are the title and description of this warning sign?

Title: _____

Description: *I know I'm in trouble with my recovery when ...*

_____

_____

_____

3-2   Review your CENAPS® Weekly Planner. What's the most important recovery activity that will help you manage this warning sign?

_____

a.   How can you use this recovery activity to help you identify this relapse warning sign if it is activated? (Remember, most warning signs are acted out in automatic and unconscious ways. A trigger is activated and we start using the old ways of thinking and acting without being consciously aware of what we're doing. To prevent relapse, it's helpful to regularly schedule recovery activities that will encourage us to talk about how we're thinking, feeling, and acting, and then receive feedback if our warning signs seem to be activated.)

_____

_____

_____

_____

b.   If you start to experience this warning sign again, how can you use this recovery activity to manage it? (Remember, managing a warning sign means changing how you think, feel, and act. How can this recovery activity help you stop thinking and doing things that make you feel like relapsing? How can it help you start thinking and doing things that make you want to get back into recovery?)

_____

_____

_____

_____

3-3   Review your CENAPS® Weekly Planner again. What's the second most important recovery activity that will help you manage this warning sign?

_____

    a.   How can you use this recovery activity to help you identify this relapse warning sign if it is activated?

_____

_____

_____

    b.   If you start to experience this warning sign again, how can you use this recovery activity to manage it?

_____

_____

_____

3-4   Review your CENAPS® Weekly Planner again. What's the third most important recovery activity that will help you manage this warning sign?

_____

    a.   How can you use this recovery activity to help you identify this relapse warning sign if it is activated?

_____

_____

_____

    b.   If you start to experience this warning sign again, how can you use this recovery activity to manage it?

_____

_____

_____

3-5   What other recovery activities can you think of that might be more effective in helping you identify and manage this warning sign if it is activated?

_____

_____

_____

Add these activities to your CENAPS® Weekly Planner.

3-6   Turn to Side 2 of your identification card for this critical warning sign. Of the recovery activities you've listed above, select the ones that would be most useful for you in managing this warning sign. Write these activities, and any important information about how you might use them, under "Recovery Activities" on your warning sign card.

Part 5:   The Final Schedule of Recovery Activities

Instructions

You might have added some activities to your recovery plan as a result of what you learned when you tested your Initial Recovery Plan. On the following page is another copy of the CENAPS® Weekly Planner. Use it to map a final weekly recovery plan that includes all the activities targeted to your critical warning signs.

CENAPS® Weekly Planner

	Sunday	Monday	Tuesday	Wednesday	Thursday	Friday	Saturday
6:00 AM							
6:30 AM							
7:00 AM							
7:30 AM							
8:00 AM							
8:30 AM							
9:00 AM							
9:30 AM							
10:00 AM							
10:30 AM							
11:00 AM							
11:30 AM							
12:00 Noon							
12:30 PM							
1:00 PM							
1:30 PM							
2:00 PM							
2:30 PM							
3:00 PM							
3:30 PM							
4:00 PM							
4:30 PM							
5:00 PM							
5:30 PM							
6:00 PM							
6:30 PM							
7:00 PM							
7:30 PM							
8:00 PM							
8:30 PM							
9:00 PM							
9:30 PM							
10:00 PM							
10:30 PM							

Part 6:   Morning Planning Inventory

The first steps in learning to avoid relapse are: (1) identifying your relapse warning signs; (2) developing management strategies for critical warning signs; and (3) developing a recovery program that will support you in the ongoing identification and management of relapse warning signs.

Warning signs often develop without our conscious awareness of them. In other words, we can experience warning signs and not know it because we're involved in other things. By using daily inventories, we can train ourselves to become aware of warning signs as they develop, and to make conscious decisions to use our warning sign management strategies.

The most effective way of taking daily inventory is to do a planning inventory every morning and a review inventory every evening. The morning planning inventory takes about fifteen minutes. It helps you plan your day, schedule your recovery activities, and stay aware of any warning signs you might experience.

The evening review inventory takes about fifteen minutes. It helps you review the activities of your day, evaluate how well you stuck to your recovery program, and notice if you experienced any relapse warning signs. It also gives you a chance to decide if you need help or support in dealing with what happened during the day.

The following forms are recommended for use during your morning and evening inventories. Make copies of these forms and use them every day.

Morning Planning Inventory

(Copyright © Terence T. Gorski, 1991, 1994, 1995)

Major Goals for Today: Day _____   Date:_____

- ☐ 1. _____
- ☐ 2. _____
- ☐ 3. _____
- ☐ 4. _____
- ☐ 5. _____

Recovery Tasks	Daily Time Plan
☐ 1.	6:00 - 7:00
☐ 2.	7:00 - 8:00
☐ 3.	8:00 - 9:00
☐ 4.	9:00 - 10:00
☐ 5.	10:00 - 11:00
Daily Tasks	11:00 - 12:00
☐ 1.	12:00 - 1:00
☐ 2.	1:00 - 2:00
☐ 3.	2:00 - 3:00
☐ 4.	3:00 - 4:00
☐ 5.	4:00 - 5:00
☐ 6.	5:00 - 6:00
☐ 7.	6:00 - 7:00
☐ 8.	7:00 - 8:00
☐ 9.	8:00 - 9:00
☐ 10.	9:00 - 10:00
☐ 11.	**Notes**
☐ 12.	
☐ 13.	
☐ 14.	
☐ 15.	

Part 7:   Evening Review Inventory

1.   **Personal and Professional Progress**

Did I make progress today toward the accomplishment of my personal and professional goals?   ❑ Yes   ❑ No   ❑ Unsure

How do I feel about that progress? _____

_____

2.   **Personal and Professional Problems**

Did I make progress today toward solving my personal and professional problems?

❑ Yes   ❑ No   ❑ Unsure

How do I feel about those problems? _____

_____

3.   **Active Warning Signs**

Did I experience warning signs of excessive stress or relapse?

❑ Yes   ❑ No   ❑ Unsure

What have I done to manage those warning signs?_____

_____

How do I feel about the presence of those warning signs?_____

_____

4.   **Decision about the Need for Outside Help**

Do I need to talk to someone about the events of the day?

❑ Yes   ❑ No   ❑ Unsure

Do I need outside help with the problems or warning signs I experienced today?

❑ Yes   ❑ No   ❑ Unsure

What feelings am I experiencing as I think about my need for outside help?

_____

_____

Relapse Prevention Therapy Workbook:
Managing Core Personality and Lifestyle Issues

Final Evaluation of Workbook Completion

Instructions

The true test of whether or not you've benefited from completing the exercises in this workbook will be your ability to avoid relapse. It may be helpful, however, to review what you've accomplished. A careful evaluation can help you identify areas in your Relapse Prevention Plan that are incomplete. By going back and completing these areas, you might avoid unnecessary relapse and the resulting pain and problems.

Here's a checklist that can help you decide if you've accomplished the objectives of completing this workbook. Read each statement and ask yourself if you've fully completed that objective, partially completed it, or not completed it at all. Remember: This is a self-evaluation designed to help you determine if you have the skills needed to avoid relapse. Be honest with yourself. If you relapse because you haven't learned the skills to stay in recovery, you're the one who will pay the price.

Phase I: Stabilization

1. *Screening:* I've honestly completed the checklists evaluating my need for stabilization and treatment, and the Assessment of Mental Status.

   Level of Completion: ❑ Full ❑ Partial ❑ None

2. *Schedule of Recovery Activities:* I've honestly and thoroughly reviewed the recovery activities I used in the past. I've identified their strengths and weaknesses and my expectations of myself in recovery.

   Level of Completion: ❑ Full ❑ Partial ❑ None

3. *Immediate Relapse Prevention Plan:* I've identified five telephone contacts, three high-risk situations, and three relapse justifications. I've identified viable ways of managing those high-risk situations and challenging those relapse justifications in the future.

   Level of Completion: ❑ Full ❑ Partial ❑ None

4. *Early Intervention Plan:* I've completed the Client Intervention Worksheet and chosen an Early Intervention Team, participated in an Intervention Team Training session according to instructions, and written an early intervention letter to myself in case I relapse in the future.

Phase II: Assessment

5. *Life and Addiction History:* I've reviewed significant relationships and events in my childhood, adolescence, and adulthood. I've identified my beliefs and expectations about alcohol and drugs during those periods.

   Level of Completion: ❑ Full ❑ Partial ❑ None

6. **Recovery and Relapse History:** I've completed a calendar showing all of my periods of recovery and relapse, a Relapse Episode List that identifies my reasons for entering each period of recovery and relapse, and a summary that identifies overall patterns in my relapse history.

Level of Completion: ❑ Full ❑ Partial ❑ None

Phase III: Warning Sign Identification

7. **Warning Sign Review:** I'm able to use the relapse warning sign list to identify personal warning signs that lead me from stable recovery to relapse. I have selected the most important warning signs that I've experienced and written personal titles and personal descriptions of those warning signs.

Level of Completion: ❑ Full ❑ Partial ❑ None

8. **Warning Sign Analysis:** I've described two past experiences with each of three personal warning signs; identified the thoughts, feelings, urges, and actions that describe my self-defeating responses to those warning signs; and identified hidden warning signs that lead me from stable recovery to relapse.

Level of Completion: ❑ Full ❑ Partial ❑ None

9. **Sentence Completion:** I've used the Sentence Completion exercises to identify hot responses and to explore how my personal warning signs lead from one to another.
Level of Completion: ❑ Full ❑ Partial ❑ None

10. **Final Warning Sign List:** I've created a final warning sign list on a series of warning sign cards and refined that list using the results of my warning sign analysis and sentence completion exercises. I've identified three critical warning signs that can serve as effective intervention points in the future.

Level of Completion: ❑ Full ❑ Partial ❑ None

Phase IV: Warning Sign Management

11. **Thought Management:** I've identified the primary irrational thoughts that lead me from stable recovery to relapse. I can translate those thoughts into mandates and injunctions and challenge my old ways of thinking. I've also developed new ways of thinking that give me new and more effective choices in managing those thoughts.

Level of Completion: ❑ Full ❑ Partial ❑ None

12. **Feeling Management:** I've identified, labeled, and learned to communicate and redirect energy from the unmanageable feelings that lead me from stable recovery to relapse. I can also identify new and more effective ways of managing those feelings.

Level of Completion: ❑ Full ❑ Partial ❑ None

13. **Behavior and Situation Management:** I've identified my high-risk situations and the critical intervention points in those situations (points where I can choose to use new behaviors that will interrupt the relapse process and reinforce my recovery and ability to live responsibly).

Level of Completion: ❑ Full ❑ Partial ❑ None

14. ***Integrated TFUAR Management:*** I've reviewed my critical warning sign cards and my answers to Processes 11-13, and used that information to complete Side 2 of the Warning Sign Identification Cards for my critical warning signs.

Level of Completion: ❑ Full ❑ Partial ❑ None

Phase V: Recovery Planning

15. ***Recovery Planing:*** I've identified five recovery goals and a preliminary schedule of recovery activities appropriate for my personal recovery needs; tested that schedule against my recovery goals and my critical warning signs; identified a final weekly schedule of recovery activities that will support the ongoing identification and management of relapse warning signs and support an early intervention should relapse occur; and learned how to use morning and evening inventory forms.

Level of Completion: ❑ Full ❑ Partial ❑ None

16. ***Overall Response:*** I've developed immediate relapse prevention and early intervention plans; identified my life, addiction, and relapse patterns; identified and learned to manage the relapse warning signs that lead me from stable recovery to relapse; and developed a schedule of recovery activities that support ongoing warning sign identification and management.

Level of Completion: ❑ Full ❑ Partial ❑ None

If you identified any areas where you feel you need more work, let your relapse prevention therapist or counselor know. Remember, it's best to be fully prepared to manage the warning signs that can lead to relapse.

A Final Word

Congratulations for all the work you've done! By now you probably feel a lot more confident about your ability to avoid relapse and to manage the stress of everyday life. You have reason to feel more confident. You know yourself much better than most people ever will, and have stronger skills for managing your thoughts, feelings, urges, and actions.

As you've probably figured out by now, your relapse prevention work isn't done. It's just beginning, but you now have the tools to be successful. If you haven't done so yet, it's time to get in contact with other people who have gone through this Relapse Prevention Planning process. You can start or join a relapse support group (your local CENAPS®-trained Relapse Prevention Specialists will know of any such groups in your area; call CENAPS® at 708-799-5000 to get a list of these people). For information on starting groups, see *How to Start Relapse Prevention Support Groups* by Terence T. Gorski (Herald House/Independence Press, 800-767-8181).

The set of Appendices that follows contains a list of relapse prevention materials and related books, booklets, and pamphlets by Terence T. Gorski (Appendix 1). It also includes the *Guidelines for Effective Feeling Management* (Appendix 8) that formed the basis for Part 3 of Process 12, *Feeling Management*. That list can be a handy tool. The other Appendices will probably be familiar as forms that your therapist or relapse prevention sponsor used while you were working through your relapse prevention sessions.

When you started Relapse Prevention Therapy, you may have felt a sense of hopelessness. Many people do, especially after years of trying to recover and falling into relapse after relapse. I trust that you've lost that sense of hopelessness and replaced it with a strong hope, faith in yourself, and the willingness to get the help you need—the help we **all** need—in order to meet life's challenges with dignity and success.

I wish you the best of luck on your journey of recovery!

Appendices

Contents

Additional Resources by Terence T. Gorski

Screening Interview Form

Strategic Treatment Plan for Relapse Prevention

Session Documentation Form

The Stress Scale

The Global Assessment of Functioning (GAF) Scale

The Magic Triangle Relaxation Technique

Guidelines for Effective Feeling Management

Books

Miller, Merlene; Gorski, Terence T.; and Miller, David, *Learning to Live Again - A Guide For Recovery from Alcoholism.* Independence, Missouri: Herald House/Independence Press, 1980.

Gorski, Terence T., and Miller, Merlene, *The Management of Aggression and Violence.* Independence, Missouri: Herald House/Independence Press, 1981.

Gorski, Terence T., and Miller, Merlene, *Counseling for Relapse Prevention.* Independence, Missouri: Herald House/Independence Press, 1982.

Miller, Merlene, and Gorski, Terence T., *Family Recovery: Growing Beyond Addiction.* Independence, Missouri: Herald House/Independence Press, 1982.

Gorski, Terence T., and Miller, Merlene, *Staying Sober: A Guide for Relapse Prevention.* Independence, Missouri: Herald House/Independence Press, 1986.

Gorski, Terence T., *The Staying Sober Workbook: A Serious Solution for the Problem of Relapse.* Independence, Missouri: Herald House/Independence Press, 1988.

Gorski, Terence T., *Do Family of Origin Problems Cause Chemical Addiction?* Independence, Missouri: Herald House/Independence Press, 1989.

Gorski, Terence T., *How to Start Relapse Prevention Support Groups.* Independence, Missouri: Herald House/Independence Press, 1989.

Gorski, Terence T., *Passages Through Recovery: An Action Plan for Preventing Relapse.* Center City, Minnesota: Hazelden, 1989.

Miller, Merlene, and Gorski, Terence T., *Staying Sober Recovery Education Modules - Exercise Manual.* Independence, Missouri: Herald House/Independence Press, 1989.

Miller, Merlene, and Gorski, Terence T., *Staying Sober Recovery Education Modules.* Independence, Missouri: Herald House/Independence Press, 1989.

Gorski, Terence T., *The Players and their Personalities.* Independence, Missouri: Herald House/Independence Press, 1989.

Gorski, Terence T., *Understanding the Twelve Steps: A Guide for Counselors, Therapists, and Recovering People.* Independence, Missouri: Herald House/Independence Press, 1989.

Gorski, Terence T., *Understanding the Twelve Steps: An Interpretation And Guide For Recovering People.* New York, New York: Prentice Hall Press, 1989.

Gorski, Terence T., *Addictive Relationships: Why Love Goes Wrong in Recovery.* Independence, Missouri: Herald House/Independence Press, 1993.

Gorski, Terence T., *Getting Love Right: Learning the Choices of Healthy Intimacy.* New York, New York: A Fireside/Parkside Book, a division of Simon & Schuster, 1993.

Gorski, Terence T.; Havens, Lisa; Kelley, John M; and Peters, Roger H. *Relapse Prevention and the Substance-Abusing Criminal Offender: An Executive Briefing.* Technical Assistance Publication Series, no. 1. Maryland: U.S. Department of Health and Human Services, Public Health Service, Substance Abuse and Mental Health Services Administration, Center for Substance Abuse Treatment, 1993.

Gorski, Terence T., and Kelley, John M., *Counselor's Manual for Relapse Prevention With Chemically Dependent Criminal Offenders.* Technical Assistance Publication Series, no. 2. Maryland: U.S. Department of Health and Human Services, Public Health Service, Substance Abuse and Mental Health Services Administration, Center for Substance Abuse Treatment, 1993.

Gorski, Terence T., and Kelley, John M., *Relapse Prevention Workbook for Chemically Dependent Criminal Offenders.* Technical Assistance Publication Series, no. 3. Maryland: U.S. Department of Health and Human Services, Public Health Service, Substance Abuse and Mental Health Services Administration, Center for Substance Abuse Treatment, 1993.

Gorski, Terence T., *Part Three: Relapse Prevention Therapy with Chemically Dependent Criminal Offenders—The Relapse Prevention Workbook for the Criminal Offender.* Independence, Missouri: Herald House/Independence Press, 1993.

Gorski, Terence T., *Keeping the Balance: A Psychospiritual Model of Growth and Development.* Independence, Missouri: Herald House/Independence Press, 1993.

Gorski, Terence T., *Part Two: Relapse Prevention Therapy with Chemically Dependent Criminal* Offenders—A Guide for Counselors, Therapists, and Criminal Justice Professionals. Independence, Missouri: Herald House/Independence Press, 1994.

Woll, Pamela, and Gorski, Terence T., *Worth Protecting: Women, Men, and Freedom From Sexual Aggression.* Independence, Missouri: Herald House/Independence Press, 1995.

Gorski, Terence T., *A Group Leader's Guide to Brief, Strategic Problem-Solving Group Therapy.* Independence, Missouri: Herald House/Independence Press, 1995.

Gorski, Terence T., *A Group Member's Guide to Brief, Strategic Problem-Solving Group Therapy.* Independence, Missouri: Herald House/Independence Press, 1995.

Booklets and Pamphlets

Gorski, Terence T., and Miller, Merlene, *The Relapse Dynamic.* Independence, Missouri: Herald House/Independence Press, 1980.

Gorski, Terence T., and Miller, Merlene, *The Phases and Warning Signs of Relapse.* Independence, Missouri: Herald House/Independence Press, 1984.

Gorski, Terence T., and Miller, Merlene, *Mistaken Beliefs About Relapse.* Independence, Missouri: Herald House/Independence Press, 1988.

Gorski, Terence T., *The Relapse Recovery Grid.* Center City, Minnesota: Hazelden, 1989. Miller, Merlene and Gorski, Terence T., *Lowering the Risk: A Self-Care Plan for Relapse Prevention.* Independence, Missouri: Herald House/Independence Press, 1990.

Gorski, Terence T., *Managing Cocaine Craving.* Center City, Minnesota: Hazelden, 1990.

Gorski, Terence T., and Miller, Merlene, *Understanding Addictive Disease.* Independence, Missouri: Herald House/Independence Press, 1990.

Gorski, Terence T., *Questionnaire of Twelve Step Completion.* Independence, Missouri: Herald House/Independence Press, 1990.

Gorski, Terence T., *Relapse Warning Signs for Criminal Behavior.* Independence, Missouri: Herald House/Independence Press, 1994.

Gorski, Terence T., *The Relapse Dynamic for Criminal Behavior.* Independence, Missouri: Herald House/Independence Press, 1994.

Relapse Prevention Therapy Workbook

Appendix 2:   Screening Interview Form

Section 1: Current Condition

1. **Presenting Problem:** Why are you seeking treatment now?

   _____

   _____

2. **Current level of ....**

   A. Intoxication: ☐ None   ☐ Mild   ☐ Moderate   ☐ Severe

   B. Withdrawal: ☐ None   ☐ Mild   ☐ Moderate   ☐ Severe

   C. Impaired Mental Status: ☐ None   ☐ Mild   ☐ Moderate   ☐ Severe

   D. Recovery Support   ☐ None   ☐ Weak   ☐ Strong   ☐ Very Strong

Section 2: Evauation of Addiction and Behavioral Health

1. **Target Disorders:**   ☐ Chemical Dependence: Stage: ☐ Early ☐ Middle ☐ Late

   ☐ Self-defeating Personality Style: _____

   ☐ Mental Disorder: _____

2. **Knowledge Of:**
   a. Chemical Dependency   ☐ Good   ☐ Fair   ☐ Poor
   b. Personality Style   ☐ Good   ☐ Fair   ☐ Poor
   c. Mental Disorder   ☐ Good   ☐ Fair   ☐ Poor

3. **Recognition Of:**
   a. Chemical Dependency   ☐ Good   ☐ Fair   ☐ Poor
   b. Personality Style   ☐ Good   ☐ Fair   ☐ Poor
   c. Mental Disorder   ☐ Good   ☐ Fair   ☐ Poor

4. **Acceptance Of:**
   a. Chemical Dependency   ☐ Good   ☐ Fair   ☐ Poor
   b. Personality Style   ☐ Good   ☐ Fair   ☐ Poor
   c. Mental Disorder   ☐ Good   ☐ Fair   ☐ Poor

5. **Recovery Skills:**
   a. Chemical Dependency   ☐ Good   ☐ Fair   ☐ Poor
   b. Personality Style   ☐ Good   ☐ Fair   ☐ Poor
   c. Mental Disorder   ☐ Good   ☐ Fair   ☐ Poor

Section 3: Evaluation of Past Recovery

1. **Periods of Recovery From Chemical Dependency:** Number: _____ Since: _____

   Describe quality, average duration, progress, and problems:

2. **Periods of Recovery From Personality Style:** Number: _____ Since: _____

   Describe quality, average duration, progress, and problems:

3.   **Periods of Recovery From Mental Disorders:** Number: _____ Since: _____
     Describe quality, average duration, progress, and problems:

Section 4: Relapse Warning Signs

1.   What set you up to relapse during past periods of recovery?

     A. Thoughts: _____

     B. Feelings: _____

     C. Behaviors: _____

     D. Situations: _____

     E. Relationships: _____

Section 5: Type of Treatment, Motivation, and Ability to Participate

1.   **Type of Treatment Needed:**   ☐ Rapid Stabilization

                                      ☐ Motivational Counseling (Denial and Resistance)

                                      ☐ Primary Recovery (Recovery Skill Building)

                                      ☐ Relapse Prevention (Warning Sign Management)

          Rationale: _____

2.   **Level of Motivation:**   ☐ Good   ☐ Fair   ☐ Poor
     Primary Motivators:

     _____

3.   **Obstacles to Effective Treatment:**   ☐ High   ☐ Moderate   ☐ Low

     _____

     _____

Section 6: Level of Functioning and Stress Levels

What Is the ...	Current	Highest In Past year	Lowest In Past Year
1. Level of functioning (GAF Score)			
2. Chronic stress level (Stress Score)			

3. **Primary Target Disorders:** _____

4. **Target Problem:**   ☐ Denial and Resistance   ☐ Lack of Recovery Skills   ☐ Pattern of Relapse

5. **Target Behaviors:**   ☐ Stop Alcohol and Drug Use   ☐ Other: _____

Section 7: Treatment Recommendations

☐ Rapid Stabilization   ☐ Motivational Counseling   ☐ Primary Recovery   ☐ Relapse Prevention

_____

_____

_____

_____   _____
Therapist   *Date*   *Client*   *Date*

Relapse Prevention Therapy Workbook

Appendix 3:   Strategic Treatment Plan for Relapse Prevention

1.   **Problem Title:** Pattern of Chronic Relapse

2.   **Date Opened:** _____

3.   **Problem Description:** The client is unable to interrupt a pattern of chronic relapse in spite of previous attempts at recovery.

4.   **Goal:** The client will be able to interrupt this pattern of chronic relapse by learning how to identify life problems that have led to relapse, to identify and manage relapse warning signs, and to develop a recovery program that supports ongoing warning sign identification and management.

5.   **Interventions:** The client will participate in a combination of group and individual therapy sessions, psychoeducational sessions, supervised study halls, and self-help group meetings, in which the following interventions will be implemented:

   (1) **Screening:** The client will provide diagnostic information, by completing a series of screening instruments eliciting detailed assessments of stabilization needs, treatment needs, and mental status. (Refer to *Relapse Prevention Therapy Workbook: Managing Core Personality and Lifestyle Issues*, Process 1.)

   (2) **Schedule of Recovery Activities:** The client will assess the effectiveness of previous recovery programs, by completing a detailed review of recovery activities and an evaluation of strengths, weaknesses, and expectations in past recovery programs. (Refer to *Relapse Prevention Therapy Workbook: Managing Core Personality and Lifestyle Issues*, Process 2.)

   (3) **Immediate Relapse Prevention Plan:** The client will develop a plan to prevent relapse during the course of relapse prevention therapy, by identifying emergency telephone contacts, immediate high-risk situations and strategies for managing those situations, and relapse justifications and strategies for challenging them. (Refer to *Relapse Prevention Therapy Workbook: Managing Core Personality and Lifestyle Issues*, Process 3.)

   (4) **Early Intervention Plan:** The client will develop a plan to intervene early if relapse occurs, by completing an early intervention worksheet, choosing intervention team members, and participating in an Intervention Team Training session and related assignments. (Refer to *Relapse Prevention Therapy Workbook: Managing Core Personality and Lifestyle Issues*, Process 4.)

   (5) **Life and Addiction History:** The client will identify lifestyle problems that increase the risk of relapse, by completing a detailed life and addiction history of childhood, adolescence, and adulthood. (Refer to *Relapse Prevention Therapy Workbook: Managing Core Personality and Lifestyle Issues*, Process 5.)

   (6) **Recovery and Relapse History:** The client will identify factors leading to past relapses by completing a relapse calendar and a detailed analysis of relapse episodes. (Refer to *Relapse Prevention Therapy Workbook: Managing Core Personality and Lifestyle Issues*, Process 6.)

   (7) **Warning Sign Review:** The client will identify the warning signs that lead from stable recovery to relapse, by reviewing a list of common warning signs and identifying three personal warning signs. (Refer to *Relapse Prevention Therapy Workbook: Managing Core Personality and Lifestyle Issues*, Process 7.)

   (8) **Warning Sign Analysis:** The client will identify the hidden warning signs that have led to past relapses, by describing past experiences with his or her personal warning signs and identifying the thoughts, feelings, urges, and actions that comprise his or her self-defeating responses to those warning signs. (Refer to *Relapse Prevention Therapy Workbook: Managing Core Personality and Lifestyle Issues*, Process 8.)

(9) **Sentence Completion:** The client will identify "hot responses" (points of emotional vulnerability or volatility) and refine the sequencing of personal warning signs, by completing a series of sentence completion exercises. (Refer to *Relapse Prevention Therapy Workbook: Managing Core Personality and Lifestyle Issues*, Process 9.)

(10) **Final Warning Sign List:** The client will develop a final list of personal warning signs that lead from stable recovery to relapse; identify the related irrational thoughts, unmanageable feelings, self-destructive urges, and self-defeating behaviors that drive those warning signs; and identify three critical warning signs. (Refer to *Relapse Prevention Therapy Workbook: Managing Core Personality and Lifestyle Issues*, Process 10.)

(11) **Thought Management:** The client will learn how to manage the thoughts that drive the critical warning signs, by learning to identify, challenge, and replace irrational mandates and injunctions with rational thoughts and choices. (Refer to *Relapse Prevention Therapy Workbook: Managing Core Personality and Lifestyle Issues*, Process 11.)

(12) **Feeling Management:** The client will learn how to manage the feelings that drive the critical warning signs by learning to identify ineffective feeling management skills, practice more effective management skills, and identify opportunities for more effective feeling management. (Refer to *Relapse Prevention Therapy Workbook: Managing Core Personality and Lifestyle Issues*, Process 12.)

(13) **Behavior and Situation Management:** The client will learn how to manage the high-risk situations and self-defeating behaviors that drive the critical warning signs, by learning to identify the intervention points within those situations and to practice effective behavior and situation management strategies. (Refer to *Relapse Prevention Therapy Workbook: Managing Core Personality and Lifestyle Issues*, Process 13.)

(14) **Integrated TFUAR (Thought, Feeling, Urge, Action, Relationship) Management:** The client will create a portable reference card for warning sign management by reviewing his or her critical warning sign list and answers to Processes 11-13, and by using that information to complete Side 2 of the Warning Sign Identification Cards for all three critical warning signs.

(15) **Recovery Planning:** The client will develop a schedule of recovery activities that will support the ongoing identification and management of relapse warning signs, test this schedule by identifying how each activity can be adapted to help him or her identify and manage critical relapse warning signs, and develop a final recovery plan that addresses all critical warning signs. (Refer to *Relapse Prevention Therapy Workbook: Managing Core Personality and Lifestyle Issues*, Process 15.)

6. **Date Closed:** _____

7. **Description of Outcome:** At the completion of Relapse Prevention Therapy, the client's ability to use the skills related to each step of the relapse prevention intervention is as follows:

(1) **Screening:** The client has successfully completed the assessment of stabilization, treatment needs, and mental status.
    Level of Completion: ☐ Full   ☐ Partial   ☐ None

(2) **Schedule of Recovery Activities:** The client has successfully completed the review of recovery activities and the evaluation of strengths, weaknesses, and expectations regarding past recovery programs.
    Level of Completion: ☐ Full   ☐ Partial   ☐ None

(3) **Immediate Relapse Prevention Plan:** The client has successfully identified emergency telephone contacts; immediate high-risk situations and strategies for managing those situations; and relapse justifications and strategies for challenging them.
    Level of Completion: ☐ Full   ☐ Partial   ☐ None

(4) **Early Intervention Plan:** The client has completed an intervention worksheet, chosen Early Intervention Team members, participated in an Intervention Team Training session, and completed all related assignments.
    Level of Completion: ☐ Full   ☐ Partial   ☐ None

(5) **Life and Addiction History:** The client has successfully completed Life and Addiction Histories of childhood, adolescence, and adulthood.

Level of Completion: ☐ Full   ☐ Partial   ☐ None

(6) **Recovery and Relapse History:** The client has successfully completed a relapse calendar and a detailed analysis of past relapse episodes.

Level of Completion: ☐ Full   ☐ Partial   ☐ None

(7) **Warning Sign Review:** The client has reviewed a list of common relapse warning signs and identified three personal warning signs that lead from stable recovery to relapse.

Level of Completion: ☐ Full   ☐ Partial   ☐ None

(8) **Warning Sign Analysis:** The client has successfully identified and examined past experiences with each of the three personal warning signs; the thoughts, feelings, urges, and actions that describe his or her self-defeating responses to those warning signs; and the hidden warning signs that lead from stable recovery to relapse.

Level of Completion: ☐ Full   ☐ Partial   ☐ None

(9) **Sentence Completion:** The client has successfully used sentence completion exercises to identify "hot responses" and to further identify the sequencing of personal warning signs.

Level of Completion: ☐ Full   ☐ Partial   ☐ None

(10) **Final Warning Sign List:** The client has created a final warning sign list, refined that list using the results of previous exercises, and identified three critical warning signs for future intervention.

Level of Completion: ☐ Full   ☐ Partial   ☐ None

(11) **Thought Management:** The client has successfully identified the irrational thoughts that drive the identified relapse warning signs, identified personal mandates and injunctions and appropriate challenges for those mandates and injunctions, and identified more effective ways of thinking.

Level of Completion: ☐ Full   ☐ Partial   ☐ None

(12) **Feeling Management:** The client has successfully identified the unmanageable feelings that drive the critical relapse warning signs, new and more effective ways of managing those feelings, and opportunities for more effective feeling management.

Level of Completion: ☐ Full   ☐ Partial   ☐ None

(13) **Behavior and Situation Management:** The client has successfully identified the high-risk situations and self-defeating behaviors that drive the critical relapse warning signs, the intervention points within those situations, and appropriate behavior and situation management strategies.

Level of Completion: ☐ Full   ☐ Partial   ☐ None

(14) **Integrated TFUAR (Thought, Feeling, Urge, Action, Relationship) Management:** The client has successfully reviewed his or her critical warning sign list and answers to Processes 11-13, and has used that information to complete Side 2 of the Warning Sign Identification Cards for all three critical warning signs.

Level of Completion: ☐ Full   ☐ Partial   ☐ None

(15) **The Final Recovery Plan:** The client has successfully developed a schedule of recovery activities that will support the ongoing identification and management of relapse warning signs, tested that schedule by identifying how each activity can be adapted to help him or her identify and manage critical relapse warning signs, and developed a final recovery plan that addresses all critical warning signs.

Level of Completion: ☐ Full   ☐ Partial   ☐ None

Relapse Prevention Workbook

Appendix 4:   Session Documentation Form

Client: _____ Therapist: _____

Type: ☐ Group ☐ Individual ☐ Psychoeducation ☐ Family ☐ Other_____

Day/Date/Time: _____

Section 1: Client Notes

1. My Target Problem is: _____

2. The most important thing I learned in this session to help solve the target problem is:

_____

_____

3. What I'm going to do differently as a result of what I learned is:

_____

_____

4. The assignment I'm working on to solve my target problem is:

_____

_____

Client Signature:_____ Date: _____

Section 2: Rating Scales and Notes

Person Completing the Rating:	Self	Leader
5. Stress Score:		
6. The Level of Functioning Outside of Sessions (GAF Score):		
7. Problem-Solving Stage Score:		
8. Problem-Solving Motivational Response Score:		
9. Session Involvement Score:		
10. Client Satisfaction Rating:		

Therapist's Progress Note: _____

_____

_____

_____

Therapist Signature: _____ Date: _____

Rating Scales
Used in Session Documentation
Developed by Terence T. Gorski

Stress Scale

0 - 3 = Mild Stress,
no inference with in-session performance

4 - 6 = Moderate Stress,
periodic interference with in-session performance

7 - 10 = Severe Stress,
consistent interference with in-session performance

Global Assessment of Functioning
(GAF) Scale

1 - 30 = Severe Impairment in Functioning

Symptoms consistently cause serious dysfunction; suicidal or homicidal risk; inability to function and care for self

31 - 50 = Moderate Impairment in Functioning:

Symptoms periodically cause dysfunction in spite of extra effort; symptoms cause serious social and occupational problems

51 - 70 = Mild Impairment in Functioning:

Symptoms are a nuisance but can always be managed with extra effort without serious social or occupational problems

71 - 100 = No Impairment in Functioning

Problem-Solving Stage Scale

0 = Not Rated

1 = No target problem has been identified

2 = Vague target problem has been identified

3 = Problem has been clarified

4 = The thoughts, feelings, and actions driving the target problem have been identified and clarified

5 = List of alternative solutions has been developed

6 = Top three alternatives have been selected after analysis of benefits and disadvantages

7 = Consequences of top three alternatives have been projected

8 = Decision to use alternative has been made

9 = Decision has been implemented

10 = Outcome has been evaluated

Problem-Solving Motivational Response Scale

0 = Did not rate

1 = Refuses to use systematic problem solving

2 = Severe denial and resistance

3 = Mild denial and resistance

4 = Passive resistance; appears to try while not fully applying self

5 = Compliance—does what is told, no more, no less

6 = Active Compliance—fully cooperates; no creative involvement

7 = Periodic creative involvement

8 = Consistent creative involvement

9 = Periodic self-directed problem solving

10 = Consistent self-directed problem solving

Session Involvement Scale

0   = Did not rate

1 - 3 = Not complying with basic responsibilities and rules

4 - 6 = Average compliance with basic responsibilities and rules

7 - 10 = Excellent use of the format to solve problems

Client Satisfaction Scale

0   = Did not rate

1 -3   = Dissatisfied with progress

4 - 7 = Satisfied with progress

8 - 10 = Very satisfied with progress

Relapse Prevention Therapy Workbook

Appendix 5:   The Stress Scale

The Stress Scale is a rating of subjectively perceived stress. The stress scale can be used to measure both acute stress levels and chronic long-term stress levels. Acute stress is the immediate stress that the client is experiencing. Chronic stress is the average day-to-day stress that the client usually experiences. The Stress Scale numerically scores the level of stress between 0 (very low) and 10 (very high).

Section 1: Rating Chronic Stress Levels

There is a standard procedure for rating chronic stress levels. The first step is to rate the level of stress at the time the current episode of treatment began. The second step is to rate the highest average level of stress experienced in the past year. This will show a comparison between current stress levels and the average level of stress prior to the onset of the current problem requiring treatment.

Using the Stress Rating Scale

Step 1:   Rate the average level of stress experienced prior to the current treatment episode.

Step 2:   Rate the highest average stress level in the past year.

Step 3:   Set outcome goals using the stress scale.

Step 4:   Use the stress scale to teach the identification and management of stress during treatment sessions.

Step 5:   Use the stress scale to report on the outcome of treatment.

The third step is to identify the average stress level that you'd like to achieve by the completion of the current episode of treatment. This sets a clearly defined outcome goal that can become one of the targets of treatment. The fourth and ongoing step is to measure the average level of stress experienced between sessions. This measure is taken at the beginning of each session during the procedure called *Reactions to Last Session*. This will show the ongoing effect that treatment has on overall stress levels. These session-by-session evaluations will keep the focus on effectively managing stress outside of sessions. When used in conjunction with the Global Assessment of Functioning Scale, the relationship between the average stress level and the level of functioning outside of sessions can be clearly seen.

Section 2: Determining the General Stress Level Using the Stress Scale

The first step in assigning a Stress Score is to determine the client's general level of stress by placing the client in one of three general stress categories: low, moderate, or severe.

A *Low Stress Level* is designated when the stress level reflects nothing more than the normal stress of day-to-day living and is managed well, without subjective distress or dysfunction. A stress rating of between 1 and 3 is assigned.

A *Moderate Stress Level* is designated when stress levels are so high that they constitute a nuisance that creates subjective distress but does not cause dysfunction.   A stress score of between 4 and 6 is assigned.

A *Severe Stress Level* is designated when the stress levels are so high that the person begins to space out, get defensive, overreact, or become dysfunctional. A stress score of between 7 and 10 is assigned.

General Stress Scale

1. *Low Stress Level (Stress Score: 0 - 3)*
   - *Normal Stress of Day-to-Day Living*
   - *Stress is Managed Well*
   - *No Subjective Distress or Dysfunction*

2. *Moderate Stress Levels (Stress Score: 4 - 6)*
   - *High Stress Levels*
   - *Stress is Managed Poorly at Times*
   - *Stress Causes Subjective Distress but No Dysfunction*

3. *Severe Stress Levels (Stress Score: 7 - 10)*
   - *Very High Stress Levels*
   - *Stress Is Usually Managed Poorly*
   - *Stress Causes Subjective Distress and Dysfunction*

   Score 7 = Space Out
   Score 8 = Get Defensive
   Score 9 = Over-React
   Score 10 = Can't Function

Notice that what is being measured is the subjective perception of stress. This subjective perception of stress is a combination of three things: (1) the intensity of the stressor (the situation activating stress); (2) the stress-coping skills of the person experiencing the stressor; and (3) the level of awareness of the client experiencing the stress.

It is possible, for example, for a client to self-score very low on a subjective stress scale in spite of very high levels of stressors and very poor management skills, if the client is numbed out and has trained him- or herself not to pay attention to the signals of stress. It is also possible for a client to experience very intense stressors but, through effective stress management skills, lower the actual level of stress.

So in teaching clients to evaluate their stress levels, focus first on teaching techniques for increasing sensitivity to and awareness of stress indicators within the body, by educating clients about typical stress reactions and teaching them to notice their own subjective physical and psychological responses to stress. Next, teach clients about typical stressors and how stress is usually an involuntary reaction to those stressors. Finally, teach clients how to effectively manage and reduce the intensity of their stress reactions by using immediate relaxation response methods.

Section 3: Measuring Levels of Acute Stress

The stress scale can also be used to measure the levels of actual here-and-now stress. This can give both the client and the therapist a tool for becoming aware of and measuring general improvement in the subjectively perceived levels of stress.

The first step is to teach the client how to become aware of subjective stress levels. One way to do this is to ask the client to:

"Imagine that you have an *internal stress thermometer* that starts at the pit of your stomach and moves on up to your throat. When the stress levels are very low (a level 0) there is no perceived tension or stress. The thermometer reads '0'."

"As the level of stress goes up, a sense of tension begins in the pit of your stomach and starts moving up the esophagus and into the throat. The stress thermometer starts to rise. When the stress hits a level seven, you have to start defending yourself against the high stress levels. You do this by spacing out, getting defensive, over-reacting, or getting dysfunctional."

"At a level 7, we temporarily space out or block awareness of our internal feelings. At a level 8, we get defensive for no apparent reason. At a level 9, we start to over-react. At a level 10, we become dysfunctional."

"Once the acute stress level reaches 7, most people are unable to respond to constructive criticism or to integrate emotional experiences. As a result, when your immediate stress level is at 7 or above, it probably won't be very productive for us to conduct therapy as usual."

"What we'll do instead is teach you to monitor your subjective stress levels. As the stress levels begin to approach or rise above a level 7, I'll ask you to use an immediate relaxation response technique to lower your stress below level 7. This will teach you to self-regulate your stress levels, so you can learn to keep your stress levels low even when you face severe stressors."

This method needs to be used consistently in all treatment sessions, including group therapy. As soon as you notice that clients are experiencing elevated stress levels, ask them to center themselves and become aware of and rate their stress levels. If a client's stress level is 7 or above, instruct the client to use immediate relaxation response techniques to lower his or her stress level.

Relapse Prevention Therapy Workbook

Appendix 6:   The Global Assessment of Functioning (GAF) Scale

The Global Assessment of Functioning (GAF) Scale is a rating of overall psychological, social, and occupational functioning used in completing a DSM IV Axis-5 evaluation. The GAF numerically scores the level of functioning between 001 (Persistent Suicidal and Homicidal Risk) and 100 (Superior Functioning).

Section 1: Standard GAF Rating Procedure

There is a standard procedure for using the GAF Rating Scale. The first step is to rate the severity of dysfunction caused by the current problems or symptoms. The second step is to rate the highest level of functioning in the past year. This will show the previous level of functioning prior to the onset of the current problem.

The third step is to set outcome goals using GAF scaling. This means that you identify the functional level using the rating scale that you would like the person to achieve by the completion of the current episode of treatment. The fourth and ongoing step is to report on progress using GAF scaling at the end of each session. This will show the effect that problem solving and treatment involvement has had on the overall functioning of the client. Session-by-session evaluations using the GAF scale keep the focus where it belongs, on improving the ability to function effectively outside of sessions.

Using The GAF Rating Scale

Step 1:   Rate the severity of dysfunction caused
            by current problems or symptoms

Step 2:   Rate the highest level of functioning
            in the past year

Step 3:   Set outcome goals using GAF scaling

Step 4:   Report on progress using GAF scaling
            at the end of each session

Section 2: Determining General Symptom Severity Using the GAF Scale

The first step in assigning a GAF score is to determine the client's general level of functional impairment. This is done by placing the client's functioning in one of four general categories of impairment: normal, mild, moderate, or severe.

- *Normal Functioning* is rated when there are no symptoms or when symptoms reflect the normal stress of day-to-day living and are managed well. The person feels good and performs well. A GAF rating between 71 and 100 is assigned.

- *Mild Impairments in Functioning* are rated when symptoms or problems are a nuisance but can always be managed successfully with extra effort. There are no serious social or occupational problems, and aside from a feeling of personal or subjective stress, the person's life is going well. A GAF score between 51 and 70 is assigned.

- *Moderate Impairments in Functioning* are rated with GAF scores between 31 and 50. The problems or symptoms periodically cause dysfunction in spite of extra efforts taken to manage them. There are also some serious social and occupational problems.

- *Severe Impairments in Functioning* are rated with a GAF score between 1 and 30. The problems or symptoms consistently cause serious dysfunction. There is suicidal or homicidal risk and the inability to function and maintain basic self-care.

Section 3: Determining General Symptom Severity

The primary tool for determining general symptom severity is to ask the following diagnostic question: When you're experiencing the problem or symptoms, how frequently are you able to manage them with extra effort and function normally? If the answer is *Almost Always,* assign a mild GAF rating; if the answer is *Sometimes*, assign a moderate GAF rating; and if the answer is *Almost Never,* assign a severe GAF rating.

General Symptom Severity

1. *Normal Functioning (GAF Score: 71 - 100)*
   - *No Serious Symptoms*
   - *Normal Day-to-Day Stress*
   - *Feels Good and Functions Well*
2. *Mild Impairments in Functioning (GAF Score: 51 - 70)*
   - *Symptoms Are a Nuisance*
   - *But Can Always Be Managed With Extra Effort*
   - *Without Serious Social or Occupational Problems*
3. *Moderate Impairments in Functioning (GAF Score: 31 - 50)*
   - *Symptoms Periodically Cause Dysfunction in Spite of Extra Effort*
   - *Symptoms Cause Serious Social and Occupational Problems*
4. *Severe Impairments in Functioning (GAF Score: 1 - 30)*
   - *Symptoms Consistently Cause Serious Dysfunction*
   - *Suicidal or Homicidal Risk*
   - *Inability to Function and Care for Self*

Section 4: Assigning Precise Severity Ratings

The table on the following page gives you guidelines for assigning precise GAF ratings.

Global Assessment of Functioning Scale

Adapted From DSM IV by Terence T. Gorski

1. Superior Functioning—GAF Score: 91 - 100 (Average Score = 95)
- *No Significant Symptoms or Problems*
- *Superior Functioning in a Wide Range of Activities*
- *Life Problems Never Seem to Get Out of Hand*
- *Is Sought Out by Others Because of Many Positive Qualities*

2. Above Average Functioning—GAF Score: 81 - 90 (Average Score = 85)
- *Absent or Minimal Symptoms*
- *Good Functioning in All Areas*
- *Interested and Involved in a Wide Range of Activities*
- *Socially Effective*
- *Generally Satisfied With Life*
- *No More Than Everyday Problems or Concerns*

3. Average Functioning—GAF Score: 71 - 80 (Average Score = 75)
- *Transient Symptoms*
- *Expectable Reactions to Psychosocial Stressors*
- *No More Than Slight Impairment to Social, Occupational, or School Functioning*

4. Mild Symptoms—GAF Score: 61 - 70 (Average Score = 65)
- *Some Mild Symptoms or Some Difficulty in Social, Occupational, or School Functioning*
- *Generally Functioning Well*
- *Has Some Meaningful Interpersonal Relationships*

5. Moderate Symptoms—GAF Score: 51 - 60 (Average Score = 55)
- *Moderate Symptoms That Create Periodic Dysfunction OR*
- *Moderate Difficulty in Social, Occupational, or School Functioning*

6. Periodic Severe Symptoms—GAF Score: 41 - 50 (Average Score = 45)
- *Serious Symptoms That Create Periodic Dysfunction and Serious Subjective Distress*
- *Serious Impairment in Social, Occupational, or School Functioning*

7. Persistent Severe Symptoms—GAF Score: 31 - 40 (Average Score = 45)
- *Some Impairment in Reality Testing and Communication OR*
- *Major Impairment in Several Areas, Such as Work or School, Family Relations, Judgment, Thinking, or Mood*

8. Inability to Control Behavior—GAF Score: 21 - 30 (Average Score = 25)
- *Behavior Influenced by Delusions or Hallucinations OR*
- *Serious Impairment to Communication or Judgment OR*
- *Inability to Function in Almost All Areas*

9. Periodic Danger to Self or Others—GAF Score: 11- 20 (Average Score = 15)
- *Some Danger to Self and Others OR*
- *Occasional Failure to Maintain Minimal Personal Hygiene (Periodic Inability to Care for Self)*
- *Gross Impairment in Communication*

10. Persistent Danger to Self or Others—GAF Score: 1 - 10 (Average Score = 5)
- *Persistent Danger of Harming Self or Others OR*
- *Complete Inability to Care for Self*
- *Suicidal Attempt With Clear Expectation of Death*
- *Threat of Injury or Death to Others*

Relapse Prevention Therapy Workbook

Appendix 7:   The Magic Triangle Relaxation Technique

Most relapse-prone people have serious stress problems that can lead to relapse. It's important to teach relaxation techniques that can be used to turn off or significantly reduce the immediate stress response when it occurs.

The Magic Triangle Relaxation Technique is one of the best techniques for teaching immediate relaxation response training, because it involves a combination of deep breathing, guided imagery, and auto-suggestion. It's called the *Magic Triangle Relaxation Technique* because it uses the focal image of a triangle to induce relaxation.

For this exercise you'll want to maintain a tone of voice that's appropriate for a guided imagery exercise. Speak in the lower register of your voice, to promote relaxation. Speak slowly, pausing between sentences and phrases, to allow your listener to absorb and visualize what you've said. Here's a detailed description.

Give a General Relaxation Suggestion

"Take a deep breath and sit back in your chair. I'm going to teach you an immediate relaxation response exercise called the *Magic Triangle Relaxation Technique*. Once you learn it, you'll be able to use this technique to help you to turn off or significantly reduce stress whenever you're tense or agitated."

Give the Suggestion of Total Control and Safety

"You'll be in total control of this relaxation process. If at any time you feel uncomfortable or frightened, all you need to do is open your eyes, sit up, and look around the room, and you'll come back to the present."

Change Your Body Posture

"Change your body posture in the chair. Sit up straight, put your feet flat on the floor and look straight ahead. Find a spot on the wall or a spot in space in front of you. You can allow your eyes to close if it's comfortable, but you can also leave your eyes open and stare blankly in front of you as you let your mind relax and wander. You can do what feels best for you."

Body Awareness and Relaxation

"Notice your feet. Notice the pressure of your feet on the floor. Notice the feeling in your feet. Now say to yourself: 'My feet are warm and comfortable. I feel a tingling sense of relaxation in my feet'." (Repeat this suggestion three to five times.)

"Now notice your legs. Notice the feelings in your lower and upper legs. Now say to yourself: 'My legs are warm and comfortable. I feel a tingling sense of relaxation in my legs'." (Repeat this suggestion three to five times.)

"Now notice your lower body. Notice the feelings in your buttocks, lower back, and lower stomach. Feel the weight of your body pressing into your chair. As you're feeling the weight of your body, say to yourself: 'My lower body is warm and comfortable. I feel a tingling sense of relaxation in my lower body'." (Repeat this suggestion three to five times.)

"Now notice your upper body. Notice the feelings in your chest and upper back. Feel the weight of your body pressing into your chair. As you're feeling the weight of your body, say to yourself: 'My upper body is warm and comfortable. I feel a tingling sense of relaxation in my upper body'." (Repeat this suggestion three to five times.)

"Now notice your arms and shoulders. Notice the feelings in your arms and shoulders. Feel the weight of your arms as they rest comfortably on your lap. Notice the feeling of your arms gently pulling down on your shoulders. Notice any tension in your arms and shoulders and, if it's comfortable to do so, adjust your arms and shoulders to release the tension and become more relaxed."

"As you're feeling the feelings in your arms and shoulders, say to yourself: 'My arms and shoulders are warm and comfortable. I feel a tingling sense of relaxation in my arms and shoulders'." (Repeat this suggestion three to five times.)

"Now notice your neck. Notice the feelings in your neck. Notice any tension in your neck and, if it is comfortable to do so, adjust your neck by rotating it gently to release the tension and become more relaxed."

"As you're feeling the feelings in your neck, say to yourself: 'My neck is warm and comfortable. I feel a tingling sense of relaxation in my neck'." (Repeat this suggestion three to five times.)

"Now notice your head and scalp. Notice the feelings in your head and scalp. Imagine your scalp tingling with a warm sense of relaxation."

"As you're feeling the feelings in your head and scalp, say to yourself: 'My head and scalp are warm and comfortable. I feel a tingling sense of relaxation in my head and scalp'." (Repeat this suggestion three to five times.)

"Notice your face. Notice any tension in your face. Notice your jaw and allow it to relax. Feel how heavy your jaw is becoming and allow your jaw to relax. If it's comfortable to do so, adjust your jaw by rotating it gently to release the tension and become more relaxed. Notice the feelings around your eyes. If it's comfortable to do so, move the muscles around your eyes to release any tension."

"As you're experiencing the feelings in your face, jaws, and eyes, say to yourself: 'My face, jaws, and eyes are warm and comfortable. I feel a tingling sense of relaxation in my face, jaws, and eyes'." (Repeat this suggestion three to five times)

Deep Breathing

"Notice your breathing. Notice how your breath flows in and out of your body. Notice that you can regulate how quickly or slowly you breathe. Take a deep breath, hold it for a moment until your lungs feel tense, then slowly exhale. Take another deep breath, hold it for a moment until your lungs feel tense, then slowly exhale. One more time. Take another deep breath, hold it for a moment, slowly exhale."

"Notice if you're breathing from high in your chest or low in the stomach. As you notice your breathing, lower the breathing deep into your stomach. Imagine your lower stomach going in and out with each breath you take."

Rhythmic Breathing

"Now, as you're listening to my voice and noticing yourself relaxing, slowly breathe in to the count of four, and out to the count of four. As you breathe in, allow your breathing to fill the lower part of your stomach. As you breathe out, feel the lower part of your stomach relax. Inhale ... one, two, three, four—exhale ... one, two, three, four ... hold it a moment." (Repeat this for five to ten breaths.)

Visualizing the Triangle and Ball

"Now picture a black background before your eyes. See a bright red triangle, pointing up, with equal sides appearing on this deep black background. See the deepness and brightness of the red color in the triangle."

"Now imagine a bright yellow ball at the bottom right-hand side of the triangle. Imagine the ball rolling slowly up to the top of the triangle as you count slowly to four. Bring the ball up ... one, two, three, four. Balance the ball at the top of the triangle. Now bring the ball down ... one, two, three, four." (Practice this five to ten times.)

Combining Breathing and the Triangle and Ball

"Now, as you see the ball rising to the top of the triangle, take a very slow and deep breath. As your lungs fill with air, imagine the ball balancing at the top of the triangle. As you slowly exhale, imagine the ball slowly moving down the other side of the triangle."

Inhale ... raise the ball to the top of the triangle ... hold it for moment—exhale ... lower the ball to the bottom of the triangle." (Practice this five to ten times)

Adding Relaxation Suggestions

"As you breathe in and imagine the ball rolling to the top of the pyramid, say to yourself: 'I am ...' As the ball rolls down the other side of the triangle, say to yourself: 'relaxing ...' 'I am ...'—Ball to the top. 'relaxing'—Ball to the bottom." (Repeat this five to ten times.)

Waking Up From Relaxation

"Imagine that you're waking up in the morning from a deep and peaceful sleep. As you awaken, you feel an urge to stretch and try to yawn. Take a deep, deep breath. Slowly come awake, feeling the urge to stretch and yawn. Open your eyes, stretch your arms over your head. Come back fully awake, feeling rested and alert."

Appendix 8:   *Guidelines for Effective Feeling Management*

1. I anticipate situations that are likely to provoke strong feelings and emotions.

2. I recognize when I'm having a strong feeling or emotion.

3. I stop myself from automatically responding to the feeling without thinking it through.

4. I call a "time out" or get away from the situation for a few minutes. (Note: Excusing yourself to go to the bathroom is a technique that can be helpful.)

5. I use an immediate relaxation technique to bring down the intensity of the feeling.

6. I take a deep breath and notice what I'm feeling.

7. I find words that describe what I'm feeling. I use the feeling list if necessary.

☐ Strong or ☐ Weak _____	☐ Safe or ☐ Threatened _____
☐ Angry or ☐ Caring _____	☐ Fulfilled or ☐ Frustrated _____
☐ Happy or ☐ Sad _____	☐ Proud or ☐ Ashamed, guilty _____

8. I rate the intensity of the feeling using a ten-point scale.

9. I consciously acknowledge the feeling and its intensity by saying to myself, "Right now I'm feeling _____ and it's okay to be feeling this way."

10. I identify what I'm thinking that's making me feel this way. I ask myself, "How can I change my thinking in a way that will make me feel better?"

11. I identify what I'm doing that's making me feel this way. I ask myself, "How can I change what I'm doing in a way that will make me feel better?"

12. I recognize and resist urges to create problems, hurt myself, or hurt other people.

13. I recognize my resistance to doing things that would help me or my situation, and I force myself to do those things in spite of the resistance.

14. I get outside of myself and recognize and respond to what other people are feeling.

15. I talk with a safe person about what I'm feeling.
    - I tell them what I'm feeling and how strong the feeling is.
    - I tell them what I have an urge to do as a result of this feeling.
    - I tell them the thoughts that are making me feel this way.
    - I tell them what I'm doing that's making me feel this way.
    - I talk about how I can change what I'm thinking and doing in order to change how I feel or the intensity of what I'm feeling.

Warning Sign Identification Card—Side 1

Title: _____

Description: I know I'm in trouble with my recovery when ...

Thought: When I experience this warning sign I tend to think ...

Feeling: When I experience this warning sign I tend to feel ...

Urge: When I experience this warning sign I have an urge to ...

Action: When I experience this warning sign what I actually do is ...

Enabling Relationships: I tend to invite others to become part of my problem by ...

Warning Sign Identification Card—Side 1

Title: _____

Description: I know I'm in trouble with my recovery when ...

Thought: When I experience this warning sign I tend to think ...

Feeling: When I experience this warning sign I tend to feel ...

Urge: When I experience this warning sign I have an urge to ...

Action: When I experience this warning sign what I actually do is ...

Enabling Relationships: I tend to invite others to become part of my problem by ...

Warning Sign Identification Card—Side 1

Title: _____

Description: I know I'm in trouble with my recovery when ...

Thought: When I experience this warning sign I tend to think ...

Feeling: When I experience this warning sign I tend to feel ...

Urge: When I experience this warning sign I have an urge to ...

Action: When I experience this warning sign what I actually do is ...

Enabling Relationships: I tend to invite others to become part of my problem by ...

THE CENAPS CORPORATION
TRAINING · CONSULTATION · RESEARCH

Please send me information on the Relapse Prevention Certification School

Name _____

Title _____

Organization _____

Work Address _____

Work City/State/Zip _____

Home Address _____

Home City/State/Zip _____

Work Phone _____ Home Phone _____

Warning Sign Identification Card—Side 2

Title:

Recovery Activities: The recovery activities I can use to manage this warning sign are ...

Managing Thoughts: A new way of thinking that will help me manage this warning sign is ...

Managing Feelings: A new way of managing my feelings is ...

Managing Urges: A new way of managing my urges is ...

Changing Actions: A new way of acting is ...

Changing Enabling Relationships: A new way of inviting people to help me is ...

Warning Sign Identification Card—Side 2

Title:

Recovery Activities: The recovery activities I can use to manage this warning sign are ...

Managing Thoughts: A new way of thinking that will help me manage this warning sign is ...

Managing Feelings: A new way of managing my feelings is ...

Managing Urges: A new way of managing my urges is ...

Changing Actions: A new way of acting is ...

Changing Enabling Relationships: A new way of inviting people to help me is ...

The Center for Applied Sciences
The CENAPS Corporation
18650 Dixie Highway
Homewood, Illinois 60430

Warning Sign Identification Card—Side 1

Title: _____

Description: I know I'm in trouble with my recovery when ...

Thought: When I experience this warning sign I tend to think ...

Feeling: When I experience this warning sign I tend to feel ...

Urge: When I experience this warning sign I have an urge to ...

Action: When I experience this warning sign what I actually do is ...

Enabling Relationships: I tend to invite others to become part of my problem by ...

Warning Sign Identification Card—Side 1

Title: _____

Description: I know I'm in trouble with my recovery when ...

Thought: When I experience this warning sign I tend to think ...

Feeling: When I experience this warning sign I tend to feel ...

Urge: When I experience this warning sign I have an urge to ...

Action: When I experience this warning sign what I actually do is ...

Enabling Relationships: I tend to invite others to become part of my problem by ...

Warning Sign Identification Card—Side 1

Title: _____

Description: I know I'm in trouble with my recovery when ...

Thought: When I experience this warning sign I tend to think ...

Feeling: When I experience this warning sign I tend to feel ...

Urge: When I experience this warning sign I have an urge to ...

Action: When I experience this warning sign what I actually do is ...

Enabling Relationships: I tend to invite others to become part of my problem by ...

Warning Sign Identification Card—Side 1

Title: _____

Description: I know I'm in trouble with my recovery when ...

Thought: When I experience this warning sign I tend to think ...

Feeling: When I experience this warning sign I tend to feel ...

Urge: When I experience this warning sign I have an urge to ...

Action: When I experience this warning sign what I actually do is ...

Enabling Relationships: I tend to invite others to become part of my problem by ...

Warning Sign Identification Card—Side 2

Title: _____

Recovery Activities: The recovery activities I can use to manage this warning sign are …

Managing Thoughts: A new way of thinking that will help me manage this warning sign is …

Managing Feelings: A new way of managing my feelings is …

Managing Urges: A new way of managing my urges is …

Changing Actions: A new way of acting is …

Changing Enabling Relationships: A new way of inviting people to help me is …

Warning Sign Identification Card—Side 2

Title: _____

Recovery Activities: The recovery activities I can use to manage this warning sign are …

Managing Thoughts: A new way of thinking that will help me manage this warning sign is …

Managing Feelings: A new way of managing my feelings is …

Managing Urges: A new way of managing my urges is …

Changing Actions: A new way of acting is …

Changing Enabling Relationships: A new way of inviting people to help me is …

Copyright © Terence T. Gorski, 1995. CENAPS®, 17900 Dixie Hwy, Homewood, IL 60430; 708/799-5000.

Warning Sign Identification Card—Side 2

Title: _____

Recovery Activities: The recovery activities I can use to manage this warning sign are …

Managing Thoughts: A new way of thinking that will help me manage this warning sign is …

Managing Feelings: A new way of managing my feelings is …

Managing Urges: A new way of managing my urges is …

Changing Actions: A new way of acting is …

Changing Enabling Relationships: A new way of inviting people to help me is …

Copyright © Terence T. Gorski, 1995. CENAPS®, 17900 Dixie Hwy, Homewood, IL 60430; 708/799-5000.

Warning Sign Identification Card—Side 2

Title: _____

Recovery Activities: The recovery activities I can use to manage this warning sign are …

Managing Thoughts: A new way of thinking that will help me manage this warning sign is …

Managing Feelings: A new way of managing my feelings is …

Managing Urges: A new way of managing my urges is …

Changing Actions: A new way of acting is …

Changing Enabling Relationships: A new way of inviting people to help me is …

Copyright © Terence T. Gorski, 1995. CENAPS®, 17900 Dixie Hwy, Homewood, IL 60430; 708/799-5000.

Warning Sign Identification Card—Side 1

Title: _____

Description: I know I'm in trouble with my recovery when ...
_____

Thought: When I experience this warning sign I tend to think ...
_____

Feeling: When I experience this warning sign I tend to feel ...
_____

Urge: When I experience this warning sign I have an urge to ...
_____

Action: When I experience this warning sign what I actually do is ...
_____

Enabling Relationships: I tend to invite others to become part of my problem by ...
_____

Copyright © Terence T. Gorski, 1995. CENAPS®, 17900 Dixie Hwy, Homewood, IL 60430; 708/799-5000.

Warning Sign Identification Card—Side 1

Title: _____

Description: I know I'm in trouble with my recovery when ...
_____

Thought: When I experience this warning sign I tend to think ...
_____

Feeling: When I experience this warning sign I tend to feel ...
_____

Urge: When I experience this warning sign I have an urge to ...
_____

Action: When I experience this warning sign what I actually do is ...
_____

Enabling Relationships: I tend to invite others to become part of my problem by ...
_____

Copyright © Terence T. Gorski, 1995. CENAPS®, 17900 Dixie Hwy, Homewood, IL 60430; 708/799-5000.

Warning Sign Identification Card—Side 1

Title: _____

Description: I know I'm in trouble with my recovery when ...
_____

Thought: When I experience this warning sign I tend to think ...
_____

Feeling: When I experience this warning sign I tend to feel ...
_____

Urge: When I experience this warning sign I have an urge to ...
_____

Action: When I experience this warning sign what I actually do is ...
_____

Enabling Relationships: I tend to invite others to become part of my problem by ...
_____

Copyright © Terence T. Gorski, 1995. CENAPS®, 17900 Dixie Hwy, Homewood, IL 60430; 708/799-5000.

Warning Sign Identification Card—Side 1

Title: _____

Description: I know I'm in trouble with my recovery when ...
_____

Thought: When I experience this warning sign I tend to think ...
_____

Feeling: When I experience this warning sign I tend to feel ...
_____

Urge: When I experience this warning sign I have an urge to ...
_____

Action: When I experience this warning sign what I actually do is ...
_____

Enabling Relationships: I tend to invite others to become part of my problem by ...
_____

Copyright © Terence T. Gorski, 1995. CENAPS®, 17900 Dixie Hwy, Homewood, IL 60430; 708/799-5000.

Warning Sign Identification Card—Side 2

Title: _____

Recovery Activities: The recovery activities I can use to manage this warning sign are …

Managing Thoughts: A new way of thinking that will help me manage this warning sign is …

Managing Feelings: A new way of managing my feelings is …

Managing Urges: A new way of managing my urges is …

Changing Actions: A new way of acting is …

Changing Enabling Relationships: A new way of inviting people to help me is …

Warning Sign Identification Card—Side 2

Title: _____

Recovery Activities: The recovery activities I can use to manage this warning sign are …

Managing Thoughts: A new way of thinking that will help me manage this warning sign is …

Managing Feelings: A new way of managing my feelings is …

Managing Urges: A new way of managing my urges is …

Changing Actions: A new way of acting is …

Changing Enabling Relationships: A new way of inviting people to help me is …

Copyright © Terence T. Gorski, 1995. CENAPS®, 17900 Dixie Hwy, Homewood, IL 60430; 708/799-5000.

Warning Sign Identification Card—Side 2

Title: _____

Recovery Activities: The recovery activities I can use to manage this warning sign are …

Managing Thoughts: A new way of thinking that will help me manage this warning sign is …

Managing Feelings: A new way of managing my feelings is …

Managing Urges: A new way of managing my urges is …

Changing Actions: A new way of acting is …

Changing Enabling Relationships: A new way of inviting people to help me is …

Copyright © Terence T. Gorski, 1995. CENAPS®, 17900 Dixie Hwy, Homewood, IL 60430; 708/799-5000.

Warning Sign Identification Card—Side 2

Title: _____

Recovery Activities: The recovery activities I can use to manage this warning sign are …

Managing Thoughts: A new way of thinking that will help me manage this warning sign is …

Managing Feelings: A new way of managing my feelings is …

Managing Urges: A new way of managing my urges is …

Changing Actions: A new way of acting is …

Changing Enabling Relationships: A new way of inviting people to help me is …

Copyright © Terence T. Gorski, 1995. CENAPS®, 17900 Dixie Hwy, Homewood, IL 60430; 708/799-5000.

Warning Sign Identification Card—Side 1

Title: _____

Description: I know I'm in trouble with my recovery when ...
_____

Thought: When I experience this warning sign I tend to think ...
_____

Feeling: When I experience this warning sign I tend to feel ...
_____

Urge: When I experience this warning sign I have an urge to ...
_____

Action: When I experience this warning sign what I actually do is ...
_____

Enabling Relationships: I tend to invite others to become part of my problem by ...
_____

Copyright © Terence T. Gorski, 1995. CENAPS®, 17900 Dixie Hwy, Homewood, IL 60430; 708/799-5000.

Warning Sign Identification Card—Side 1

Title: _____

Description: I know I'm in trouble with my recovery when ...
_____

Thought: When I experience this warning sign I tend to think ...
_____

Feeling: When I experience this warning sign I tend to feel ...
_____

Urge: When I experience this warning sign I have an urge to ...
_____

Action: When I experience this warning sign what I actually do is ...
_____

Enabling Relationships: I tend to invite others to become part of my problem by ...
_____

Copyright © Terence T. Gorski, 1995. CENAPS®, 17900 Dixie Hwy, Homewood, IL 60430; 708/799-5000.

Warning Sign Identification Card—Side 1

Title: _____

Description: I know I'm in trouble with my recovery when ...
_____

Thought: When I experience this warning sign I tend to think ...
_____

Feeling: When I experience this warning sign I tend to feel ...
_____

Urge: When I experience this warning sign I have an urge to ...
_____

Action: When I experience this warning sign what I actually do is ...
_____

Enabling Relationships: I tend to invite others to become part of my problem by ...
_____

Copyright © Terence T. Gorski, 1995. CENAPS®, 17900 Dixie Hwy, Homewood, IL 60430; 708/799-5000.

Warning Sign Identification Card—Side 1

Title: _____

Description: I know I'm in trouble with my recovery when ...
_____

Thought: When I experience this warning sign I tend to think ...
_____

Feeling: When I experience this warning sign I tend to feel ...
_____

Urge: When I experience this warning sign I have an urge to ...
_____

Action: When I experience this warning sign what I actually do is ...
_____

Enabling Relationships: I tend to invite others to become part of my problem by ...
_____

Copyright © Terence T. Gorski, 1995. CENAPS®, 17900 Dixie Hwy, Homewood, IL 60430; 708/799-5000.

Warning Sign Identification Card—Side 2

Title: _____

Recovery Activities: The recovery activities I can use to manage this warning sign are ...

Managing Thoughts: A new way of thinking that will help me manage this warning sign is ...

Managing Feelings: A new way of managing my feelings is ...

Managing Urges: A new way of managing my urges is ...

Changing Actions: A new way of acting is ...

Changing Enabling Relationships: A new way of inviting people to help me is ...

Warning Sign Identification Card—Side 2

Title: _____

Recovery Activities: The recovery activities I can use to manage this warning sign are ...

Managing Thoughts: A new way of thinking that will help me manage this warning sign is ...

Managing Feelings: A new way of managing my feelings is ...

Managing Urges: A new way of managing my urges is ...

Changing Actions: A new way of acting is ...

Changing Enabling Relationships: A new way of inviting people to help me is ...

Copyright © Terence T. Gorski, 1995. CENAPS®, 17900 Dixie Hwy, Homewood, IL 60430; 708/799-5000.

Warning Sign Identification Card—Side 2

Title: _____

Recovery Activities: The recovery activities I can use to manage this warning sign are ...

Managing Thoughts: A new way of thinking that will help me manage this warning sign is ...

Managing Feelings: A new way of managing my feelings is ...

Managing Urges: A new way of managing my urges is ...

Changing Actions: A new way of acting is ...

Changing Enabling Relationships: A new way of inviting people to help me is ...

Copyright © Terence T. Gorski, 1995. CENAPS®, 17900 Dixie Hwy, Homewood, IL 60430; 708/799-5000.

Warning Sign Identification Card—Side 2

Title: _____

Recovery Activities: The recovery activities I can use to manage this warning sign are ...

Managing Thoughts: A new way of thinking that will help me manage this warning sign is ...

Managing Feelings: A new way of managing my feelings is ...

Managing Urges: A new way of managing my urges is ...

Changing Actions: A new way of acting is ...

Changing Enabling Relationships: A new way of inviting people to help me is ...

Copyright © Terence T. Gorski, 1995. CENAPS®, 17900 Dixie Hwy, Homewood, IL 60430; 708/799-5000.

Warning Sign Identification Card—Side 1

Title: _____

Description: I know I'm in trouble with my recovery when ...

_____

Thought: When I experience this warning sign I tend to think ...

_____

Feeling: When I experience this warning sign I tend to feel ...

_____

Urge: When I experience this warning sign I have an urge to ...

Action: When I experience this warning sign what I actually do is ...

Enabling Relationships: I tend to invite others to become part of my problem by ...

Copyright © Terence T. Gorski, 1995. CENAPS®, 17900 Dixie Hwy, Homewood, IL 60430; 708/799-5000.

Warning Sign Identification Card—Side 1

Title: _____

Description: I know I'm in trouble with my recovery when ...

_____

Thought: When I experience this warning sign I tend to think ...

_____

Feeling: When I experience this warning sign I tend to feel ...

_____

Urge: When I experience this warning sign I have an urge to ...

Action: When I experience this warning sign what I actually do is ...

Enabling Relationships: I tend to invite others to become part of my problem by ...

Copyright © Terence T. Gorski, 1995. CENAPS®, 17900 Dixie Hwy, Homewood, IL 60430; 708/799-5000.

Warning Sign Identification Card—Side 1

Title: _____

Description: I know I'm in trouble with my recovery when ...

_____

Thought: When I experience this warning sign I tend to think ...

_____

Feeling: When I experience this warning sign I tend to feel ...

_____

Urge: When I experience this warning sign I have an urge to ...

Action: When I experience this warning sign what I actually do is ...

Enabling Relationships: I tend to invite others to become part of my problem by ...

Copyright © Terence T. Gorski, 1995. CENAPS®, 17900 Dixie Hwy, Homewood, IL 60430; 708/799-5000.

Warning Sign Identification Card—Side 1

Title: _____

Description: I know I'm in trouble with my recovery when ...

_____

Thought: When I experience this warning sign I tend to think ...

_____

Feeling: When I experience this warning sign I tend to feel ...

_____

Urge: When I experience this warning sign I have an urge to ...

Action: When I experience this warning sign what I actually do is ...

Enabling Relationships: I tend to invite others to become part of my problem by ...

Copyright © Terence T. Gorski, 1995. CENAPS®, 17900 Dixie Hwy, Homewood, IL 60430; 708/799-5000.

Warning Sign Identification Card—Side 2

Title: _____

Recovery Activities: The recovery activities I can use to manage this warning sign are ...

Managing Thoughts: A new way of thinking that will help me manage this warning sign is ...

Managing Feelings: A new way of managing my feelings is ...

Managing Urges: A new way of managing my urges is ...

Changing Actions: A new way of acting is ...

Changing Enabling Relationships: A new way of inviting people to help me is ...

Warning Sign Identification Card—Side 2

Title: _____

Recovery Activities: The recovery activities I can use to manage this warning sign are ...

Managing Thoughts: A new way of thinking that will help me manage this warning sign is ...

Managing Feelings: A new way of managing my feelings is ...

Managing Urges: A new way of managing my urges is ...

Changing Actions: A new way of acting is ...

Changing Enabling Relationships: A new way of inviting people to help me is ...

Copyright © Terence T. Gorski, 1995. CENAPS®, 17900 Dixie Hwy, Homewood, IL 60430; 708/799-5000.

Warning Sign Identification Card—Side 2

Title: _____

Recovery Activities: The recovery activities I can use to manage this warning sign are ...

Managing Thoughts: A new way of thinking that will help me manage this warning sign is ...

Managing Feelings: A new way of managing my feelings is ...

Managing Urges: A new way of managing my urges is ...

Changing Actions: A new way of acting is ...

Changing Enabling Relationships: A new way of inviting people to help me is ...

Copyright © Terence T. Gorski, 1995. CENAPS®, 17900 Dixie Hwy, Homewood, IL 60430; 708/799-5000.

Warning Sign Identification Card—Side 1

Title: _____

Description: I know I'm in trouble with my recovery when ...
_____

Thought: When I experience this warning sign I tend to think ...
_____

Feeling: When I experience this warning sign I tend to feel ...
_____

Urge: When I experience this warning sign I have an urge to ...
_____

Action: When I experience this warning sign what I actually do is ...
_____

Enabling Relationships: I tend to invite others to become part of my problem by ...
_____

Copyright © Terence T. Gorski, 1995. CENAPS®, 17900 Dixie Hwy, Homewood, IL 60430; 708/799-5000.

Warning Sign Identification Card—Side 1

Title: _____

Description: I know I'm in trouble with my recovery when ...
_____

Thought: When I experience this warning sign I tend to think ...
_____

Feeling: When I experience this warning sign I tend to feel ...
_____

Urge: When I experience this warning sign I have an urge to ...
_____

Action: When I experience this warning sign what I actually do is ...
_____

Enabling Relationships: I tend to invite others to become part of my problem by ...
_____

Copyright © Terence T. Gorski, 1995. CENAPS®, 17900 Dixie Hwy, Homewood, IL 60430; 708/799-5000.

Warning Sign Identification Card—Side 1

Title: _____

Description: I know I'm in trouble with my recovery when ...
_____

Thought: When I experience this warning sign I tend to think ...
_____

Feeling: When I experience this warning sign I tend to feel ...
_____

Urge: When I experience this warning sign I have an urge to ...
_____

Action: When I experience this warning sign what I actually do is ...
_____

Enabling Relationships: I tend to invite others to become part of my problem by ...
_____

Copyright © Terence T. Gorski, 1995. CENAPS®, 17900 Dixie Hwy, Homewood, IL 60430; 708/799-5000.

Warning Sign Identification Card—Side 1

Title: _____

Description: I know I'm in trouble with my recovery when ...
_____

Thought: When I experience this warning sign I tend to think ...
_____

Feeling: When I experience this warning sign I tend to feel ...
_____

Urge: When I experience this warning sign I have an urge to ...
_____

Action: When I experience this warning sign what I actually do is ...
_____

Enabling Relationships: I tend to invite others to become part of my problem by ...
_____

Copyright © Terence T. Gorski, 1995. CENAPS®, 17900 Dixie Hwy, Homewood, IL 60430; 708/799-5000.

Warning Sign Identification Card—Side 2

Title: _____

Recovery Activities: The recovery activities I can use to manage this warning sign are ...

_____

Managing Thoughts: A new way of thinking that will help me manage this warning sign is ...

_____

Managing Feelings: A new way of managing my feelings is ...

_____

Managing Urges: A new way of managing my urges is ...

_____

Changing Actions: A new way of acting is ...

_____

Changing Enabling Relationships: A new way of inviting people to help me is ...

_____

Warning Sign Identification Card—Side 2

Title: _____

Recovery Activities: The recovery activities I can use to manage this warning sign are ...

Managing Thoughts: A new way of thinking that will help me manage this warning sign is ...

Managing Feelings: A new way of managing my feelings is ...

Managing Urges: A new way of managing my urges is ...

Changing Actions: A new way of acting is ...

Changing Enabling Relationships: A new way of inviting people to help me is ...

Copyright © Terence T. Gorski, 1995. CENAPS®, 17900 Dixie Hwy, Homewood, IL 60430; 708/799-5000.

Warning Sign Identification Card—Side 2

Title: _____

Recovery Activities: The recovery activities I can use to manage this warning sign are ...

Managing Thoughts: A new way of thinking that will help me manage this warning sign is ...

Managing Feelings: A new way of managing my feelings is ...

Managing Urges: A new way of managing my urges is ...

Changing Actions: A new way of acting is ...

Changing Enabling Relationships: A new way of inviting people to help me is ...

Copyright © Terence T. Gorski, 1995. CENAPS®, 17900 Dixie Hwy, Homewood, IL 60430; 708/799-5000.

Warning Sign Identification Card—Side 2

Title: _____

Recovery Activities: The recovery activities I can use to manage this warning sign are ...

Managing Thoughts: A new way of thinking that will help me manage this warning sign is ...

Managing Feelings: A new way of managing my feelings is ...

Managing Urges: A new way of managing my urges is ...

Changing Actions: A new way of acting is ...

Changing Enabling Relationships: A new way of inviting people to help me is ...

Copyright © Terence T. Gorski, 1995. CENAPS®, 17900 Dixie Hwy, Homewood, IL 60430; 708/799-5000.

Warning Sign Identification Card—Side 1

Title: _____

Description: I know I'm in trouble with my recovery when ...
_____
_____

Thought: When I experience this warning sign I tend to think ...
_____
_____

Feeling: When I experience this warning sign I tend to feel ...
_____
_____

Urge: When I experience this warning sign I have an urge to ...
_____
_____

Action: When I experience this warning sign what I actually do is ...
_____
_____

Enabling Relationships: I tend to invite others to become part of my problem by ...
_____
_____

Copyright © Terence T. Gorski, 1995. CENAPS®, 17900 Dixie Hwy, Homewood, IL 60430; 708/799-5000.

Warning Sign Identification Card—Side 1

Title: _____

Description: I know I'm in trouble with my recovery when ...
_____
_____

Thought: When I experience this warning sign I tend to think ...
_____
_____

Feeling: When I experience this warning sign I tend to feel ...
_____
_____

Urge: When I experience this warning sign I have an urge to ...
_____
_____

Action: When I experience this warning sign what I actually do is ...
_____
_____

Enabling Relationships: I tend to invite others to become part of my problem by ...
_____
_____

Copyright © Terence T. Gorski, 1995. CENAPS®, 17900 Dixie Hwy, Homewood, IL 60430; 708/799-5000.

Warning Sign Identification Card—Side 1

Title: _____

Description: I know I'm in trouble with my recovery when ...
_____
_____

Thought: When I experience this warning sign I tend to think ...
_____
_____

Feeling: When I experience this warning sign I tend to feel ...
_____
_____

Urge: When I experience this warning sign I have an urge to ...
_____
_____

Action: When I experience this warning sign what I actually do is ...
_____
_____

Enabling Relationships: I tend to invite others to become part of my problem by ...
_____
_____

Copyright © Terence T. Gorski, 1995. CENAPS®, 17900 Dixie Hwy, Homewood, IL 60430; 708/799-5000.

Warning Sign Identification Card—Side 1

Title: _____

Description: I know I'm in trouble with my recovery when ...
_____
_____

Thought: When I experience this warning sign I tend to think ...
_____
_____

Feeling: When I experience this warning sign I tend to feel ...
_____
_____

Urge: When I experience this warning sign I have an urge to ...
_____
_____

Action: When I experience this warning sign what I actually do is ...
_____
_____

Enabling Relationships: I tend to invite others to become part of my problem by ...
_____
_____

Copyright © Terence T. Gorski, 1995. CENAPS®, 17900 Dixie Hwy, Homewood, IL 60430; 708/799-5000.

Warning Sign Identification Card—Side 2

Title: _____

Recovery Activities: The recovery activities I can use to manage this warning sign are ...

Managing Thoughts: A new way of thinking that will help me manage this warning sign is ...

Managing Feelings: A new way of managing my feelings is ...

Managing Urges: A new way of managing my urges is ...

Changing Actions: A new way of acting is ...

Changing Enabling Relationships: A new way of inviting people to help me is ...

Warning Sign Identification Card—Side 2

Title: _____

Recovery Activities: The recovery activities I can use to manage this warning sign are ...

Managing Thoughts: A new way of thinking that will help me manage this warning sign is ...

Managing Feelings: A new way of managing my feelings is ...

Managing Urges: A new way of managing my urges is ...

Changing Actions: A new way of acting is ...

Changing Enabling Relationships: A new way of inviting people to help me is ...

Warning Sign Identification Card—Side 2

Title: _____

Recovery Activities: The recovery activities I can use to manage this warning sign are ...

Managing Thoughts: A new way of thinking that will help me manage this warning sign is ...

Managing Feelings: A new way of managing my feelings is ...

Managing Urges: A new way of managing my urges is ...

Changing Actions: A new way of acting is ...

Changing Enabling Relationships: A new way of inviting people to help me is ...

Copyright © Terence T. Gorski, 1995. CENAPS®, 17900 Dixie Hwy, Homewood, IL 60430; 708/799-5000.

Warning Sign Identification Card—Side 2

Title: _____

Recovery Activities: The recovery activities I can use to manage this warning sign are ...

Managing Thoughts: A new way of thinking that will help me manage this warning sign is ...

Managing Feelings: A new way of managing my feelings is ...

Managing Urges: A new way of managing my urges is ...

Changing Actions: A new way of acting is ...

Changing Enabling Relationships: A new way of inviting people to help me is ...

Copyright © Terence T. Gorski, 1995. CENAPS®, 17900 Dixie Hwy, Homewood, IL 60430; 708/799-5000.

Warning Sign Identification Card—Side 1

Title: _____

Description: I know I'm in trouble with my recovery when ...
_____

Thought: When I experience this warning sign I tend to think ...
_____

Feeling: When I experience this warning sign I tend to feel ...
_____

Urge: When I experience this warning sign I have an urge to ...
_____

Action: When I experience this warning sign what I actually do is ...
_____

Enabling Relationships: I tend to invite others to become part of my problem by ...
_____

Copyright © Terence T. Gorski, 1995. CENAPS®, 17900 Dixie Hwy, Homewood, IL 60430; 708/799-5000.

Warning Sign Identification Card—Side 1

Title: _____

Description: I know I'm in trouble with my recovery when ...
_____

Thought: When I experience this warning sign I tend to think ...
_____

Feeling: When I experience this warning sign I tend to feel ...
_____

Urge: When I experience this warning sign I have an urge to ...
_____

Action: When I experience this warning sign what I actually do is ...
_____

Enabling Relationships: I tend to invite others to become part of my problem by ...
_____

Copyright © Terence T. Gorski, 1995. CENAPS®, 17900 Dixie Hwy, Homewood, IL 60430; 708/799-5000.

Warning Sign Identification Card—Side 1

Title: _____

Description: I know I'm in trouble with my recovery when ...
_____

Thought: When I experience this warning sign I tend to think ...
_____

Feeling: When I experience this warning sign I tend to feel ...
_____

Urge: When I experience this warning sign I have an urge to ...
_____

Action: When I experience this warning sign what I actually do is ...
_____

Enabling Relationships: I tend to invite others to become part of my problem by ...
_____

Copyright © Terence T. Gorski, 1995. CENAPS®, 17900 Dixie Hwy, Homewood, IL 60430; 708/799-5000.

Warning Sign Identification Card—Side 1

Title: _____

Description: I know I'm in trouble with my recovery when ...
_____

Thought: When I experience this warning sign I tend to think ...
_____

Feeling: When I experience this warning sign I tend to feel ...
_____

Urge: When I experience this warning sign I have an urge to ...
_____

Action: When I experience this warning sign what I actually do is ...
_____

Enabling Relationships: I tend to invite others to become part of my problem by ...
_____

Copyright © Terence T. Gorski, 1995. CENAPS®, 17900 Dixie Hwy, Homewood, IL 60430; 708/799-5000.

Warning Sign Identification Card—Side 2

Title:

Recovery Activities: The recovery activities I can use to manage this warning sign are …

Managing Thoughts: A new way of thinking that will help me manage this warning sign is …

Managing Feelings: A new way of managing my feelings is …

Managing Urges: A new way of managing my urges is …

Changing Actions: A new way of acting is …

Changing Enabling Relationships: A new way of inviting people to help me is …

Copyright © Terence T. Gorski, 1995. CENAPS®, 17900 Dixie Hwy, Homewood, IL 60430; 708/799-5000.

Warning Sign Identification Card—Side 2

Title:

Recovery Activities: The recovery activities I can use to manage this warning sign are …

Managing Thoughts: A new way of thinking that will help me manage this warning sign is …

Managing Feelings: A new way of managing my feelings is …

Managing Urges: A new way of managing my urges is …

Changing Actions: A new way of acting is …

Changing Enabling Relationships: A new way of inviting people to help me is …

Copyright © Terence T. Gorski, 1995. CENAPS®, 17900 Dixie Hwy, Homewood, IL 60430; 708/799-5000.

Warning Sign Identification Card—Side 2

Title:

Recovery Activities: The recovery activities I can use to manage this warning sign are …

Managing Thoughts: A new way of thinking that will help me manage this warning sign is …

Managing Feelings: A new way of managing my feelings is …

Managing Urges: A new way of managing my urges is …

Changing Actions: A new way of acting is …

Changing Enabling Relationships: A new way of inviting people to help me is …

Copyright © Terence T. Gorski, 1995. CENAPS®, 17900 Dixie Hwy, Homewood, IL 60430; 708/799-5000.

Warning Sign Identification Card—Side 2

Title:

Recovery Activities: The recovery activities I can use to manage this warning sign are …

Managing Thoughts: A new way of thinking that will help me manage this warning sign is …

Managing Feelings: A new way of managing my feelings is …

Managing Urges: A new way of managing my urges is …

Changing Actions: A new way of acting is …

Changing Enabling Relationships: A new way of inviting people to help me is …

Warning Sign Identification Card—Side 1

Title: _____

Description: I know I'm in trouble with my recovery when ...

_____

Thought: When I experience this warning sign I tend to think ...

_____

Feeling: When I experience this warning sign I tend to feel ...

_____

Urge: When I experience this warning sign I have an urge to ...

_____

Action: When I experience this warning sign what I actually do is ...

_____

Enabling Relationships: I tend to invite others to become part of my problem by ...

_____

Copyright © Terence T. Gorski, 1995. CENAPS®, 17900 Dixie Hwy, Homewood, IL 60430; 708/799-5000.

Warning Sign Identification Card—Side 1

Title: _____

Description: I know I'm in trouble with my recovery when ...

_____

Thought: When I experience this warning sign I tend to think ...

_____

Feeling: When I experience this warning sign I tend to feel ...

_____

Urge: When I experience this warning sign I have an urge to ...

_____

Action: When I experience this warning sign what I actually do is ...

_____

Enabling Relationships: I tend to invite others to become part of my problem by ...

_____

Copyright © Terence T. Gorski, 1995. CENAPS®, 17900 Dixie Hwy, Homewood, IL 60430; 708/799-5000.

Warning Sign Identification Card—Side 1

Title: _____

Description: I know I'm in trouble with my recovery when ...

_____

Thought: When I experience this warning sign I tend to think ...

_____

Feeling: When I experience this warning sign I tend to feel ...

_____

Urge: When I experience this warning sign I have an urge to ...

_____

Action: When I experience this warning sign what I actually do is ...

_____

Enabling Relationships: I tend to invite others to become part of my problem by ...

_____

Copyright © Terence T. Gorski, 1995. CENAPS®, 17900 Dixie Hwy, Homewood, IL 60430; 708/799-5000.

Warning Sign Identification Card—Side 1

Title: _____

Description: I know I'm in trouble with my recovery when ...

_____

Thought: When I experience this warning sign I tend to think ...

_____

Feeling: When I experience this warning sign I tend to feel ...

_____

Urge: When I experience this warning sign I have an urge to ...

_____

Action: When I experience this warning sign what I actually do is ...

_____

Enabling Relationships: I tend to invite others to become part of my problem by ...

_____

Copyright © Terence T. Gorski, 1995. CENAPS®, 17900 Dixie Hwy, Homewood, IL 60430; 708/799-5000.

Warning Sign Identification Card—Side 2

Title:

Recovery Activities: The recovery activities I can use to manage this warning sign are ...

Managing Thoughts: A new way of thinking that will help me manage this warning sign is ...

Managing Feelings: A new way of managing my feelings is ...

Managing Urges: A new way of managing my urges is ...

Changing Actions: A new way of acting is ...

Changing Enabling Relationships: A new way of inviting people to help me is ...

Warning Sign Identification Card—Side 2

Title:

Recovery Activities: The recovery activities I can use to manage this warning sign are ...

Managing Thoughts: A new way of thinking that will help me manage this warning sign is ...

Managing Feelings: A new way of managing my feelings is ...

Managing Urges: A new way of managing my urges is ...

Changing Actions: A new way of acting is ...

Changing Enabling Relationships: A new way of inviting people to help me is ...

Warning Sign Identification Card—Side 2

Title:

Recovery Activities: The recovery activities I can use to manage this warning sign are ...

Managing Thoughts: A new way of thinking that will help me manage this warning sign is ...

Managing Feelings: A new way of managing my feelings is ...

Managing Urges: A new way of managing my urges is ...

Changing Actions: A new way of acting is ...

Changing Enabling Relationships: A new way of inviting people to help me is ...

Copyright © Terence T. Gorski, 1995. CENAPS®, 17900 Dixie Hwy, Homewood, IL 60430; 708/799-5000.

Warning Sign Identification Card—Side 2

Title:

Recovery Activities: The recovery activities I can use to manage this warning sign are ...

Managing Thoughts: A new way of thinking that will help me manage this warning sign is ...

Managing Feelings: A new way of managing my feelings is ...

Managing Urges: A new way of managing my urges is ...

Changing Actions: A new way of acting is ...

Changing Enabling Relationships: A new way of inviting people to help me is ...

Copyright © Terence T. Gorski, 1995. CENAPS®, 17900 Dixie Hwy, Homewood, IL 60430; 708/799-5000.

Warning Sign Identification Card—Side 1

Title: _____

Description: I know I'm in trouble with my recovery when ...

Thought: When I experience this warning sign I tend to think ...

Feeling: When I experience this warning sign I tend to feel ...

Urge: When I experience this warning sign I have an urge to ...

Action: When I experience this warning sign what I actually do is ...

Enabling Relationships: I tend to invite others to become part of my problem by ...

Copyright © Terence T. Gorski, 1995. CENAPS®, 17900 Dixie Hwy, Homewood, IL 60430; 708/799-5000.

Warning Sign Identification Card—Side 1

Title: _____

Description: I know I'm in trouble with my recovery when ...

Thought: When I experience this warning sign I tend to think ...

Feeling: When I experience this warning sign I tend to feel ...

Urge: When I experience this warning sign I have an urge to ...

Action: When I experience this warning sign what I actually do is ...

Enabling Relationships: I tend to invite others to become part of my problem by ...

Copyright © Terence T. Gorski, 1995. CENAPS®, 17900 Dixie Hwy, Homewood, IL 60430; 708/799-5000.

Warning Sign Identification Card—Side 1

Title: _____

Description: I know I'm in trouble with my recovery when ...

Thought: When I experience this warning sign I tend to think ...

Feeling: When I experience this warning sign I tend to feel ...

Urge: When I experience this warning sign I have an urge to ...

Action: When I experience this warning sign what I actually do is ...

Enabling Relationships: I tend to invite others to become part of my problem by ...

Copyright © Terence T. Gorski, 1995. CENAPS®, 17900 Dixie Hwy, Homewood, IL 60430; 708/799-5000.

Warning Sign Identification Card—Side 1

Title: _____

Description: I know I'm in trouble with my recovery when ...

Thought: When I experience this warning sign I tend to think ...

Feeling: When I experience this warning sign I tend to feel ...

Urge: When I experience this warning sign I have an urge to ...

Action: When I experience this warning sign what I actually do is ...

Enabling Relationships: I tend to invite others to become part of my problem by ...

Copyright © Terence T. Gorski, 1995. CENAPS®, 17900 Dixie Hwy, Homewood, IL 60430; 708/799-5000.

Warning Sign Identification Card—Side 2

Title: _____

Recovery Activities: The recovery activities I can use to manage this warning sign are ...

Managing Thoughts: A new way of thinking that will help me manage this warning sign is ...

Managing Feelings: A new way of managing my feelings is ...

Managing Urges: A new way of managing my urges is ...

Changing Actions: A new way of acting is ...

Changing Enabling Relationships: A new way of inviting people to help me is ...

Warning Sign Identification Card—Side 2

Title: _____

Recovery Activities: The recovery activities I can use to manage this warning sign are ...

Managing Thoughts: A new way of thinking that will help me manage this warning sign is ...

Managing Feelings: A new way of managing my feelings is ...

Managing Urges: A new way of managing my urges is ...

Changing Actions: A new way of acting is ...

Changing Enabling Relationships: A new way of inviting people to help me is ...

Copyright © Terence T. Gorski, 1995. CENAPS®, 17900 Dixie Hwy, Homewood, IL 60430; 708/799-5000.

Warning Sign Identification Card—Side 2

Title: _____

Recovery Activities: The recovery activities I can use to manage this warning sign are ...

Managing Thoughts: A new way of thinking that will help me manage this warning sign is ...

Managing Feelings: A new way of managing my feelings is ...

Managing Urges: A new way of managing my urges is ...

Changing Actions: A new way of acting is ...

Changing Enabling Relationships: A new way of inviting people to help me is ...

Copyright © Terence T. Gorski, 1995. CENAPS®, 17900 Dixie Hwy, Homewood, IL 60430; 708/799-5000.

Warning Sign Identification Card—Side 2

Title: _____

Recovery Activities: The recovery activities I can use to manage this warning sign are ...

Managing Thoughts: A new way of thinking that will help me manage this warning sign is ...

Managing Feelings: A new way of managing my feelings is ...

Managing Urges: A new way of managing my urges is ...

Changing Actions: A new way of acting is ...

Changing Enabling Relationships: A new way of inviting people to help me is ...

Copyright © Terence T. Gorski, 1995. CENAPS®, 17900 Dixie Hwy, Homewood, IL 60430; 708/799-5000.